Sanctifying Suburbia

Sanctifying Suburbia

How the Suburbs Became the Promised Land for American Evangelicals

BRIAN J. MILLER

OXFORD
UNIVERSITY PRESS

Oxford University Press is a department of the University of Oxford.
It furthers the University's objective of excellence in research, scholarship,
and education by publishing worldwide. Oxford is a registered trade mark of
Oxford University Press in the UK and certain other countries.

Published in the United States of America by Oxford University Press
198 Madison Avenue, New York, NY 10016, United States of America.

© Oxford University Press 2025

All rights reserved. No part of this publication may be reproduced, stored in a retrieval system, transmitted, used for text and data mining, or used for training artificial intelligence, in any form or by any means, without the prior permission in writing of Oxford University Press, or as expressly permitted by law, by license or under terms agreed with the appropriate reprographics rights organization. Inquiries concerning reproduction outside the scope of the above should be sent to the Rights Department, Oxford University Press, at the address above.

You must not circulate this work in any other form
and you must impose this same condition on any acquirer

Library of Congress Cataloging-in-Publication Data
Names: Miller, Brian J. (Brian Jonathan), author.
Title: Sanctifying suburbia : how the suburbs became the promised land for
American evangelicals / Brian J. Miller.
Description: New York, NY, United States of America : Oxford University Press, [2025] |
Includes bibliographical references and index.
Identifiers: LCCN 2024034708 (print) | LCCN 2024034709 (ebook) |
ISBN 9780197679630 (pb) | ISBN 9780197679623 (hb) | ISBN 9780197679661 |
ISBN 9780197679647 (epub)
Subjects: LCSH: Evangelicalism—United States—History. | Suburbs—
United States—History. | Christianity and culture—United States—History. |
Suburbanites—United States—Religious life.
Classification: LCC BR1642.U5 M557 2025 (print) | LCC BR1642.U5 (ebook) |
DDC 370.8/20973—dc23/eng/20240904
LC record available at https://lccn.loc.gov/2024034708
LC ebook record available at https://lccn.loc.gov/2024034709

DOI: 10.1093/oso/9780197679623.001.0001

Paperback printed by Marquis Book Printing, Canada
Hardback printed by Bridgeport National Bindery, Inc., United States of America

Contents

Acknowledgments   vii

Introduction: Evangelicals in Jesusland   1

1. Evangelicals, Suburbs, and the American Dream   14
2. Evangelicals and Suburbs: A Short History   38
3. Evangelicals (and Other Protestant Groups) Leave Chicago for the Suburbs   60
4. United Evangelicals Across (Parts of) America: The Locations of the National Association of Evangelicals   81
5. The Holy Suburb of Wheaton, Illinois   103
6. "Evangelical Meccas": Clusters of Evangelical Organizations in Suburbs and Cities
   with Benjamin E. Norquist   122
7. Where Evangelicals and Other Religious Traditions Live, 1972–2016   142
8. Evangelical Cultural Toolkits and Changing Suburbs   162
9. Conclusion   182

References   203
Index   227

Acknowledgments

This book was years in the making and benefitted from the encouragement and support of many. This includes the following:

Wheaton College; my colleagues in the Department of Anthropology, Sociology, and Urban Studies; Ben Norquist (co-author of Chapter 6) and Opus: The Art of Work (at Wheaton College); and students in multiple classes. Numerous colleagues listened patiently and offered valuable feedback. Students thoughtfully engaged with these ideas in courses.

The participants in the American Sociological Association, the Society for the Scientific Study of Religion, and the Association for the Sociology of Religion meetings who responded graciously and provided helpful critiques to portions of the book.

The museum staff, archivists, local historians, and librarians who helped in researching communities and obtaining materials.

Student research assistants who helped with data organization and finding sources for various parts of the book, including Matthew Porter, Marielle Merry, Jessica Mohkami, Jasmine Stein, Bethany Thomas, Maurice Bokanga, Rebecca Carlson, and Isabella Wallmow.

Chapter 3 is adapted from my article "Growing Suburbs, Relocating Churches: The Suburbanization of Protestant Churches in the Chicago Region, 1925–1990," *Journal for the Scientific Study of Religion* 56, no. 2 (2017): 342–364.

Ryan Burge for the data for Chapter 7.

Theo Calderara and Oxford for believing in and carrying out this project.

My immediate and extended family, particularly my wife and sons, who listened to me talk about these topics, provided time and space to write, and participated in numerous suburban adventures during the process.

The errors in the text are mine alone.

Introduction
Evangelicals in Jesusland

Naming and Praying for Suburban Evangelicals

In April 2005, quirky and sardonic singer-songwriter Ben Folds released the album *Songs for Silverman*. In his second solo album, after time in the 1990s with the Ben Folds Five, Folds plumbed similar musical and thematic grounds: piano-driven songs with Folds commenting on American society as well as individual lives. The third track on the album is titled "Jesusland." What Folds describes in the song could easily fit a suburban landscape. A driver keeps going by structures that diminish in size over a distance. The suburbs are full of McMansions, highways, billboards, parking lots, and offices. With all this activity, few people are visible on the street or outside buildings. What does the suburban landscape have to do with Jesus?

There is also a religious element to the landscape: crosses are present. Folds dubs these spaces "Jesusland," and the chorus consists of this word repeated. And at the end of the third verse, Folds suggests this is not just a landscape imbued with religiosity, it is a space that needs prayer: "You hang your head and pray / For Jesusland." Jesusland needs divine help.

When he released this song, Ben Folds was no stranger to music about suburban settings. His first solo album—*Rockin' the Suburbs*, from 2001—was widely reviewed (McClain and McClain 2016). The songs on that album told of tragic suburban lives amidst the adolescent anger of the title track. Folds later created kid-friendly lyrics for the song "Rockin' the Suburbs" when he contributed to the soundtrack for the 2006 animated film *Over the Hedge*, which follows the lives of multiple animals living in the suburbs. The first chorus of the child-appropriate version of the song echoes decades of suburban critiques where it is hard to tell the similar houses apart and the neighbors on the cul-de-sac have better looking grass.

In his 2019 memoir, Folds told of moving from neighborhood to neighborhood as a kid and having difficulty settling in within different contexts. In

Sanctifying Suburbia. Brian J. Miller, Oxford University Press. © Oxford University Press 2025.
DOI: 10.1093/oso/9780197679623.003.0001

one instance, he describes a run-in his family had with a professor regarding their dog: "These were the kinds of surreal middle-class suburban scenes that informed so much of my songwriting, and not just on the album entitled *Rockin' the Suburbs*" (Folds 2019, 27).

But "Jesusland" added a new element to consideration of the stereotypical suburbs dominated by single-family homes. Numerous cultural works have addressed suburban life, ranging from novels like *Cracks in the Picture Window* to *Gone Girl*, films like the Oscar-winning *American Beauty* or the comedic *The 'Burbs*, television shows including *Leave It to Beaver* and *The Sopranos*, both popular and serious poetry, and rock and pop music (Haralovich 1992; Leibman 1995; Beuka 2004; Jurca 2001; Spigel 2001; Gill 2013; Huq 2013; Coon 2014; Vermeulen 2014; Rowley 2015; Miller 2017a; Miller 2018). Missing from many of these works is the element of religious faith, a regular and influential feature of American life. Religion is particularly important in the suburbs and particular regions of the United States.

In the wake of the 2004 presidential election where incumbent president and avowed evangelical George W. Bush defeated John Kerry, Jesusland was a meme denoting the states in the middle of the country that supported Bush. While a simplification of voting patterns that continued to diverge in subsequent presidential elections (with urban residents leaning Democratic, residents of rural and exurban areas leaning Republican, and people in middle suburbs divided; Sellers 2013), Jesusland offered a shorthand for political and cultural patterns in the United States. And the designation was not just noting social patterns or poking in good fun; Folds's call for prayer for this part of the country was rooted in a desire for change.

Religion and the Suburbs

The American suburbs are not exclusive to heartland ("Jesusland") states, but they do resonate with values and images of middle-America as well as the larger American Dream to which Americans aspire: suburbs feature single-family homes, cars, lawns, strip malls and big box stores, parents seeking a better life for their children with family life, good schools, safe settings, and local governments responsive to local needs and protective of the quality of life. Often overlooked is that suburbs are also full of places of worship. Suburban street corners, main roads, and highways throughout the United States are dotted with churches and synagogues as well as an increasing number of temples and mosques. The suburban landscape well-known for individualism, private property, and the American Dream also is home to thousands of religious groups seeking to worship and meet together. The American suburban dream rarely comes with any explicit religious connotations—except perhaps a near-religious belief in middle-class meritocracy, consumerism, individualism, or exclusion—and yet the United States is unusually religious among developed nations.

This book is about one large religious group in the United States—evangelicals—and how they have embraced and been shaped by the most common place for Americans to live: the suburbs. These phenomena are both quintessentially American phenomena; while suburbs and evangelicals exist elsewhere in the world, in the United States they are both numerous and take particular influential forms. The suburbs developed from an escape from burgeoning city life in the mid to late-1800s to the dominant geographic space in the twentieth century due to social policy, cultural ideology, and racial exclusion and residential segregation (Jackson 1985; Fishman 1987; Sugrue 1996; Hayden 2003; Wiese 2004; Kruse 2005; Teaford 2008). Evangelicals, as they are understood today, emerged in the second half of the twentieth century from conservative and fundamentalist religious groups who wanted to engage society and politics while holding to particular orthodox Christian beliefs (Henry 1947; Smith 1998).

At first glance, these large categories, one a place and another a religious group, might not seem like they go together, or are worth considering at the same time. Religious and nonreligious residents of the United States live in many different places and regions. Even with clusters of different religious groups in different locations, such as members of the Church of Jesus Christ of Latter-day Saints in Utah or Orthodox Jews in New York City and the surrounding region, American religious groups and congregations are often spread throughout the country.

At the same time, when considering geography, evangelicals are often associated with particular parts of the country. This could be the Bible Belt, running roughly from Virginia to Texas, or rural areas and small towns far away from big cities or the coasts. In other words, "Jesusland." Evangelicals are not associated with urban life (Mulder and Smith 2009; Elisha 2011b), particularly not some of the biggest coastal cities in the United States such as New York, Los Angeles, San Francisco, and Seattle. The occasional exceptions to the rule, whether a successful evangelical pastor in a global city like Tim Keller or the presence of evangelicals returning to cities (Bielo

2011a), help reinforce the normality of the evangelical embrace of suburbia. According to Pew Research (2015) in the Religious Landscape Survey, 25.4% of Americans are evangelical. Often defined by four theological traits—an emphasis on Jesus Christ's work on the cross, the need for a conversion experience, the authority of the Bible, and living out the gospel (Bebbington 1989; Lifeway 2015)—evangelicals are well-known for their religious beliefs and practices. There is also an important cultural component to their identity beyond a theological definition: evangelicals in the twentieth and twenty-first century have particular political beliefs and actions, patterns of behavior, and even a whole subculture of books, movies, television, radio, schools, and organizations.

Suburbs are also widespread, even if they take some different forms outside varied American cities. For instance, the sprawl of Houston and other fast-growing Sun Belt cities differs from the dense, inner-ring suburbs initially created in part by streetcars outside cities in the Northeast and Midwest. In the United States, just over 50% of Americans live in the suburbs, according to the US Census Bureau, while roughly 30% live in cities and 18% live in rural areas (US Census Bureau 2002; Mather et al. 2011). Suburbs are also now home to all kinds of Americans. They are increasingly diverse in race and ethnicity (Frey 2022), social class (Kneebone and Berube 2013), and religious traditions (Numrich and Wedam 2015). The Census Bureau's definitions of suburbs mean that they are quick definition of the suburbs from the Census Bureau is that they are the places between big cities and rural areas that have significant regular connections to urban areas ("2010 Standards" 2010). But the suburbs are more than a geographic designation on a map; in the United States, the suburbs are part of the American Dream, the pursuit of a single-family home for the enrichment of one's family and a private, car-dominated lifestyle with the ability to keep others and urban issues away from the community. Many presentations of the suburban ideal— the single-family home, a happy nuclear family, a well-off neighborhood or community—provide little hint regarding the influence of religion.

A Road to Studying the Suburbs and Evangelicals

In this book, I argue that the connections between evangelicals and suburbs are deeper than previously articulated, with evangelicals embracing suburban values and locations with consequences for evangelical belief and action as well as communities. By analyzing multiple sources of data—historical, current, quantitative, and qualitative—regarding evangelicals and suburbs, I show how the spatial context of the suburbs has shaped and influenced one of the larger US religious traditions. I add to existing explanations of how religious groups reside where they do: the ecological approach emphasizes competition; the political economy approach emphasizes uneven settlement due to decisions made by powerful leaders; and the "cultural toolkit" approach (Swidler 1986) examines how evangelicals have made numerous choices to settle in suburbs rather than other geographic options.

An academic cottage industry is devoted to studying evangelicals, and numerous scholars examine suburbs. Few study both or the intersection of the place and the socioreligious group addressed here. I argue that the typical approaches to evangelicals and suburbs fail to reckon with an influential factor in the study of evangelicals: where they live and how these spaces shape their beliefs, behavior, and belonging. Those who study evangelicals often examine their religious activity or their political actions and rarely consider the communities in which evangelicals are commonly situated. More broadly, these connections suggest that scholars studying religious groups and traditions must account for their spatial contexts.

Similarly, evangelicals as a group can influence communities and suburbs. Those who study suburbs may acknowledge religious congregations or groups, but rarely is religion a formative variable in the analysis of suburban communities or suburban lifestyles. The cultural dimensions of suburban life are well-known, while religion, a social force that also influences how people make meaning of their surroundings, receives less attention. Those studying places, particularly suburbs, should consider the impact of religious groups and organizations.

This study of the connections between religion and suburbs has a personal component in addition to a scholarly motivation. Suburban landscapes and evangelical beliefs, practices, and organizations have shaped much of my life. I was largely raised in suburbs, living in single-family homes, townhomes, and condos in quiet neighborhoods, attending public schools in a relatively diverse school district, and residing roughly 10–15 minutes via car from interstates and all sorts of suburban amenities. I am currently a faculty member at an evangelical college located in the suburbs of Chicago. The founding of the school in the mid-1800s was influenced by the nearby presence of the first railroad line into and out of a booming Chicago (and that railroad line existed because the initial settlers of the town granted the railroad a right of way after a nearby larger suburb refused to do so). I have attended religious congregations in suburban settings where driving to church was required and congregants came from a 15-mile radius. I study the suburbs, publishing articles on suburban growth and development as well as depictions of suburban homes on television and housing often found in suburbs. I regularly teach an urban sociology course where we discuss the relationship between cities and suburbs, and I have also taught courses specifically about suburbs. One alum of our sociology program recently reminded me that I told their class, "I was raised in the suburbs, I live in the suburbs, I will likely die in the suburbs."

As both an undergraduate and graduate student, I was drawn to the study of places through the subfield of urban sociology. After growing up visiting cities, drawing cities, playing countless hours of SimCity, and observing suburban life, a field that examined both broad and particular patterns across communities appealed to me. For my dissertation, I examined suburban growth and development among the three Chicago suburbs of Naperville, West Chicago, and Wheaton. There, I explored how three suburban communities roughly the same distance from Chicago, located in the same corner of a suburban county, and settled around the same time in the 1830s, came to be so different today as the result of external pressures, internal decisions, and the influential yet malleable character of each community (Miller 2013; Miller 2016b). Comparative analysis of cities is common, yet the method is less commonly applied to the thousands of suburban communities across the United States.

One of the communities in my dissertation research—Wheaton, Illinois—had a unique character: although it could be characterized as a classic bedroom suburb dominated by single-family homes, little manufacturing and limited retail, and relatively high levels of wealth with primarily white residents, it was widely known in the Chicago region and across the United States for its concentration of evangelical residents, organizations, and norms. For example, older residents in the area still know the suburb of Wheaton as the place where liquor could not be sold. After Prohibition ended in 1933, the suburb voted to ban the sale of alcohol until a local referendum overturned this in 1985 (and now, the city hosts an Ale Fest each year). The suburb was also home to numerous churches and parachurch groups. One sociologist who taught at Wheaton College in the 1970s and 1980s dubbed the community "Christiantown, U.S.A." (Stellway 1990). In the late 1970s, a reporter for the *New York Times* named the community "a

Protestant Vatican" as he described the collection of churches and religious organizations in and around the suburb (Vescey 1978). Even as the evangelical character of the suburb of over 50,000 people has waned with an influx of new residents and changes to the community, its name is still recognizable as a Christian center.

This unique character of Wheaton, created through a history full of particular decisions, raised sociological questions: What does it mean to have a suburb that is known for its religiosity? How did such clustering of religious residents and organizations develop and then continue over decades? Does Wheaton simply have a collection of evangelical individuals and organizations, or is the community shaped in tangible ways by the evangelicals and vice versa?

While this was not a primary question in my dissertation research, I continued to think about its implications. This question about a particular suburb connected to a larger question: What links religion and place? In a country known for geographic mobility, sprawl, and individualism, how do religion and place intersect? My previous work considering cities, suburbs, and places had little overlap with this literature. I spent several years learning from the work of historians, sociologists, geographers, and others who had broached this topic. I found a robust set of literature that connects spaces and religion with work addressing both past and current American contexts. Yet outside of several key works (cited often in this book), previous studies are primarily concerned with religion in cities and urban neighborhoods and a limited number of works consider religion across suburban contexts.

With some knowledge of the literature, I sought data that could help me both understand the uniqueness of Wheaton as well as more broadly link evangelicals and suburbs. Finding good data proved both invigorating and frustrating, as a good puzzle can be. Finding all the congregations in a populated place can be difficult (see the example of Zelinsky and Matthews 2011 in Cook County, Illinois). The US Census is prohibited from asking about religion, and the Association of Statisticians of American Religious Bodies (Grammich et al. 2023) provides data about religious traditions at the county level. Few surveys involving religion link location and religiosity beyond a simple question of where the individual respondent is located with broad response categories (see Miller 2016a). Studies that did address the connection between suburbs and religion often focused on a particular religious tradition (e.g., Cutler 1996; Gamm 1999; Diamond 2000; Mulder 2015), a particular metropolitan region (Diamond 2003; Miller 2017b), and/or relied on case studies (Dochuk 2003; Brenneman and Miller 2020).

Thus, the arguments and findings in this book are a culmination of sociological efforts encompassing various theories, methodologies, and years of analysis. I build on excellent work from a multidisciplinary group of scholars—in particular, Etan Diamond's *Souls of the City*, Paul Numrich and Elfriede Wedam's *Religion and Community in the New Urban America*, Mark Mulder's *Shades of White Flight*, the work of Darren Dochuk—that gave me hope that this sociological puzzle about evangelicals and suburbs could be put together. As far as I know, there is not a smoking gun—or holy text?—where white male evangelical leaders in the early 1950s met and said they were going to pursue a suburban strategy while abandoning central cities. At the same time, the preponderance of evidence I considered in conjunction with existing work strengthens my confidence that evangelicalism is strongly linked to and shaped by suburbs. Going further, the suburbanization of evangelicalism is a key feature of the religious tradition that affects numerous other aspects of the group. It is not enough for researchers and pundits to consider the theological positions and political behavior of evangelicals; accounting for their spatial context is part and parcel to understanding the whole package of white evangelicalism.

Making the Case for Connecting Evangelicals and Suburbs

Ben Folds's musical output would not lead observers to mistake him for an evangelical even if he spent time as a child in the Bible Belt. A contrast to Folds's biting analysis of Jesusland might be a 1993 song from the Christian rock group Audio Adrenaline. The Christian music industry, particularly marked by Contemporary Christian Music (CCM), grew in the 1990s and the early years of the twenty-first century (Payne 2024). "Big House" reached number one on the Christian charts, and one publication named it the Christian song of the decade for the 1990s (Jones 2009). Instead of Folds's concern about suburban life infused with religion, Audio Adrenaline celebrates heaven with depictions of a large home that could be set in suburbia.

The song invokes Jesus's claim in John 14: 2–4 that he is preparing God's house with many rooms for his followers. Even as Christians interpret Jesus as talking about heaven, the song lyrics can be read as invoking an American suburban dream: playing football with family in a big yard, plenty of food on hand, and lots of space for living. All is well. With this positive image and bubbly guitar line, the Christian group asks later in the song, "why not come with me" to the big house?

I argue that this combination of evangelicalism and suburbs found in this song or throughout evangelical settings in the United States since World War II is not accidental, and did not "naturally" emerge. Through a series of decisions involving migration, overlapping value systems, exclusion, and particular cultural toolkits, the suburbs and American evangelicalism are intertwined today in such a way that the two go together. Put another way, imagining white evangelicalism as rooted in American cities in the near future seems far-fetched, even as major population centers offer evangelicals opportunities for evangelism and engaging with and influencing culture. While numerous scholars and religious practitioners explored whether this is a marriage made in heaven or suburban hell, few have undertaken the task of explaining how and why suburbs and evangelicals came together.

The argument of this book unfolds in several sections: this introduction, followed by three chapters focused on historical relationships between evangelical and suburbs; three chapters examining multiple sets of geographies from a single suburb, to four communities, to different types of communities where people of different religious traditions reside; a chapter on evangelical cultural toolkits regarding suburbs and place; and a conclusion highlighting the multiple lessons learned from this analysis.

Chapter 1 introduces the argument of the book. I define suburbs in the United States—places in between cities and rural areas with a particular way of life—and evangelicals, a religious group definable by theological distinctives as well as a unique set of social practices and engagement with society after World War II. I then illustrate the intersection of evangelicals and suburbs using the cases of influential suburban megachurches, critiques of suburban faith, the cultural affinities between suburban and evangelical life, and voting patterns with evangelicals supporting particular presidential candidates and the suburbs emerging as the primary political battleground. The third section discusses existing academic work on evangelicals and suburbs before the last section adds to the two theoretical lenses often used to link geography and religion, ecological arguments and political economy, the perspective of "cultural toolkits" (Swidler 1986) where evangelicals deploy cultural processes of meaning-making (Spillman 2020) and make choices about geographies and communities.

Chapter 2 reviews the history of evangelicals and the suburbs going back to the late 1700s. This history stretches beyond the mass suburbia of the second half of the twentieth century; English parliamentarian, abolitionist, and evangelical William Wilberforce pushed for suburban living in response to a growing and morally corrupt London. At the same time, by the early twentieth century, numerous important evangelical congregations and institutions were located in major cities in the United States as they pursued evangelism and social action. As mass suburbanization began before the Great Depression and restarted at a faster pace after World War II, evangelicals joined other white religious groups in moving to the suburbs as populations changed in cities. The chapter concludes with a brief case study of how prominent evangelist Billy Graham addressed cities and suburbs in hundreds of speeches delivered after World War II.

In Chapter 3, I analyze white flight after World War II in the Chicago area among 10 different Protestant groups, including several evangelical denominations. Drawing on a database of church addresses collected by the Church Federation of Greater Chicago for decades, I look at the locations of congregations in two conservative Protestant denominations (CRC, LCMS), three mainline Protestant denominations (Episcopalian, Methodist, and Presbyterian), and one Black Protestant denomination (AME) to more closely examine neighborhoods that they left and communities in which new congregations began. In this analysis, I find that white denominations moved to largely white suburbs and left Chicago neighborhoods with growing numbers of Black residents, while AME congregations spread in both increasingly Black Chicago neighborhoods as well as in suburbs with pockets of Black residents. The congregations of different denominations did not necessarily move at the same rate to the suburbs, and their resettlement in the suburbs took place among already established congregations and where suburbanization was in full swing.

Chapter 4 examines data from the National Association of Evangelicals (NAE) to analyze the locations of the organization's headquarters and where leaders in the organization—delegates and board members—lived and/or worked in their roles with evangelical organizations. At the 1942 meeting of the group that later became the National Association of Evangelicals, a majority of the delegates represented evangelical congregations and institutions in big cities. This included multiple members from Philadelphia, New York City, Boston, and Chicago. As population patterns changed and more Americans and organizations moved to the suburbs, evangelical organizations, including leaders in the National Association of Evangelicals themselves and the office of the NAE, also changed their locations. The NAE maintained headquarters in the Chicago suburbs and Washington, DC, with a short-lived and unsuccessful attempt to operate from the Los Angeles suburbs. These findings highlight a tension among evangelicals regarding where they are willing to locate: suburban locations offer proximity to cities and their resources and networks but not necessarily access; smaller big cities offer a more urban experience, but they are not the centers of power and influence; Washington, DC offers access to political influence but not necessarily to other spheres of influence; and a limited presence in or outside the biggest cities in the United States limits evangelical financial, cultural, and global influence.

Shifting from a look at the National Association of Evangelicals to a suburban case study, Chapter 5 considers the role of evangelical faith and organizations in the development of Wheaton, Illinois, a suburb 25 miles west of Chicago. While the suburb shares characteristics with many other American suburbs with its emphasis on single-family homes and a stable and high quality of life, its own religious character from the beginning—religious founders, the establishment of Wheaton College early on—affected subsequent decisions. After World War II, Wheaton added numerous subdivisions and many evangelical organizations and businesses located in the community or in adjacent newly founded Carol Stream, where evangelical leaders provided land and financing. Among multiple possible explanations for this concentration of evangelical residents and organizations, I discuss three factors that stand out: race and class within a whiter and wealthier suburb, the bedroom suburb and evangelical celebration of single-family homes and nuclear family life, and the opportunities for evangelicals to engage in a growing and concentrated evangelical network.

Adding to the case of Wheaton, Chapter 6 analyzes three other communities that became home to concentrations of evangelical parachurch organizations with a national or international focus: Grand Rapids, Michigan; Colorado Springs, Colorado; and the suburbs east of Los Angeles and Orange County, California. When these parachurch groups with a broad scope of operations could locate anywhere in the internet age, why select these evangelical centers? Each community has a particular history as to how evangelicals converged there—Grand Rapids was home to Dutch Reformed residents, Orange County emerged as an evangelical center in the postwar era, and Colorado Springs explicitly encouraged evangelical organizations to move—yet these organizations find similar value in these locations, including having a pool of employees, interacting with other organizations, and drawing on resources from evangelical congregations and residents. These findings regarding these four centers have implications for how religious clusters come to be as well as to how other locations might become a new concentration.

Chapter 7 broadens in scope from specific communities and concentrations of evangelicals to national data by utilizing General Social Survey data from 1972 to 2016. The data allows for the analysis of where adherents of different religious types live, defined as different community types including cities, suburbs, and rural areas measured two different ways and the population of communities. Analysis across 31 waves of data reveals that evangelicals were more likely to live in smaller suburbs, small towns, and rural areas than Americans as a whole. However, the percentage of evangelicals in rural areas declined in this time, and the percentage living in suburbs and smaller cities increased. The GSS data reveals additional patterns involving other religious groups: mainline Protestants echo the locations of evangelicals, Black Protestants and Jews were more likely to reside in the largest cities and their suburbs, and the percentage of suburban adherents in almost all religious traditions increased. These findings suggest settlement patterns of religious traditions are connected to race and ethnicity and the nonreligious are spread across all kinds of communities.

In Chapter 8, I consider the cultural toolkits evangelicals deployed when considering places and suburbs in a changing United States during the twentieth century. In looking at patterns in 29 books written by Billy Graham, I show how this influential evangelist discussed cities, suburbs, and rural places, applied lessons from cities in the Bible and the future city of heaven to his time, and showed affinity for New York City. In these books, Graham utilized an individualistic evangelical approach to social problems and salvation, and his critiques of cities suggested that despite the ways they displayed human progress, they were not the hope for humanity. Adding this analysis of cultural toolkits to ecological theories emphasizing competition and explanations of uneven settlement patterns based on social inequalities stemming from race, class, and gender demonstrates how evangelicals made sense of places in an unsettled period when millions found homes in suburbia.

Chapter 9 sums up how evangelicals are shaped by suburbs, discusses how the book contributes to the ongoing conversation regarding religion and place, and includes five implications for scholars, religious practitioners and adherents, and policymakers. These takeaways include: understanding evangelicals requires analyzing their suburban lives and patterns; how evangelicals interact with race, class, and gender is shaped by suburban contexts; the suburbs and evangelicals provide in-between spaces in society that also produce difficult to resolve tensions; evangelicals can engage more deeply with place and suburbs; and cultural toolkits and their deployment in regard to how religious groups consider and choose locations help scholars better understand the dynamic intersection of religion and place.

American evangelicals are a potent force in society, yet rarely examined is their connection to and adoption of the suburbs as the places best suited for their daily activities and societal goals. The different approaches to studying evangelical suburban life in this book show how evangelicals became suburban and how this shaped their life and activity. This book does not consider all evangelical places or organizations in the United States, but based on patterns from multiple data sources, it considers the ways evangelicals came to embrace the American suburbs. The anticipated home for American evangelicals may not only be a future heaven in a spacious "Father's house"; it could be the same kinds of communities idealized in the American Dream, the Jesusland of the American suburbs.

1
Evangelicals, Suburbs, and the American Dream

In the beginning of *The Great Divorce*, medieval scholar and Anglican writer C. S. Lewis provided a description of hell. Aboard a bus flying away from "grey town," a fellow rider provides the main character a description of the community visible from the bus window:

> As soon as anyone arrives he settles in some street. Before he's been there twenty-four hours he quarrels with his neighbor. Before the week is over he's quarreled so badly that he decides to move. Very likely he finds the next street empty because all the people there have quarreled with *their* neighbors—and moved. So he settles in. If by any chance the street is full, he goes further. But even if he stays, it makes no odds. He's sure to have another quarrel pretty soon and then he'll move on again. Finally he'll move right out to the edge of the town and build a new house. You've only got to *think* a house and there it is. That's how the town keeps on growing. (Lewis 1946, 18–19, emphasis in original)

To the many critics of the American suburbs, this description from a patron saint of American evangelicals today may sound like a fitting description of the suburbs: distance between people and homes, people avoiding each other, a "greyness," and the endless construction of houses. To the millions of Americans that moved to suburbs during the twentieth century, this description may strike them as cold and too focused on conflict. How could the suburbs be a grey hell when so many Americans have sought out the American Dream among single-family homes, private property, green lawns, and family-friendly settings?

While the passage from Lewis appears to provide a bleak assessment of suburban life, it combines analysis of places with religious themes. *The Great Divorce* contrasts the "grey town" with a heaven that is more real than what humans had considered real with items "made of some different substance,

Sanctifying Suburbia. Brian J. Miller, Oxford University Press. © Oxford University Press 2025.
DOI: 10.1093/oso/9780197679623.003.0002

so much solider than things in our country that men were ghost by comparison" (Lewis 1946, 28). Without explicitly allegorizing American locations in a Christian narrative, Lewis hints at the religiosity of particular places, suburbs or otherwise. Had he been located in the United States, Lewis may have been prompted to ask: What about suburbs makes them so amenable to be described as hell, and if this is the case, why do so many American Christians claim the suburbs as home?

This book details how a particular religious group—American evangelicals—came to be associated with and embraced a particular spatial setting: the American suburbs. When evangelicals use the theological term sanctification, they refer to being set apart for religious uses or the process of becoming more holy. I argue that a similar process occurred with the American suburbs: evangelicals saw it as a place set apart, a place where they could best pursue their religious and social goals. In a suburban setting marked by racial homogeneity, pursuing a middle-class lifestyle, and the ideal of a nuclear family living in single-family homes, the cultural toolkits (Swidler 1986) of evangelicalism emphasizing individualism and anti-structuralism (Emerson and Smith 2000) found a home. By examining the history of evangelical organizations in suburbs, the white flight of evangelicals, case studies of evangelicals clustering in certain communities, and evangelical cultural toolkits, I find evangelical and suburban realms overlapped and influenced each other as evangelicals and suburbanites sought meaning (Spillman 2020) in a changing society and world. These two social spheres, one a religious tradition (conservative Protestants as defined by Steensland et al. 2000 and evangelicals defined by historians such as Bebbington 1989) and one a spatial arrangement that according to the US Census Bureau is home to more than 50% of American residents (Hobbs and Stoops 2002; Parker et al. 2018), coexist and mutually reinforce each other. To understand American evangelicalism today is to also engage with the American suburbs and the ways these places have shaped religious identity and practice.

Examining the intertwining of evangelicals and suburbia contributes to productive ongoing conversations between sociologists, historians, social scientists, and other scholars about the important intersections between religion and place. While sociologists have often examined religion in terms of the three components of belief, behavior, and belonging, their analysis rarely deeply engages with the places in which religious beliefs, behaviors, and belonging occur and how they are shaped by these settings. Material settings, such as religious buildings (Brenneman and Miller 2020) and the meanings and practices associated with them, matter for subsequent practices. Addressing whiteness and Christian nationalism among evangelicals (e.g., Whitehead and Perry 2020; Butler 2021; Emerson and Bracey 2024)? Considering issues of gender and patriarchy (e.g., Du Mez 2020; Barr 2021; Swartz 2023)? The ways evangelicals have pursued particular social issues and policies and not others (Swartz 2012; Melkonian-Hoover and Kellstedt 2019; Sutton 2024)? These lines of inquiry are connected to a suburban context born out of white flight and excluding other racial and ethnic groups, ideas about households and gender roles, and the preferred version of suburban life, including helping children get ahead, avoiding the issues of big cities, and private, nuclear family life. Evangelicals in the United States may have ended up following similar paths if they had largely lived in big cities or rural areas, but the particular combination of suburban and evangelical life helped lead to the evangelicalism known today.

This chapter proceeds in four parts to lay the foundation for the argument that evangelicals embraced and were shaped by the American suburbs. First, I define suburbs and evangelicals. Both phenomena are easily identifiable in the United States entering the third decade of the twenty-first century yet each are complex. Next, I briefly discuss four examples that illustrate the convergence of evangelicals and suburbs: suburban megachurches, critiques of the combination of suburban life and faith, evangelical politicians and the importance of suburban voters, and cultural affinities between suburbs and evangelicals. In the third section, I review the existing research on evangelicals and suburbs that helped inspire this book. At the same time, I highlight how this book moves the conversation about evangelicals in new directions. Finally, I discuss how adding the concept of "cultural toolkits" to existing theories of urban and suburban development helps provide a stronger explanation of evangelicals embracing suburbs and for studying the connections between religion and places.

Defining Suburbs and Evangelicals

The US Census Bureau officially designates places as suburban as part of larger efforts to identify and define metropolitan areas and distinguish urban and rural areas. The Census Bureau first defined these areas with the 1950 Census. Boundaries of metropolitan regions changed over time as communities grew or changed. In 2010, the Census laid out definitions for metropolitan and micropolitan areas ("2010 Standards" 2010). A metropolitan statistical area (MSA) contains an urban center of at least 50,000 residents and includes counties "containing the core, plus adjacent outlying counties having a high degree of social and economic integration with the central county or counties as measured through commuting." Thus, the New York City metropolitan region includes the central city of New York City with over eight million residents in the five boroughs plus residents of suburban counties on Long Island, New York counties north of the city, plus counties in Connecticut and New Jersey to add up to a metropolitan population of over 19 million. Such large land areas and populations lead to more complexity: the New York City MSA also has central cities of Newark and Jersey City, Combined Statistical Areas can contain multiple MSAs, and different areas within a metropolitan area can feel or appear more urban and rural yet still be part of counties defined as suburban.

The definition of suburbs can vary according to methodology. For example, households were asked in the 2017 American Community Survey (administered by the Census Bureau) to describe their neighborhood as urban, suburban, or rural. This resulted in 52% suburban households, 27% urban, and 21% rural. These responses did not always line up with earlier definitions of metropolitan areas, central cities, and outside central cities (Bucholtz 2020). In 2020, the Bureau of Justice Statistics decided to use weighted housing-unit density (rather than population density) and define "urban places are those that are densely populated, are at the center of a major metropolitan area, or some combination of these." With these changes, they reported "12% of the population lives in urban areas, 69% in suburban areas, and 19% in rural areas" (Anderson 2020).

In addition to definitions based on geography or density, the American suburbs also have a cultural component. Distance from the city or the number of residents who commute to the city does not fully capture a lifestyle revolving around single-family homes, family life, driving, excluding or living apart from undesirable others, and an emphasis on local government and control over land use. As mass-produced suburbia exploded after the end of World War II, building on decades of suburban development prior to the Great Depression, sociologists and others investigated these new communities. They found an emphasis on the nuclear family and helping secure advantages for children (Seeley et al. 1956), suburbanites who came from different communities and urban neighborhoods found ways to work together to reach mutual goals such as setting up schools and community associations (Gans 1967), and working-class and middle-class suburban residents expressed happiness with the homes and consumer products they could acquire (Berger 1960). At the same time, other observers critiqued the new suburban life. For example, William Whyte (1956) lamented the rise of "organization man" who traded his individuality for work in large corporations. Novels, poetry, film, and television looked behind the happy façade of suburbia and portrayed troubled lives (e.g., Beuka 2004; Gill 2013; Coon 2014). These early studies of mass suburbia often contained limited data on religious patterns though religious practitioners (e.g., Greeley 1959; Winter 1961; Shippey 1964) expressed concern about what religion might be in this sprawling setting.

As residents settled in postwar suburbs, later studies added to scholarly knowledge of what comprises suburban life and how suburbs have changed over time. In contrast to some portrayals of conformist and similar suburbs, subsequent research examined multiple kinds of suburban communities that developed throughout the United States. Bedroom suburbs featured large subdivisions and residents worked elsewhere (Gans 1967). In contrast, edge cities have millions of square feet of office space and hundreds of thousands of square feet of retail space (Garreau 1991). Working-class suburbs have smaller homes and blue-collar jobs (Nicolaides 2002). "Boomburbs" are suburbs largely in the South and West with rapid population growth over several decades (Lang and Lefurgy 2007). Contra the image of white suburbia, ethnoburbs are suburbs with significant or majority-minority populations (Li 2009). Necessary due to exclusion from white suburbs, Black residents founded and developed suburban communities (Wiese 2004; Haynes 2001; Lacy 2007). Inner-ring suburbs are adjacent to big cities with higher density levels and facing many big city issues (Hanlon 2010), while exurbs sit at the edges of metropolitan regions (e.g., Eiesland 2000). Across all suburbs, populations changed from the image of white middle- to upper-class residents as minority suburban populations increased (Frey 2022) and more people in poverty moved to suburbs (Kneebone and Berube 2013).

Multiple accounts detail modern day-to-day suburban life. Regarding community life and interacting with neighbors, an attitude of "moral minimalism" contingent on suburbanites leaving each other alone and avoiding direct conflict helps develop suburban community (Baumgartner 1988). More public conflict and tension between suburban residents, such as about development (Miller 2013) or differences in how schools should educate children (Warikoo 2022), can last years and reinforce existing patterns and inequalities. Suburbanites with more resources work to maintain advantages and status markers compared to nearby suburbanites (Heiman 2015). Maintaining symbolic and moral boundaries between suburban groups is important (Lacy 2007). Some suburbanites look to live in gated communities where symbolic and physical barriers reduce anxiety about safety (Low 2003). Minority racial and ethnic groups develop suburban community amidst threats from others in the community or from nearby locations (Li 2009).

As social conditions both changed and stayed the same in suburbs, these communities became home to more varied religious traditions beyond the known quantities of Protestants, Catholics, and Jews of the early postwar era (Herberg 1955). After World War II, Jews moved to the suburbs and established synagogues and communities (Cutler 1996; Diamond 2003). With increases in immigration from new areas of the world after the passing of the Immigration and Nationality Act of 1965, new religious groups arrived in the suburbs. This included Muslims and Hindus who sought to develop masjids and temples (Numrich and Wedam 2015; Howe 2018), as well as immigrant Christian groups. The suburbia of today is more complex than the common image of white, wealthy suburban enclaves that keep others out and worship in established religious traditions—though such communities do still exist and normative ideas of what the suburbs are continue.

As suburbs changed and experienced multiple waves of development beginning in the mid-1800s through today (Hayden 2003), they became an essential part of the American Dream. From an early desire for a small home close to nature (Archer 2005) to the modern interest in a large suburban home that is a good investment (McCabe 2016) located in a high-status community with good schools and amenities (Heiman 2015), the suburban American Dream received support from American presidents, the federal government, advertisers, builders and developers, zoning, and multiple generations of the American public. The popularity of suburbs is not a flash in a pan or simply a postwar phenomenon; the suburbs have deep roots and many social forces contributed to their rise.

The ascendency of suburbs also impacted the popularity of big cities in the United States. There are both anti-urban sentiments in the United States (Conn 2014) and a renewed interest in cities around the turn of the twenty-first century (Ehrenhalt 2012). Now, a suburban lifestyle is well established and is often depicted in a particular form: sprawling metropolitan regions composed largely of single-family homes and dependent on driving (Duany et al. 2000). Surveys from recent years suggest millennials desire to live in the suburbs, even if there are barriers to doing so or they also want to live in urban neighborhoods (Sisson 2016; Capps 2018). Numerous American big cities are important global centers for economic and cultural activity (Sassen 2001) and continue to attract residents from the United States and around the globe. Big cities and metropolitan areas could work together to address common social issues, but they often do not as they compete over resources and status (e.g., Orfield 2002; Florida 2017). The American suburbs are still attractive to many people even as cities offer cultural scenes, diversity, and economic opportunities.

Entering the third decade of the twenty-first century, suburbs are firmly part of American society. American evangelicals also have an established history in the United States with a set of beliefs, belonging, and behavior. Their roots stretch to evangelical movements in the 1700s and 1800s in Great Britain (Larsen 2007; Kidd 2019). However, evangelicals as they are known today emerged in the postwar decades and particularly arrived as a cohesive group in the late 1970s. When noted pollster George Gallup named 1976 "the year of the evangelical" and *Newsweek* in October of the same year led with a cover story profiling the evangelical movement (Woodward 1976), the group had fully emerged as a group with a cohesive identity and a sizable influence on American society. Marked by consistent religious beliefs, practices, and social engagement while also beset by fragmentation, a lack of hierarchy, and internal and external criticism, evangelicals attracted much attention from social observers and scholars.

Some of this research interest is due to the size of the group: according to the Pew Research Religious Landscape Study, 25.4% of Americans are evangelical Protestant (Pew Research 2015). This makes evangelicals the largest religious tradition in the United States compared to 22.8% of Americans with no religious affiliation, Catholics comprising 20.8% of the population, mainline Protestants comprising 14.7%, and Black Protestants comprising 6.5% of the population.

Evangelicals have a unique set of beliefs that help animate their worship and practices. Scholars often define evangelicals by theological beliefs or doctrines: an emphasis on Jesus Christ's work on the cross, the need for a conversion experience, the authority of the Bible, and a focus on evangelism (Bebbington 1989; National Association of Evangelicals 2015). While these beliefs separately or collectively could overlap with those of other

Christians, the particular bundle of and emphasis on these four doctrines plus how they have put these into practice mark evangelicals as unique. Within the American religious landscape, evangelicals or conservative Protestants (terms used interchangeably in this text while fundamentalists refers to a subset of this group and Pentecostal and nondenominational Christians are also considered part of evangelicalism) are distinct from mainline Protestants who hold more liberal or progressive theological and social views, and Black Protestants who share some theological beliefs with evangelicals but have a very different social history (Steensland et al. 2000; Shelton and Emerson 2012).

Similar to the suburbs, these more technical definitions of evangelicals based on theological distinctions do not capture the full day-to-day reality of evangelicalism. They may not describe particular congregational or individual religious experiences. They do not include the alternative institutions set up by evangelicals, ranging from media universes (including radio and TV stations and publishing houses) to schools (from preschool to postgraduate education) to independent congregations and networks of influential pastors. The single term does not easily capture the various strands of evangelicalism or the disagreements over both central and more peripheral issues. Beliefs about God and the Bible may lead to conflict with science and other authorities in American social life, contributing to particular political and social stances. Perhaps more so in recent years, evangelicals are closely tied to support for the Republican Party and conservative causes (see Martí 2020), even with some evangelicals from the early 1970s pushing for more left-leaning political positions and collaborations (Swartz 2012).

Modern evangelical history begins in the early 1940s as conservative Christians in the United States considered how to engage society. In the early decades of the twentieth century, these believers felt pushed to the margins of American society. Modernist religion emerged in the late 1800s, dividing denominations and religious institutions. Higher criticism of the Bible threatened the authority of scripture and a social gospel promoted work toward social change in line with a vision of God's kingdom on earth. After retreating to fundamentalist circles and institutions for several decades, a gathering in St. Louis in 1942 brought together evangelical leaders. In a group that eventually became the National Association of Evangelicals, pastors and leaders of evangelical institutions called for more engagement with American society (Executive Committee 1942). Several years later, theologian Carl F. H. Henry (1947) articulated a robust vision for social engagement by conservative Protestants. Subsequent actions and leaders built on this. For example, increasingly popular evangelical evangelist Billy Graham founded *Christianity Today* as a counter to mainline magazine *Christian Century*, and the magazine's headquarters in Washington, DC helped evangelicals engage with the country's big issues (Wacker 2014). The Jesus Movement of more charismatic and culturally engaged young Christians promoted Jesus amid the protests of the late 1960s (Eskridge 2013).

Unlike some fundamentalists, evangelicals wanted to engage society, hoping to hold to their faith and participate in discussing and addressing social issues. At the same time, the evangelical energy of the twentieth century often depended on fundamentalist values and practices (Carpenter 1997, 237). Even as they sought broader engagement with society, evangelicals privileged some issues such as abortion, prayer in school, and gay marriage (Smith 1998), in contrast to other causes evangelicals might have picked up such as anti-materialism or creation care (Swartz 2012). Evangelicals have an individualistic theology, which then affect other areas of life such as race relations and leadership by clergy (Emerson and Smith 2000) or interactions with cities and their problems (Bielo 2011a; Elisha 2011a).

In terms of organizational structure, evangelicals are not bound to other congregations, or loosely bound, even if they are within a denomination. While some large denominations are considered evangelical (such as the Southern Baptist Convention), evangelicalism has a number of smaller denominations (such as the Presbyterian Church in America or the Nazarene Church) as well as many independent congregations. The nondenominational church is often an evangelical congregation. The National Association of Evangelicals purports to represent evangelicals as a whole but the leadership of the religious tradition often falls to a collection of well-known pastors, political figures, and certain institutions and their leaders. Despite this fragmentation, evangelical congregations often have a similar routine, liturgy, lingo, and set of beliefs familiar to those within the evangelical universe.

Both suburbs and evangelicals contain complexity and variation and each has experienced change over time. Both phenomena are broad and influential enough to attract the interest of numerous scholars who continue to bring forth new arguments about their past, present, and future. Yet to this point, few scholars have examined how these two phenomena have influenced each other and how evangelicals have reckoned with and been shaped by place.

Megachurches, Critiques of Suburban Faith, Politics, and Cultural Affinities

With clearer definitions of suburbs and evangelicals, four particular manifestations of postwar evangelical faith illustrate the tight connections between evangelicals and suburbs. Each of these four examples are widely known, yet the connection between faith and places is not always made.

Megachurches

If outsiders were to connect evangelicals to any one specific place, they might pick the suburban megachurch on Sunday mornings. These supersized congregations that emerged in the decades after World War II often meet in relatively nondescript yet large buildings in suburban areas near major highways (Thumma and Travis 2007). Offering emotional energy to attendees (Wellman, Corcoran, and Stockly 2020), these structures and communities became increasingly visible in evangelical circles. While megachurches do exist and flourish in urban neighborhoods, a number of suburban megachurches have risen to national prominence.

The prominent evangelical congregation Willow Creek Community Church in South Barrington, Illinois demonstrates the convergence of suburbs, megachurches, and evangelicalism. The church started in the living room of long-time pastor Bill Hybels. The focus on growth led to a suburban campus with over 10,000 attendees each weekend, satellite congregations throughout the Chicago region, and the Willow Creek Association, which loosely ties together numerous congregations, Willow Creek became paradigmatic of the evangelical phenomenon that emerged in the United States in the late 1970s with the number of Americans identifying as "born-again," the rise of the "Moral Majority," and the emergence of evangelicals as a category. And Willow Creek has suffered some of the same problems that emerged among evangelicalism: a high-profile sex scandal involving the charismatic pastor, an emphasis on getting people in the doors but setbacks in promoting sustained spiritual growth among attendees, and critiques from other evangelicals and outsiders.

When examining this well-known megachurch, it would be a mistake to consider the congregation, its leaders, and its impacts without seriously examining its geographic location and interaction with suburban life. Start with the building. When Willow Creek sought to build a large sanctuary, Hybels said it should be constructed not following traditional architectural conventions but rather look more like a suburban office park to be more inviting to potential attendees. The church is surrounded by a large parking lot that provides room for cars pulling in off two major arterial roads and the nearby interstate. There is no steeple or bell tower. A Starbucks is located inside. The sanctuary looks like a theater (Loveland and Wheeler 2003, 127–179).

Beyond the church building, the church grew alongside the suburbs northwest of Chicago. The church is in South Barrington, Illinois, a suburb located on a corridor including Schaumburg (an edge city; see Garreau 1991) and Hoffman Estates along Interstate 90. Within a short drive are corporate headquarters and major retailers and restaurants. The suburb is small and wealthy: in 1980, the community had 1,168 residents and today has roughly 5,000 residents while the median household income is over $200,000. Subdivisions, office parks, shopping areas, and roads stretch in all directions from Willow Creek.

The style and approach of Willow Creek may not have been possible without the development of suburbs. Expanding suburban populations provided possible attendees and easy highway access allowed suburbanites from far and wide to come. The informal style of many nondenominational evangelical churches fit with the informality of middle-class suburban life. When the church moved to develop neighborhood or community-based congregations to accompany the large-scale church services and small groups promoted by the church, the venture lasted only a few years (Mundey 2009). A service based on popular-sounding worship music, charismatic preachers, and limited stuffiness appealed to middle-class suburbanites. Suburban megachurches provided myriad options for potential worshippers including a menu of weekend services and small groups and satellite locations spread throughout a metropolitan region (Wilford 2012). Social scientists have discussed the marketplace of American religion where due to the freedom of religious worship and the separation of church and state religious groups compete with each other for attendees and other resources (e.g., Finke and Stark 2005). In the suburbs with readily available cars and access to hundreds of churches within a metropolitan region, potential churchgoers can consume church or church shop just as they might a single-family home or a SUV.

Bill Hybels and other important evangelical leaders, including Rick Warren with his own influential suburban megachurch in Orange County, California, learned and implemented principles from earlier suburban megachurches like Garden Grove Community Church in Orange County. In a booming suburban area in the 1950s, pastor Robert Shuller transformed a growing drive-in church into a large church campus and television ministry with an appeal to hope, middle-class values, increasingly impressive building projects, and an imperative for ongoing growth (Mulder and Martí 2020).

In short, suburbs shape some of the leading megachurches of evangelicalism, congregations whose leaders, programs, and direction help guide a fragmented evangelical movement. As the suburbs grew, so did megachurches. The context of suburbia is woven through and through Willow Creek, Saddleback, and additional suburban congregations that anchor religious life for many suburban attendees.

Suburban Faith and Critiques

Even as megachurches flourished and an increasing number of Americans came to worship in larger congregations, not all religious practitioners applauded the suburbanization of faith. In 2017, a church planter from South Africa named Ross Lester spoke in Nashville to the Acts 29 global conference, a group of Calvinist congregations devoted to church planting. Although Lester spoke from his experiences in Johannesburg, the difficulties he encountered could come from any metropolitan area in the United States: how to bring evangelical faith to the suburbs with the suburban emphasis on "the cult of the stand-alone nuclear family unit," trying to teach about diversity, justice, and God's work in a setting aimed at comfort and homogeneity, and teaching about grace and surrender in an environment celebrating individualism and self-sufficiency. He concluded his talk saying, "The suburbs are essentially an attempt to create an alternate Kingdom. A place of peace and security here on earth. As such, it is a noble endeavor, but it does it through exclusion and not through the power of God's grace and truth" (Lester 2017). How might American evangelicals reconcile these competing interests of the suburban good life and the life of faith?

The concerns Lester expressed are not new. The mixing of the suburban American Dream and religious commitments was not confined solely to conservative Protestants. Since the blooming of mass suburbia after World

War II, numerous people of faith asked how Christian faith and the suburbs would intersect. University of Chicago ethicist Gibson Winter (1961) criticized Protestants for leaving the city. Sociologist and Catholic priest Andrew Greeley (1959) said the new suburban Catholic parishes would struggle to reconcile the competing interests of Sunday morning and the rest of the week. Sociologist and evangelical David Moberg (2007 [1972], 41) noted that evangelicals often respond to poor Black and white residents moving into neighborhoods by moving to suburbs to "avoid direct confrontation with 'those incompatible people whom it is impossible to reach with the gospel.'"

The religious fervor of the postwar era mixed with mass suburbanization in multiple important ways. Innovative congregations in booming suburban areas grew (e.g., Mulder and Martí 2020). Multiple white religious traditions moved from changing urban neighborhoods to the suburbs, including Protestants, Catholics, and Jews (McGreevy 1996; Gamm 1999; Diamond 2000; Dochuk 2003; Cutler 1996; Mulder 2015; Miller 2017b), and established new congregations. Religious groups discussed how to approach new suburban communities; should it be with comity plans that would space out mainline congregations through hierarchical planning coordinated across denominations or where any tradition or congregation could move where they desired (Diamond 2003)? More recently, religious traditions newer to the United States moved to the suburbs in increasing numbers (Numrich and Wedam 2015; Howe 2018).

The specific concerns raised about a religious suburban existence echo larger concerns evangelicals and other religious commentators have about life in the United States. Since the early 2000s, multiple evangelical authors explored how suburban Christians should act given their faith and lifestyle commitments in books with titles like *The Suburban Church, Death by Suburb, Justice in the Burbs, The Jesus of Suburbia, Suburbianity,* and *The Holy Suburbs*. My analysis of these texts (Miller 2021) shows that these authors have similar concerns: separating the suburban American Dream from Christian faith, waking up to God's action in the suburbs, thinking beyond the private and consumeristic suburban emphases, and developing Christian practices and beliefs to counter suburban life. Yet these texts struggle to fully comprehend suburban life with its emphasis on private space and exclusion while also being hindered by the lack of theological and theoretical resources within evangelicalism to engage with place.

Evangelical Politicians and Suburbs

A third example of the interaction of evangelicals and suburbs emerges from voting patterns and evangelical politicians in the United States in recent decades. When considering social change, evangelicals often desire to see evangelical leaders at the top who they then believe can influence society (Hunter 2010). Democrat Jimmy Carter, a Southern Baptist peanut farmer from small town Georgia, was elected as the first evangelical president in 1976. Carter's campaign helped bring to the forefront of American life the sizable evangelical population who mobilized around a collective identity that included being "born-again" and holding particular views about social, economic, and political life. These newly discovered voters were often said to reside in suburbs and rural areas in middle America, not in big cities. Even as Carter devoted his life to a number of causes that evangelicals could identify with—such as working with Habitat for Humanity to provide housing—evangelicals disliked his sympathies for and work with nonevangelicals and largely switched their allegiance to Ronald Reagan in the 1980 election. It was at this point that the social concerns of evangelicals came to be more associated with right-wing politics and other social concerns, such as combatting poverty or promoting peace, was relegated to a small evangelical left often linked to the Democratic Party (Swartz 2012).

While the presidents and presidential candidates after Carter appealed to evangelicals in different ways, it was not until the 2000 presidential election that another evangelical ran for the highest office in the land. George W. Bush spoke of his relationship with Jesus, his conversion to faith after a rougher young adulthood, and his personal relationship with Billy Graham. In his close victory, the suburbs played an important role. Bush eked out a close victory, in part due to suburban voters in key states. At the same time, the suburban vote, once assumed to be solidly Republican in many places, continued to tilt toward more Democratic voters, a trend that continued for subsequent election cycles (Sellers 2013).

Bush himself was the product of multiple places. He was born in New Haven, Connecticut to a family with long Connecticut political roots. He grew up in Midland and Houston, Texas with family ties to the oil industry. As an adult, he lived in a neighborhood of large single-family homes in a Dallas neighborhood north of downtown (even though it was within city limits, the neighborhood looks suburban) as well as called home a ranch northwest of Waco, Texas. In these latter locations, Bush represented the sprawling growth of Texas and the emphasis on single-family homes.

A number of the policies promoted by George W. Bush appealed to evangelicals and suburbanites. His support for business and free markets appealed to conservatives worried about government regulations. His tough stance on terrorism exemplified in invasions of Afghanistan and Iraq was attractive to evangelicals worried about global order. His promotion of international policies to aid the poor and sick, such as monetary support from the US government to fight AIDS in Africa, helped highlight evangelicals' role as "powerful internationalists" (Kristof 2008; King 2019).

Bush also emphasized suburban life through promoting homeownership and an ownership society. After September 11, 2001, Bush pushed for more homeownership opportunities for Blacks and Latinos in order to close a "homeownership gap" (Sobieraj 2002). In a 2004 speech, Bush said, "This administration will constantly strive to promote an ownership society in America. We want more people owning their own home. It is in our national interest that more people own their own home. After all, if you own your own home, you have a vital stake in the future of our country" (The White House 2003). While this emphasis on homeownership was not explicitly suburban, Bush's connection to evangelicals, residences, and promotion of homeownership connected to suburban values and ideology.

After Bush's time in office, subsequent presidential elections continued to hinge on suburban and evangelicals. For example, the election of Donald Trump in 2016 depended on high levels of evangelical support as well as suburban voters in key states (Kotkin 2016). At several points during the summer of 2020, Trump made several appeals via Twitter claiming his opponents would "abolish suburbs" (Badger and Cohn 2020). Combined with work to end federal efforts to desegregate suburban housing (Capps 2020; Shanahan 2020), Trump attempted to appeal to white suburbanites who might fear new residents of color and lower-income residents. Such suggestions fit long-term patterns of white suburbanites separating themselves from racial change and perceived crises in cities (e.g., Sugrue 1996; Kruse 2005; Gotham and Greenberg 2014).

Cultural Affinities Between Suburban Life and Evangelical Life

A fourth example of the overlap of evangelicalism and suburbs involves multiple social and cultural dimensions of suburban life and evangelical life. Just as suburbs promote private homes for families and raising children, evangelicals support nuclear families and family values (Wilcox 2009) with evangelical congregations often promoting programs for children and young adults. The evangelical emphasis on individual faith resonates with suburban preferences for single-family homes and private residences. This individualistic approach also affects how evangelical address social issues such as race (Emerson and Smith 2000) in locations that often have histories of exclusion by race and ethnicity.

The middle-class meritocracy and milieu often promoted and protected in suburbs fits with a number of evangelical practices. This includes evangelical populism (Hatch 1989, 219; Carpenter 1997, 240–242), attempting to link American and Christian values and appealing to a broad audience of people who might need Jesus while attempting to remain distinct from the broader culture. Evangelicals engage regularly with popular culture (Luhr 2009), often producing similar but different evangelical versions of cultural products. More broadly, evangelicals want to engage society even as they experience the tension of "being in the world but not of it" (Smith 1998). This populist approach also applies to strategies for social change. For evangelicals, change often begins with changed hearts of individuals and moves upward to congregations and religious groups and then broader dimensions of society (Bean 2014; Miller 2022). Rather than work through elite power structures, evangelicals often promote anti-intellectualism and pragmatic, action-oriented strategies executed by evangelical leaders to address social issues (Hunter 2010; Noll 1994).

Evangelicals have also tended to hold anti-urban sentiments since the early 1900s. This reaction to cities stems from several factors (Mulder and Smith 2009). Cities are home to a diverse population and white evangelical moved away from these changing demographics. Many large cities have had Democratic leaders in recent decades, contrasting with evangelical preferences for Republican officials and smaller or fewer units of government. Cities emphasize culture and cosmopolitanism and this clashes with evangelical preferences for family life, private spaces, and lowbrow or mass culture as opposed to highbrow culture (let alone possible objections to the content of urban cultural displays and performances). Cities can have many single-family homes but not quite in the same lower-density and private formats that many suburbs offer.

This is not to say that an evangelical lifestyle cannot be lived outside of the suburbs. Many evangelicals live in small towns or rural areas while some also live in big cities. Yet the overlap between the suburban and evangelical lifestyle is strong—perhaps too strong according to multiple evangelical critics. As evangelical author and suburbanite David Goetz (2006) says in *Death by Suburb: How to Stop the Suburbs from Killing Your Soul*, the good life of the American suburbs can lull the Christian to sleep and dull their faith.

Previous Studies of Evangelicals and Suburbs

Even as evangelicals worship in suburban megachurches, the suburbs present certain dangers to believers, evangelical and suburban voting blocs are intertwined, and evangelical and suburban day-to-day preferences overlap, relatively few studies suggest place is an important causal factor in the history of and current life of American evangelicals. Research that does link evangelicals and suburbs tends to paint with broad strokes or connect evangelicals to particular geographies and suburban locations within certain time periods.

Sociologist H. B. Cavalcanti (2007) provides an example of arguing for a broad connection between suburbs and evangelicals. He suggests that modern conservative Christians embraced the suburban lifestyle and redefined holy living. The evangelical life of today does not require sacrifice or adherence to the hard sayings of Jesus. The new vision of "the God-filled life" allows for suburban comfort while holding Christian beliefs. Even as evangelicals may affirm a marginal status in American public life—rooted in a history of working-class religion—many are firmly ensconced in comfortable suburban settings. The ability to engage in the culture wars waged since the 1980s (see Hunter 1991) provide evidence of how far suburban American evangelicals have come and the resources they can draw on.

More common are studies of particular suburban locations with concentrations of evangelicals. One such location is Orange County, California. Historians, sociologists, and political scientists have examined how Orange County faith wedded modern evangelical attitudes with an affluent Sun Belt suburban lifestyle and conservative politics. A former home to orange groves and ranches southeast of Los Angeles, the county quickly grew in population as the size of Los Angeles expanded rapidly in the mid-twentieth century (Starr 2009). The population boom brought numerous religious conservatives from other parts of the country who combined suburban life and conservative faith and then exported it to other parts of the country including the new Republican South (Dochuk 2011). In subsequent political debates and movements, these white and affluent conservative Christians exercised their power in the Christian Right and other conservative political causes (McGirr 2001).

The sprawling county with many conservative Protestants helped give rise to influential congregations and megachurches of different kinds. Into this sprawl spoke pastors like Robert Schuller, who started with a drive-in church and developed a national and global ministry at the Crystal Cathedral (Mulder and Martí 2020). Calvary Chapel in Costa Mesa helped spread the approach of the Jesus People Movement (Eskridge 2013). Schuller helped inspire Rick Warren and his work at Saddleback Church (Mulder and Martí 2020; Wilford 2012). Numerous ministries and congregations contributed to youth programs and evangelization (Luhr 2009). As more areas of the country mirrored the suburban sprawl of affluent Orange County, megachurches and suburban evangelical culture spread.

Orange County was not the only place home to a concentration of evangelicals. Scheitle, Dollhopf, and McCarthy (2017) examined clusters of evangelical parachurch organizations in Colorado Springs, Tulsa, Nashville, and Washington, DC. While these spaces included central cities, they are also sprawling Sun Belt or heartland metropolitan areas. Wheaton, Illinois is home to a leading evangelical college and numerous evangelical organizations are located nearby (Maas and Weber 1976; Stellway 1990; Call 2006. One analysis of counties in the United States highlighted "Evangelical epicenters," places with household incomes below the national average for counties and "full of young families and evangelical Christians" (Chinni and Gimpel 2010, 9). The majority of these locations are in an area bounded by Texas on the southwest, northern Missouri on the north, western North Carolina on the east, and northern Florida on the south.

Furthermore, mass postwar suburbanization included evangelical residents and congregations. Historians and sociologists provide multiple cases where conservative Protestant church attendees moved to the suburbs from urban neighborhoods, prompting their urban congregations to follow. While this did not occur instantaneously but rather happened as a process involving race, theology, and church authority (Dochuk 2003; Mulder 2015), many evangelical congregations left cities for suburbia. With growing populations in suburban areas, evangelicals relocated some congregations and founded new congregations (Eiesland 2000; Miller 2017b).

This book adds significantly to this research by expanding the analysis of evangelicals and suburbs. This includes examining a longer time period including the actions of British legislator and evangelical William Wilberforce in the late 1700s, the birth of suburbs in the United States in the mid-1800s, the start of mass suburbanization in the early 1900s, and postwar suburbia alongside the history of American evangelicalism. This book also includes analysis of multiple locations throughout the United States, including the Chicago region and evangelical centers such as Grand Rapids, Michigan; Wheaton and Carol Stream, Illinois; Orange County and suburbs east of Los Angeles in California; and Colorado Springs, Colorado. Additionally, I study the intertwining of evangelicals and suburbs in the United States as a whole with analysis of the locations of the National Association of Evangelicals, data from the General Social Survey on where religious traditions are located, and the books of Billy Graham where he discussed suburbs and places. Drawing on sociological and historical data plus incorporating qualitative and quantitative methods, I show how evangelicals came to embrace the American suburbs as their promised land.

Adding to Theories of Religion and Place

Explaining why evangelicals or other religious groups are in a particular setting, suburban or not, draws on theories of religious organization, competition, and locations. Sociologists have often applied ecological theory to explain why religious groups are located where they are. The emphasis in ecological theory is on competition between religious groups for people, resources, and land. This might be as simple as seeking cheap land on which to construct a religious building (Zelinsky and Matthews 2011, 54, 57), or multiple congregations in the same community looking to attract residents to their flock (Eiesland 2000).

Within the broader United States, the search for religious resources takes place within conditions enabling religious competition. The prohibition on a state-sponsored religion and the freedom to worship are both enumerated in the First Amendment of the Bill of Rights. These two conditions mean that religious groups compete with other religious groups or nonreligious groups for adherents. This competition prompts religious groups to innovate, to find new ways of attracting just as businesses might seek an edge or niche in markets (e.g., Finke and Stark 2005). This competition is not completely open—for example, congregations face concerns and opposition to plans for buildings and land from local residents and governments (Miller 2019; Miller 2020)—but there is room for congregations, denominations, and traditions to jockey for physical and social position. In this competitive landscape, evangelicals have competed effectively in recent decades.

Religious ecology models echo the Chicago School model of urban settlement patterns. First proposed in the 1920s, sociologist Robert Park and others (1925) argued that different actors compete for space just as organisms look for resources. Land prices drop the further the property is from the city center, providing opportunities for groups and giving rise to zones of land use. This led to the image of the Chicago area overlaid with concentric circles representing different zones of development.

This religious competition can play out in different ways in communities. Sociologist Nancy Eiesland (2000) showed how the exurban community of Dacula, Georgia changed with the introduction of new religious congregations. As the population grew, new congregations began and competed with existing religious groups. The pressure of suburbanization plus the introduction of new groups led to changes in existing congregations, a new religious landscape, and implications for community life. Or, when religious groups make proposals regarding land or buildings, communities can welcome the group or residents and leaders might present objections to the proposal or the presence of the group itself (Miller 2019; Miller 2020).

Looking across a metropolitan area, congregations within a denomination can compete with each other or with other religious groups for adherents. In the decades after World War II, historian Etan Diamond (2003) documented how a variety of religious groups made their way to the suburbs of Indianapolis. Some religious groups worked together; mainline Protestants developed comity plans where they strategically located church buildings from different denominations so that they would not compete with each other. However, other religious groups operated outside of this system and located where they could find a home and congregants. In Grand Rapids, sociologists Kevin Doughtery and Mark Mulder (2009) examined how different Christian Reformed Church congregations inside and outside the city developed different niches within the same religious tradition in an attempt to attract worshippers. In Columbus, Ohio, congregations looked for locations that would make it easy for people to attend church (Form and Dubrow 2008). Different congregations might also engage with the communities around them in different ways and for different purposes: evangelicals have started congregations in urban neighborhoods to reengage cities (Bielo 2011a), while a number of evangelical congregations embrace intentionally engaging with the communities around them (Mulder and Jonason 2017).

Missing in the religious ecology argument is an explanation for how settlement patterns, which then affect where religious congregations can and do locate, develop in the first place. The political economy or growth machine model commonly utilized in urban sociology helps explain where development takes place as well as the uneven settlement patterns present in metropolitan regions. This approach considers how production relationships are spatialized and who has rights to the city (Lefebvre 1991 [1974]), the role of labor power in cities (Castells 1979), which actors come together to promote growth—often local business and political leaders—and who benefits (Logan and Molotch 1987), and who guides urban development and how this is affected by race, class, and gender domination (Feagin 1998). In other words, development does not simply spread at an even pace from the center of a city or region according to the price of land and which actors have resources; powerful actors and capital push for development where it is advantageous for some and there are profits to be made. This disadvantages other groups who have limited access to economic and political resources.

Religious actors rarely feature in growth machines perspective even as religious congregations and denominations are often involved in civic activity, may own and control significant amounts of property, and could be influential within local groups of powerful actors. Religious congregations and groups do not pay property taxes, an annual benefit calculated by several researchers of over $26 billion (Cragun et al. 2012). However, they do often seek to contribute to their communities (Numrich and Wedam 2015). By owning land and participating in local conversations about development and land use, religious groups benefit from and help shape spatial patterns even as race, class, and gender set the conditions under which there may be space for religious gatherings in the first place.

The consistent patterns involving white religious groups and white flight in the postwar era highlight the role of race and capital in influencing the location decisions of religious groups. On the one hand, white congregations wanted to compete in growing suburban areas. On the other hand, they chose not to compete in urban neighborhoods as more Black residents moved in. The suburban religious competition was premised on long-standing patterns of racial exclusion connected to places.

To more fully explain the evangelical choices to move to, remain in, and embrace the suburbs, I add a third theory: cultural toolkits. Religious ecology's competition fits with evangelical interest in engaging society, gaining market share, and evangelism and uneven settlement patterns highlight the role of race and class in helping anchor evangelicals in suburbs. Yet examining the cultural toolkits (Swidler 1986) of evangelicals highlights the processes of meaning-making (Spillman 2020) deployed by both evangelicals and suburbanites. As noted above in the discussion of the cultural affinities between evangelicals and suburbanites, including emphases on nuclear family life and individual or private activity, evangelical and suburban meaning-making overlap significantly. The unique cultural toolkit among evangelical Christians in the United States, particularly when compared to other Christian traditions in the United States or around the world, allows evangelicals to both celebrate suburban life and downplay the importance of places for their faith.

How the evangelical cultural toolkit intersected with place, specifically suburbs, also helps make sense of the examples of megachurches, critiques of suburban faith, and evangelical voting patterns. When presented with "unsettled times" (Swidler 1986) that included changing American settlement patterns, social and political change, and internal issues among conservative Protestants, evangelicals made choices that aligned with suburban ideals and ways of life. In the postwar era of prosperity and growing populations, megachurches built on large properties and near major roads provided a path through which to reach many new suburbanites. The model of the neighborhood church may have already been on the way out, but megachurches provided a way to proclaim the spoken Gospel efficiently and impressively. While critics suggested suburban faith was shallow and abandoned cities, evangelicals chose not to stay in or return to cities where they had numerous established churches and ministries. Rather, evangelicals made decisions to leave for suburbia and the ways of life that involved. Finally, the coalescing of evangelicals behind a politically conservative agenda in the late 1970s included turning against other political options that would have highlighted urban and/or particular societal concerns. Within the battles between the two major political parties over suburban voters, conservative Protestants felt well-positioned given suburban and evangelical emphases on family life, safety, and local government and choices.

Religious competition and innovation, the manifestation of economic and social capital and power in geographies and places, and evangelicals deploying their particular cultural and theological toolkit all matter for understanding the evangelical embrace of suburbs. Evangelicals in the suburbs, in their engagement with society at large and communities at the local level, both are the result of and contribute to spatialized social and religious patterns.

Conclusion

Reflecting in 2005 on the influential text on American fundamentalism he had authored in 1980, historian George Marsden highlighted several themes from the decades after the initial release. Marsden (2006, 254) noted how conservative Protestant teaching could coincide with self-fulfillment ideologies in the United States. In commenting on "perplexing mixes of the spiritual and the materialistic," Marsden said, "it is usually assumed, and sometimes advertised, that the comforts of the suburbs, ability to vacation in exotic places, and economic security may well be added benefits of 'Seeking first the kingdom of God.'" In the early twenty-first century, Marsden suggests the mixing of suburbanization and evangelicalism was an established part of American life.

Over the course of multiple decades, evangelicals sanctified the American suburbs by settling into them as individuals, congregations, and organizations and embracing their practices and logics. This evangelical embrace of the suburbs affected numerous social institutions, including higher education. When colleague Ben Norquist and I (2021) examined the locations of the governing members of the Council for Christian Colleges & Universities (CCCU), we found that many of the schools, just over 43% of the 111 institutions, were located in suburbs. In terms of regions, more CCCU institutions are located in the South and Midwest. The evangelical presence in numerous colleges located outside the biggest cities, a limited presence in and around some of the biggest cities, like New York City, and multiple colleges in or around smaller big cities, influences how evangelicals can engage with and exert influence in American society.

One case in our data helps illustrate the argument of this book. The commemorative book *Biola University: Rooted for One Hundred Years* (Biola University 2007) details the story of an influential Los Angeles religious school that turned to the suburbs. Biola, the Bible Institute of Los Angeles, was founded in 1908 in the growing city of Los Angeles. At Biola's founding, Los Angeles was growing rapidly: with a population of just over 11,000 in 1880, the city grew to over 319,000 residents in 1910. The main funder of the school's founding, Lyman Stewart, also helped fund the publication of *The Fundamentals*, a foundational text of essays for the fundamentalist movement (Neumann 2019). The Bible Institute expanded in subsequent decades, moving to four-year degrees and adding a seminary, as Los Angeles grew to nearly two million people in 1950.

But like many residents of the region, the college too decided to move to the suburbs. The commemorative book describes multiple reasons for the move: "But to become the bold and vibrant college its leaders envisioned, Biola needed more room to expand ... Both the city congestion and the pollution were among the deciding factors of Biola's move towards a calmer, cleaner suburban city" (Biola University 2007, 69). In 1957, the school broke ground in La Mirada and the school opened in the suburban location in 1959. La Mirada was not just any suburban community. Roughly 20 miles southeast of Los Angeles, the land was originally a ranch that produced olive oil, lemons, and grapefruit. The property was sold several times after World War II and by 1956 was a planned community with nearly 8,000 homes (City of La Mirada 2020). In one move, Biola moved from a booming and sprawling city to a master-planned suburban community. A recent Biola web page for students (Biola University 2019) highlights some of the features of their home suburb: "A recent CNN/Money Magazine poll on the "Best Places to Live" ranked La Mirada third in California and 34th in the nation. La Mirada has one of the lowest crime rates in the region and remains one of the safest cities in L.A. County."

While Biola University lists its own reasons for moving from its vibrant ministry in Los Angeles to the new and rapidly expanding suburbs, how widespread was interest among evangelicals in moving to the suburbs? Did Biola make a singular decision, or was it part of a broader pattern after World War II? The next chapter reviews the history of evangelicals and suburbs, starting with ideology about cities and morals in late eighteenth-century London and advancing the twin histories of evangelicals and suburbs into the early twenty-first century.

2
Evangelicals and Suburbs
A Short History

The 2008 book *The Suburban Church: Practical Advice for Authentic Ministry* includes a foreword by Leith Anderson, suburban megachurch pastor and then president of the National Association of Evangelicals. Leading into his discussion of the importance of suburbs for evangelical ministry, Anderson begins with the example of Jesus visiting Bethany:

> Bethany was Jesus' favorite suburb. He often commuted the 1.8 miles into the city of Jerusalem where much of his ministry took place. Bethany was home to three of his best friends—Mary, Martha, and Lazarus. Jesus ate there, slept there, and performed his top miracle in Bethany when he brought Lazarus out of the grave alive. (DeKruyter and Schultze 2008, ix)

This is an example of the evangelical practice of connecting Biblical texts to modern realities. Bethany was certainly close to Jerusalem. The *Dictionary of Jesus and the Gospels* suggests Bethany was three kilometers east of Jerusalem near the Mount of Olives (Green, Brown, and Perrin 2013, 52–53). In addition to his interactions with Mary, Martha, and Lazarus, Jesus had other important experiences in Bethany including Martha's concern with her sister Mary paying more attention to Jesus than the meal preparation, Jesus having a meal in Simon the Leper's home, and Mary anointing Jesus's feet with oil (Nesbitt 1961). In an era before engines, Bethany was within the orbit of Jerusalem.

Yet viewing Bethany as a suburb of Jerusalem risks taking an anachronistic approach to the small community and the scale of cities and their regions two millenniums ago. By today's popular understanding of suburbs, the proximity of Bethany to Jerusalem would warrant calling it a suburb. The people of Bethany could easily walk or travel to Jerusalem. Jerusalem was a notable city in Palestine due to its economic, symbolic, religious, and political activity. But the big city nearby was modest by today's reckoning; Green et al. (2013, 408) say the city had a population of 25,000–80,000, with significant population increases during festival times. Did Jesus regularly commute? Did the people of Bethany consider themselves as living in a bedroom suburb? Did life in Bethany offer the best of city and rural life in a location between both? Did Bethany residents prize their private single-family homes while Jerusalem residents lived in more dense, multifamily dwellings? Did Jerusalem have the kind of urban problems the residents of Bethany did not wish to deal with?

As Anderson links Jesus's ministry with contemporary manifestations of suburbs in the United States (with a final adage in the foreword of "as the suburbs go, so goes the nation"; see DeKruyter and Schultze 2008, xiv), he highlights a feature of many cities in human history: they often had small communities surrounding the denser population center. Sometimes these communities were just outside city walls, while others were a short travel away. However, the suburbs as known today in the United States are a unique phenomenon with a particular history and development path. Furthermore, American evangelicals have a specific trajectory over time and this involved living in, interacting with, and influencing different kinds of places.

This chapter places two histories side by side: the rise of suburbs and suburbanization in the United States and the story of evangelical Protestants in the United States. This overview includes the interaction of evangelicals with places as well as the numerous significant social forces that shaped suburbs and evangelicalism: urbanization, industrialization, migration patterns, changing transportation technologies, emerging cultural ideologies regarding single-family homes, racial attitudes, and debates about how religious groups should engage with society. The outcome of these conjoined historical processes is that within a country with a long strain of antipathy toward cities (e.g., Conn 2014; Macek 2006), evangelicals fully embraced suburbs and disassociated themselves from large cities (Conn 1994; Mulder and Smith 2009). American evangelicals emerged from wrestling with these historical and social forces and embraced the suburbs in ways that influenced evangelical life.

The Emergence of American Cities and Suburban Retreats

In the first two centuries of European settlement in the United States, American cities were relatively small places compared to cities of the early twenty-first century (Monkkonen 1988). Even as late as the early decades of the 1800s, residents could walk across the largest American cities in just an hour or two (Jackson 1985). Denser population centers emerged in the Northeast and mid-Atlantic and not the South, with its greater emphasis on an agrarian economy and commitment to slavery.

New cities in North America were centers of worship, government, markets, and protection. When Puritan leader John Winthrop considered what would happen if members of the Massachusetts Bay Colony followed God, he said, "we shall be as a city on a hill." A Puritan vision of a joined civil and ecclesial union through local communities and government competed with other conceptions of how communities and religious bodies should interact (Conn 1994, 32). In contrast to the Puritan vision, the Dutch founded New Amsterdam as an economic center that encouraged religious pluralism (Burrows and Wallace 1999).

Suburbs in the United States have their roots in English plans for communities outside burgeoning cities. Transformed by the Industrial Revolution, rapid and massive changes in English cities helped give rise to small communities within a short distance of major economic and industrial centers like London and Manchester. Wealthy landowners constructed country villas where they could retreat from urban life yet stay connected to urban life. These country homes could be elaborate and broadcast the status of their owners (Archer 2005).

These English patterns had deeper roots. In the Roman Empire, those with means and status could access country villas. In times of plagues and unrest, the wealthy could flee to the country. Sociologist Rodney Stark (1996) suggests that when Christians in the Roman Empire stayed in cities and cared for others in times of sickness rather than just caring for their own or leaving cities, this marked them as different and helped boost interest in their way of life. For centuries, rulers and the wealthy continued to have country estates. As an example, King Louis XVI of France developed Versailles as a property with extensive lavish dwellings and gardens in what now could be considered a suburb of the burgeoning city of Paris.

Some historians trace the roots of American evangelicalism to English religious movements that emerged roughly at the same time as urbanization and small suburban settlements. These evangelicals were noted for their public activity and particular causes, their anti-Catholicism, and their standing as a group in the Church of England (Bebbington 1989; Noll 2003; Larsen 2007; Kidd 2019). The life of William Wilberforce helps illustrate the growing interest in suburbs and religious motivations for settling in them. Wilberforce was elected as a Member of Parliament at 21 years old in 1780. As a young legislator, Wilberforce enjoyed making connections with other leaders, building on an existing friendship with future prime minister William Pitt, and a lively social life that included gambling. In 1785, Wilberforce converted to a more evangelical faith and these convictions shaped his subsequent political and public activity. Revered today in evangelical circles for his decades-long opposition to slavery, Wilberforce pursued other concerns as well, including proper "manners" that could support an evangelical understanding of good and evil within society (Fishman 1987; Tomkins 2010; Stott 2012).

This new understanding of faith had consequences for where Wilberforce lived and spent his time (Fishman 1987; Tomkins 2010; Stott 2012). Wilberforce believed the city and its various vices were dangerous for women and that women should run the domestic household. This contributed to Wilberforce and others joining in the move of wealthier English to the outskirts of cities. In the 1790s, one of Wilberforce's friends, Henry Thornton, constructed a home for his family and provided a vision of a community built around Wilberforce and their common causes. By 1800, Clapham, roughly five miles southwest of London, was home to dozens of wealthy evangelical families who lived in homes around an improved common. The husbands traveled regularly to London to conduct business and the women and children could be safe and attend to the domestic sphere in the new community. As a growing suburban community with a concentration of religious residents, Clapham served as a physical center for an interlocking set of relationships and activity motivated by evangelical Anglican faith. Historian Robert Fishman (1987, 53) describes how evangelicals viewed the new arrangement:

> A location like Clapham gave them the ability to take the family out of London without taking leave of the family business. Equally importantly, it provided a whole community people who shared their values ... The Evangelicals never tired of repeating that, if all urban social life must be rejected, the truly godly recreations were family life and direct contact with nature. (Fishman 1987, 53)

Additionally, single-family homes allowed for familial religious practices in common spaces and bedrooms for each household member allowed for private religious activity (Tosh 1999, 36–38).

This way of life spread quickly in England and found its way across the Atlantic into the growing American colonies. Those with money and land could develop villas and estates. For those with more modest means, the ideal of a humble cottage in the woods spread. While this home might have few rooms and relatively few amenities, it could sit on a plot of land close to nature and away from other dwellings. With less stated emphasis on social class compared to the English, Americans could idealize the frontier and individualism. The private home away from others yet within a short journey to resources and/or amenities had particular appeal.

As American cities grew and faster transportation emerged, single-family homes outside the city became more desirable, possible, and profitable (Archer 2005; Hayden 2003). In addition to the growing support for putting distance between developing cities and residences, changing transportation technologies from the third decade of the 1800s onward helped alter the form and size of cities. The development of railroads enabled residents and goods to travel longer distances at higher rates of speed.

American Protestantism developed as cities and suburbs emerged. Different Protestant strands emerged in different colonies and states yet coalesced over time to create a narrative of a Christian nation, albeit one where evangelicals could engage in sharp disagreements such as over slavery (Kidd 2019; Whitehead and Perry 2020). Relatively few residents attended church regularly (Finke and Stark 2005). The First and Second Great Awakening, the first in the 1730s to the 1750s and the second from 1800 to 1830, affected American cities and rural areas as thousands responded to Protestant calls for revival and repentance (Conn 1994, 33–40; Noll 2019). Denominations and congregations spread into new lands and growing population centers required more assemblies.

Growing American Urbanism and Religious Fundamentalism and Modernism

After the Civil War, American cities grew at a tremendous pace. Established cities like New York continued to grow through immigration and annexation. New York attracted Irish, German, Italian, and Jewish immigrants.

When New York City annexed Brooklyn in the 1890s, then the third largest city in the United States, it firmly established itself as the biggest American city. New frontier cities also grew quickly; St. Louis boomed in the 1820s, Chicago boomed from the 1850s onward, undeterred by a major fire, and San Francisco became a sizable American city on the Pacific. Cities grew within their expanding boundaries and expanded their reach across regions. For example, commodities and resources flowed to Chicago via railroad and water to contribute to a booming metropolis and region (Cronon 1991).

Railroads connected the entire country plus linked city centers to suburban hinterlands, making suburban land more valuable. Horse-drawn streetcars followed by electric streetcars enabled development to fill in between railroad lines and at higher densities (e.g., Warner 1978; Keating 2005). Developers saw opportunities to purchase land and sell it along transportation lines that offered easy access to urban centers (Keating 2002). New suburban communities emerged as did subdivided residential lots with access to city centers in under an hour. Industrial suburbs, like East St. Louis, Illinois, or Gary, Indiana, provided cheap industrial land and thousands of jobs for residents (Taylor 1915).

In the same period, the frontier continued to expand. After California was admitted as a state prior to the Civil War, white settlers streamed westward, indigenous groups were forcibly confined to small areas, and new states emerged. With this expansion came the idea that true morality and faith were contained by farmers and rural residents—harkening back to Thomas Jefferson's pastoral ideal—while cities were centers of vice and sin (Mendieta 2009). New cities were also founded, some free of the models of big cities in the Northeast and Midwest. New cities in the South, such as Atlanta, grew and attracted residents and commerce. As a different example, Los Angeles offered a new path forward: "The white, middle-class, midwestern protestants who wrested Los Angeles from its original settlers had the opportunity to create the kind of city that they believed represented the hopes and dreams of people like themselves" (Marsh 1990, 165).

As cities grew, so did the number of suburban residents. By the end of the nineteenth century, fewer suburban residents desired that their community be annexed into the big city. By then, smaller communities could be more easily provide their own municipal services such as water and electricity. Municipal boundaries in numerous Northeast and Midwestern cities became relatively fixed (Rusk 2013). Expanding suburban regions started to envelop what had once been small towns or rural areas just a few decades before. The final decades of the 1800s gave rise to a number of paradigmatic suburbs, such as Riverside, Illinois, which featured single-family homes on winding streets and among nature but within a short trip to the city.

In big cities, downtown commercial interests pushed out religious buildings and activity to different neighborhoods. Whereas English communities and early American communities often contained religious and government activities in their centers, American cities centered their central physical and social spaces on economic activity. In Chicago, churches moved to quieter residential locations to be closer to their attendees as well as escape the land prices and noise of downtown life (Lowe 2010). Urban religious life boomed with existing congregations adapting to changing conditions and new immigrant groups starting new congregations and providing anchors for urban enclaves: Catholics, from Ireland, Italy, Poland, and elsewhere, attended newly formed urban parishes and established practices leading to national parishes where specific Catholic churches became home to Catholics hailing from different countries; Jews, from eastern Europe and Russia, started synagogues in major cities; Protestants of different kinds, both formal denominations and independent traditions, spread out across American cities.

The growth of American cities coincided with sizable religious shifts in the American landscape. Even with the acknowledgment that cities could be centers of vice, religious congregations and organizations in big cities encouraged residents and communities toward religious belief and practice. Important fundamentalists and revivalists of the late nineteenth century operated out of Northeastern cities: "While fundamentalism has been called a 'Bible Belt' phenomenon of the South and Midwest, its origins and organizational centers were in the cities of the northeastern quadrant, from Chicago and St. Louis to Philadelphia and Boston" (Carpenter 1997, 6). New evangelical organizations providing for both physical and spiritual needs formed in big cities (Magnuson 1977). The Salvation Army cared for the poor, shared the gospel, and sought the attention of the public in big cities like New York (Winston 1999). A national Sunday School movement emerged in cities to help teach Christian virtue, civic responsibility, and middle-class norms (Conn 1994, 39).

At the same time, certain religious denominations, now considered mainline Protestant groups, embraced science, downplayed miracles, and advocated for social activism to address the growing issues of urban centers. The idea of natural selection and evolution—formally argued by Charles

Darwin in *The Origin of Species* in 1856 and quickly supported by other scientists and thinkers—swept through cities and society. Some religiously motivated actors, ranging from Walter Rauschenbach to Jane Addams, promoted solving urban issues and furthering humanity's progress. Higher criticism and applying the scientific method to biblical texts and narratives threatened the primary source of authority for evangelicals (Marsden 2006, 17–21). Providing an explanation for human development and achievement alongside or in opposition to religious and supernatural explanations, the new ideas led to conflict. Cities were home to scientific and social progress while "fundamentalists seemed to be trying to recreate the religious culture of earlier small-town America, where people of different classes had extensive contact" (Carpenter 1997, 10). Cities could appear to offer the best of humanism and progress while religion could seem like it was suited for previous, less urbanized, eras.

By the early 1900s, this conflict led to a split between religious modernism and religious fundamentalism in the United States. Fundamentalists returned to what they considered fundamental doctrines including the inerrancy of the Bible and a need for individual conversion (Sutton 2014; Carpenter 1997). These convictions could lead to supporting some social causes, such as opposition to alcohol, and not others, such as lynching (Kidd 2019, 62–66). Evangelical leaders like Dwight Moody, a religious leader in Chicago who founded Moody Bible Institute in the same city, and Billy Sunday, baseball player turned prominent preacher, called for Americans to turn to God amidst technological achievements and a rapidly changing society. Moody was ambivalent about cities over the course of his career; after leading successful urban revivals, he later spoke disparagingly of cities. Sunday spent more time in smaller cities (Conn 1994, 60–61, 73). In his work, Sunday's focus on "individual virtue" could help evangelicals not focus on societal conditions contributing to problems in cities (Morgan 2002, 49–50). The approaches and practices of fundamentalists, often based in the Northeast and Midwest, spread to the South and West (Hummel 2023).

After the outcome of the Scopes Monkey Trial in 1925—a court case regarding teaching evolution conducted in small town Tennessee that was a legal victory for fundamentalists but a cultural victory for modernists—the two sides appeared split by beliefs and practices as well as geographies. Conservative Protestantism had moved from mainstream American society to alienated outsiders over the course of half a century (Marsden 2006, x). Fundamentalists were identified as living in more rural areas and modernists in more urban areas. The lines were not entirely clear-cut; numerous fundamentalist Bible schools and seminaries were located in big cities (Carpenter 1997, 17–20), but cities were no longer viewed as the best keepers of a conservative Protestant tradition.

Urbanization and the start of suburbanization affected men and women differently. Marsh (1990, 8) found that women focused on domesticity as embodied by the family, which "offered an alternative to the conflict and competition of the marketplace economy." Initially considered possible in all sorts of settings, including in the rapidly changing city, women by the end of the 1800s increasingly tied domesticity to the physical setting of suburbia. In contrast, men focused on homeownership in the suburbs as a means to "preserve the republican dream of a nation governed by small property owners" (Marsh 1990, 2). After several decades in practice, these gendered experiences came together to form "suburban familism" (Marsh 1990, 16). This gendered vision became part of a later linking of the growing suburbs with heavenly or sacred experiences (Hayden 2003, 6–8).

For those who could access them, the suburbs provided an escape from the rapid urban change of the preceding decades and built on the American ideals of private property ownership. Periods of economic prosperity, including the 1920s, and increasing access to automobiles, helped suburbs expand. This was not quite mass suburbia yet; some suburbanites still constructed their own homes and used the suburban yard for growing food (Nicolaides 2002). Additionally, the number of large builders was limited. Some suburbanites were fleeing the other. This included immigrants who poured into American cities (the Immigration Act of 1924 then slowed immigration for decades), including the concerning numbers of immigrant Catholics (Bendroth 2005, 5) and the hundreds of thousands of Black migrants who moved North seeking jobs and housing in the Great Migration (Hirsch 1983; Wilkerson 2010). White leaders and residents restricted nonwhites, including Black people, Jews, Chinese residents, and others, from suburban communities and denied them opportunities to buy homes (Glotzer 2020). This led to the formation of some minority suburbs (Wiese 2004).

Historian Margaret Bendroth (2005) shows the complexities of evangelical Protestant life in Boston from the 1880s through the 1940s. The experiences of "militant evangelicalism" included conflict with Boston leaders after three prominent pastors were arrested in Boston Common in early 1885 and multiple urban revivals, including those led by Billy Sunday and Billy Graham, that ended up in "an increasingly generalized attachment to Boston, less as a place and more as a symbolic launching site for world wide revival" (Bendroth 2005, 8). Yet even with all of the activity in the city and the durability of evangelical institutions in Boston, "they resisted the pull of the suburbs for only so long" (Bendroth 2005, 189), and Catholic institutions and life dominated the city. The opportunities cities could provide evangelicals, such as access to large populations for evangelical missions, were not enough to stop the move to suburbs.

Postwar Suburban and Evangelical Growth Through the Early 1960s

The mass suburbanization that took place after World War II occurred due to multiple factors. The United States had over a decade and a half of pent-up demand for housing due to limited construction during the Great Depression and World War II, plus an expanding population with the emergence of the baby boomer generation after the war. The federal government promoted homeownership with changed mortgage guidelines during the Great Depression and cheaper mortgages for returning veterans. Additionally, starting in the 1950s, the federal government provided billions of dollars for a national system of interstates that connected cities but also provided suburbanites quick driving access to urban cores. Builders and developers operated at a larger scale; prewar building was often conducted by small-scale operators, while postwar construction could happen thousands of homes at a time in places like Levittown, New York and Lakewood, California. Postwar prosperity enabled more people to purchase homes and goods for them. This expansion of mass consumerism helped define a middle-class suburban lifestyle with particular amenities. Increasing populations of Black residents as well as residents of other racial and ethnic minority groups prompted increased levels of white flight as many whites left for suburban locales that limited Black, Asian, Mexican, Jewish, and other minority residents from living there. The mass exodus of white residents pulled jobs and resources to the suburbs, isolating poor urban neighborhoods. Due to these changes, suburbs outside older cities in the Northeast and Midwest expanded, as did new suburbs outside growing cities in the South and West. During the 1960s, the percentage of Americans living in suburbs first surpassed that of those living in cities. A number of cities, particularly in the Northeast and Midwest, started to experience population decline (Jackson 1985; Fishman 1987; Wilson 1996; Hayden 2003; Archer 2005).

Several traits marked the newly booming suburbs. The single-family home was no longer a "cottage in the woods" but often a mass-produced structure within a subdivision of similar looking homes at similar price points. The balloon-frame homes could be constructed quickly by larger developers and builders who could erect dozens or hundreds of homes within months. Zoning, a local government prerogative developed in cities in the early 1900s to separate land uses, protected single-family homes from perceived threats (Hirt 2014). Limited regional cooperation in planning privileged local interests in various suburbs over metropolitan needs (Gottdiener 1977). With suburban expansion taking place between railroad and streetcar lines (which rapidly disappeared), residents needed cars for commuting to work and accessing other regular sites. This reliance on cars gave rise to features of life that quickly became normal: commuting longer distances, fast food, shopping malls, and development structured around major highways and roadways. Local social life revolved around children and helping them succeed. Communities were largely white, middle- or upper-class, and patriarchal (Seeley, Sim, and Loosely 1956; Gans 1967). Working-class suburbs existed as places where even auto workers could feel they had achieved success (Berger 1960). Racial and ethnic minorities still had limited access to suburban communities due to a system of laws, regulations, and community-level practices (Rothstein 2017; Kushner 2009).

Multiple forms of mass media, including novels, films, television, and poems, depicted the expanding suburbs and life therein. This regularly included images of nuclear families in single-family homes facing everyday issues or encountering problems that threatened the happy façade of suburban life (e.g., Haralovich 1992; Beuka 2004; Jurca 2001; Spigel 2001; Gill 2013; Huq 2013; Coon 2014; Vermeulen 2014; Rowley 2015; Miller 2017a). These displays helped highlight the role of women in mass suburbs. In many of these narratives suburban women stayed at home, helped their husbands and children, and had limited power and influence. In contrast, men worked outside the home providing for their families, and children attended school and engaged in local hijinks. Such depictions could match rhetoric from conservative Protestants who, amid fears of communism and an immoral American culture, extolled the virtues of the Christian nuclear family life in growing suburbia (Neumann 2019).

These depictions did not always accurately reflect women in suburbia, who often worked and exercised agency as they tackled personal, familial, and community concerns. In response to the tension that women often felt between idealized suburban roles and lived realities, Betty Friedan (1963) helped launch the modern feminist movement from the suburbs of Long Island. Based on her own experiences and conversations with suburban women, she described the ways the suburbs and their proscribed gender roles did not fulfill women. The domesticity of women had shifted as conditions changed, including an increasing number of suburban women working and suburbia becoming less homogenized (Marsh 1990, 182–189). Evangelical women could work yet still articulate the larger importance of maintaining certain gender roles and family structures, oppose feminism, and give birth to and raise children (Gallagher 2003; McGowin 2018). Even fundamentalist women pursued work outside the home in order to enable purchasing a home in the suburbs (Ammerman 1987, 207).

This period of mass suburbanization happened at the same time as an increase in religious activity and affiliation in the United States. From 1945 through 1960, church attendance rose (Finke and Stark 2005). Civil religion was encoded further in the 1950s and 1960s with the addition of "under God" to the Pledge of Allegiance and "In God We Trust" on currency as well as references to God in presidential speeches (Bellah 1967). American religious faith and its connections to capitalism and democracy were clearly contrasted with communism, which was perceived to threaten it at a global scale. Evangelicals contributed to these efforts in sponsoring a "Declaration of Seven Divine Freedoms" signed by President Eisenhower and Vice President Nixon in 1953 (Sutton 2014, 324), highlighting the kind of Christian nationalism evangelicals would promote strongly in subsequent decades (Whitehead and Perry 2020). In 1955, scholar Will Herberg (1955) described a "triple melting pot" of Protestants, Catholics, and Jews with Protestants as the largest religious constituency. The increased religious fervor and suburbanization contributed to a religious building boom with the architectural styles of the new buildings ranging from traditional forms to modernist structures (Price 2013).

This was also a time of significant changes among conservative Protestants. Emerging from a fundamentalist withdrawal from society, the National Association of Evangelicals formed in the early 1940s as an effort to collectively represent the concerns of evangelicals and engage with particular social issues (National Association of Evangelicals 1942). Not all conservative Protestants were interested in such social engagement. Fundamentalists, represented by Carl McIntire who stressed separatism, and the "neo-evangelicals," represented by Boston pastor Harold Ockenga who desired engagement, sparred over a series of theological and social concerns. The two sides split by the late 1950s with a détente not coming for several decades (Marsden 1987). The "revivalist individualism" of fundamentalists, emphasizing personal salvation leading to social reform (Carpenter 1997, 118), undergirded approaches to suburban life.

Evangelist Billy Graham illustrated these tendencies. He learned his craft in the suburbs at Wheaton College outside of Chicago and in his first role as a suburban pastor. Even as he rose to prominence with notable crusades in cities like Los Angeles (1949) and New York City (1957), Graham presented an attractive image of a revived evangelicalism focused on addressing societal needs through personal salvation (Miller 2022). At the same time, evangelicals showed limited appetite for addressing certain societal concerns or changing structural conditions (Moberg 2007 [1972]). In particular, evangelicals resisted addressing structural racism and inequalities (Emerson and Smith 2000; Butler 2021). Evangelist Tom Skinner (1970), speaking at the 1970 Urbana conference for evangelical college students, described the consequences of the evangelical temerity toward civil rights this way: "Make no bones about it: the difficulty in coming to grips with the evangelical message of Jesus Christ in the black community is the fact that most evangelicals in this country who say that Christ is the answer will also go back to their suburban communities and vote for law-and-order candidates who will keep the system the way it is."

Multiple American religious groups adjusted to suburban contexts as both adherents and congregations moved to or were founded in suburbs. Even with an emphasis on consecrated altars at existing urban parishes, Catholics left cities for new suburban parishes, leaving behind urban parishes that served new populations (Gamm 1999; McGreevy 1996). More mobile because of congregations' anchoring to the Torah, Jews moved to suburban neighborhoods (Gamm 1999; Cutler 1996). As they gained broader acceptance in American society, success was also measured by living in the suburbs. Historian Etan Diamond (2000, 66) found particular adaptations to their new context: "the development of the congregation as social center; the bureaucraticization of the synagogue; the introduction of middle-class styles of decorous worship; and the construction of architecturally modern sanctuaries." Jewish residents in cities were some of the few leaving cities that sold homes and religious buildings to Black residents.

Congregations in numerous Protestant denominations moved to the suburbs (Miller 2017b), though their experiences could vary. Christian Reformed Church congregations, used to a tight-knit connection between a local congregation and religious school, moved out of the south side of Chicago to white suburbs while similar groups tied to more hierarchical denominations took a bit longer to reach the suburbs. Efforts at the denominational level to retain churches and missions in the city did not gain much purchase from rank-and-file members or individual congregations (Mulder 2015). It could take time for congregations to move to the suburbs, even after large numbers of members had made the move. The Highland Park Baptist congregation in Detroit debated the move for years and needed theological justification for leaving their city location (Dochuk 2003).

Different religious groups approached the task of finding suburban locations in varied ways. Mainline Protestants pursued joint plans to space out congregations with the idea that their different denominations did not want to directly compete and could offer attendees similar features. On the other hand, conservative and independent Protestants allowed congregations to make their own choices. These moves and foundings helped transform metropolitan religious landscapes (Diamond 2003). Existing suburban communities could contain congregations already active for decades as well as numerous new congregations in the same or different traditions that offered both old and new residents new options.

Evangelicals appeared to have few problems in adapting to suburban contexts. Compared to rural and urban contexts, suburbs offered opportunities for growth and success (O'Brien 2019, 143). Racially segregated suburbs provided space to celebrate and protect the nuclear family with the particular power structure of family relationships reinforcing evangelical understandings of society at large (Bjork-James 2021, 137). Evangelical congregations and ideology developed in new areas where Americans were moving. For example, Orange County, California, became home to residents from across the country, particularly the traditional Bible Belt. This presented new opportunities for innovative evangelical leaders (Dochuk 2011; Mulder and Martí 2020). Urban congregations experienced members moving to the suburbs and deliberated on whether and/or when to join them before often doing so (Dochuk 2003; Mulder 2015). Congregations in different evangelical denominations closed urban churches and started new suburban churches over the course of several decades (Miller 2017b). Multiple influential suburban evangelical institutions that exemplified the neo-evangelical emergence—including Fuller Seminary, Wheaton College, Gordon College, Trinity Evangelical Divinity School, and Biola College—helped shape the growing evangelical movement by educating students, training pastors and leaders, and providing centers for evangelical thought and action.

The religious move to the suburbs did not go without comment or concern from those interested in religion. The demographic shift presented both opportunities and challenges. Denominations and independent religious groups built new buildings, reached new populations, and developed plans amongst themselves or worked independently to operate in the new context (Douglass 1925; Diamond 2003). However, critics suggested a suburban context refocused religious attention in less than helpful ways, such as diverting attention from pressing urban issues as Protestants fled cities (Winter 1961) or lulling suburbanites into a cocoon of pleasant consumerism with little need for faith (Greeley 1959). These "suburban jeremiads" lamented what was lost in suburban faith even as religion as a whole in the United States was booming (Hudnut-Beumler 1994).

Ending the Twentieth Century and Entering the Twenty-First Century

Following postwar prosperity, growing suburbs, and increasing religious fervor, the mid-1960s signaled a shift in religious life. Religious attendance stopped growing by the late 1960s, theologian Harvey Cox published the bestseller *The Secular City* in 1965, and a famous 1965 *Time* cover asked, "Is God Dead?" While evangelicalism grew in some ways, such as through the emergence of "Jesus People" in California's growing suburbs (Eskridge 2013) and the emergence of influential megachurches, it also changed in significant ways.

Historians and social scientists (e.g., Noll, Bebbington, and Marsden 2019) mark 1976 as a critical year for evangelical emerging as a collective on the American scene. With successful presidential candidate Jimmy Carter, a Southern Baptist Democrat from Georgia, and the pronouncement from pollster George Gallup that it was "the year of the evangelical" (Woodward 1976), evangelicals appeared as a unified and potentially powerful group. In the following years, many evangelicals would sour on Carter and by 1980 evangelicals became associated with more conservative politics. Evangelicals rallied with the "Moral Majority," the Republican Party, and a host of Christians turned political leaders like Jerry Falwell, James Dobson, and Pat Robertson while pushing away more progressive or left-leaning evangelical options (Swartz 2012). Evangelicals took advantage of a shift toward parachurch religious groups (Wuthnow 1988) to found many important evangelical organizations addressing particular political issues, promoting missions and evangelism, and providing alternatives to secular institutions. Evangelicals actively engaged American society and politics and did so confidently, if not combatively. This included supporting particular political candidates, such as evangelical presidential candidate George W. Bush, with the idea that having moral leaders in key positions would lead to social change (Hunter 2010). Additionally, evangelicals advocated for certain positions regarding social and cultural issues such as with abortion, gay marriage, and prayer in schools (Smith 1998).

In the final decades of the twentieth century, Southerners became more incorporated in evangelicalism as a larger collective. Prompted in part by a shift in politics, including Nixon's "southern strategy" and a more vocal evangelical conservatism plus a doubling down on racism and segregationism (Lassiter 2006; Butler 2021), this represented a shift away from antipathy toward Northerners and separatist impulses in the immediate aftermath of World War II. This coincided with the tremendous suburban growth in the Sun Belt, ranging roughly from Virginia to Texas, and the West. Sun Belt cities grew rapidly: in 1950, Houston was the largest Sun Belt city and was the fourteenth largest city in the United States. According to the 2020 Census, Houston ranked as the fourth largest city in the United States, Phoenix was fifth, San Antonio was seventh, and Dallas was ninth. "Regional boosterism, the mobilization of capital, and the transformation of American religion" helped evangelicalism grow in Sun Belt communities (Atkins 2019, 229). Suburban evangelicals in Texas coalesced in opposition to perceived liberal causes (Sandul 2019, 8) while evangelical congregations could reflect regional interests, such as the cowboy churches in the Texas suburbs that featured a seeker-sensitive approach appealing to rural life (McAdams 2019). Additionally, millions of Southerners moved to other parts of the United States (Marsden 2006, 236–239). This geographical mobility could be influential in particular places, such as Southern California, where evangelical activity and conservative political fervor combined in the postwar decades (McGirr 2001; Dochuk 2011; Mulder and Martí 2020). Finally, fundamentalists both found a home in suburbia and had an improving relationship with evangelicals (Ammerman 1987).

By the turn of the millennium, the United States was firmly established as a suburban country. Even as American big cities were essential for economic activity, political movements, and cultural life, suburbs were the most common place of residence for Americans. The 2000 Census showed that 50% of Americans lived in cities versus 30% living in central cities (Hobbs and Stoops 2002). Suburban populations continued to grow as Americans expressed their preferences for suburban living (Teaford 2008). Metropolitan areas continued to expand outward, even as numerous big cities grappled with population loss, significant economic changes, and concentrated poverty (Wilson 1996).

The suburbs continued to symbolize success and "a distinction from the city" rather than "a relationship with the city" (Conn 1994, 137). Cities provided different experiences and amenities but were not necessary for the daily lives of many as the suburbs encompassed more economic, cultural, and social activity. Suburban communities could contain many jobs, including in edge cities with concentrations of office and retail space (Garreau 1991), and significant levels of economic activity (Muller 1981). Positive social interactions between middle-class suburbanites involved leaving each other alone and limiting moments of conflict (Baumgartner 1988). Women could both exercise agency amid multiple suburban possibilities (England 1993) and be described as "soccer moms" shuttling kids to sports and extracurriculars (Swanson 2003). Large McMansions attempted to provide a lot of square footage for less money, impress onlookers, and mimic and combine traditional architectural styles (Miller 2012).

The suburban dream of homeownership and a better life for families extended to new residents. More people of color and immigrants moved to the suburbs (Frey 2015; Frey 2022). Black residents moved to suburbs in increasing numbers, sometimes residing in suburban areas with significant Black populations (Lacy 2007). "Ethnoburbs," majority-minority suburbs, emerged in places like the suburbs just east of Los Angeles. While these communities looked like suburbs in form—single-family homes, strip malls—they were home to newer ethnic groups, who came to the United States after the Immigration and Nationality Act of 1965, particularly Asian immigrants (Li 2009). Inner-ring suburbs, more mature suburbs adjacent to or very near big cities, also contained diverse populations (Hanlon 2010).

At the same time, practices reinforced racial, ethnic, and class differences in the suburbs. The passage of the Fair Housing Act of 1968 that outlined discriminatory practices due to race, ethnicity, and national origin did not eliminate ongoing residential segregation (Massey and Denton 1993). Whites shifted talk from racial residential preferences to economic residential preferences (Freund 2007). Real estate practices reinforcing residential segregation continued (Korver-Glenn 2022). Asian Americans did not necessarily find welcoming environments in suburban settings (Lung-Amam 2017; Matsumoto 2018; Warikoo 2022). The presence of undocumented immigrants in suburbs could prompt local responses and tensions (Vicino 2013).

Poverty became more common in the suburbs such that a larger number of Americans living in poverty resided in suburbs than big cities (Kneebone and Berube 2013). Different suburban communities had varying levels of ability and organizations to address suburban poverty (Murphy 2010). Wealthier residents worked to limit access to particular communities and institutions through the construction of gated communities and debates over boundaries within school districts (e.g., Low 2003; Heiman 2015). A preference for local governmental control (Teaford 1997) limited the ways suburbs could work together to effectively address unevenness in resources, services, and opportunities across metropolitan regions (Orfield 2002; Rusk 2013).

These new geographic patterns also included new religious groups in suburbs. Immigrants moved to suburbs in increasing numbers. An earlier model of spatial assimilation suggested that immigrants to the United States first moved to big-city ethnic enclaves and subsequent generations moved to the suburbs (Portes and Zhou 1993; Singer et al. 2008). More recently, Muslims gathered in mosques and community centers and negotiated the intersection of work and faith (Howe 2018). Buddhist and Hindu temples emerged in suburbia (Numrich 1997; Li 2009; Padoongpatt 2015). As religious groups sought out buildings and land, communities responded more negatively to proposals from Muslim and Orthodox Jewish groups (Miller 2019; Miller 2020). Congregations adopted different orientations toward engaging local communities with some choosing higher levels of community action and others focusing elsewhere (Numrich and Wedam 2015).

Broader changes in American religion affected faith in the suburbs. More Americans found attractive private faith or faith rooted in an individual self (Bellah et al. 1985). Educated suburbanites sought freedom and rootedness in their spiritual lives, resulting in a "spiritual pastiche" (Brooks

2000, 241) while middle-class suburbanites of varied religious backgrounds pursued alternative healing outside of scientific medicine approaches (McGuire 1987). Increasing numbers of Americans did not identify with any religious groups, becoming known as religiously unaffiliated or "religious nones" (Smith 2021). These large changes coupled with different populations in the suburbs helped lead to a suburban religious landscape in the early twenty-first century that looked different than the "Protestant-Catholic-Jew" consensus of the 1950s (Herberg 1955).

Evangelicals continued to embrace and adapt to the changing suburbs. The ongoing expansion of suburban communities further from the city could lead to interactions between new and established suburban religious congregations competing for a growing number of residents (Eiesland 2000). Suburban megachurches rose to prominence as did many of their leaders. While megachurches are not exclusively in suburban settings, important suburban congregations appealed to and adapted to suburban settings with easy access to major roads, informal presentations and expectations, buildings often designed not to look like traditional churches, Christian blessings of suburban norms, and emotional appeals (Loveland and Wheeler 2003; Dickinson 2015, 125–153; Wellman, Corcoran, and Stockly 2020). Willow Creek Community Church in South Barrington, Illinois drew thousands each weekend for services, became the anchor of the Willow Creek Association, a loose affiliation of evangelical congregations, and created multiple satellite congregations throughout the Chicago region. Saddleback Church in Lake Forest, California hosted numerous services in different styles each weekend on its main suburban campus and its hundreds of small groups in sprawling suburbia helped anchor people to a decentralized congregation in a sprawling region (Wilford 2012). The rise in satellite congregations enabled evangelical congregations based in suburbs or cities to spread broadly throughout metropolitan regions with one to dozens of additional locations (Thumma and Bird 2015).

In contrast to the evangelical mass in the suburbs, a small group of evangelicals moved to big cities and encouraged other evangelicals to follow. Some evangelicals formed intentional communities in urban neighborhoods, including in Philadelphia and Midwestern cities, with an emphasis on simpler communal living amid diverse populations in order to better follow the requirements of Christian faith (Claiborne 2006; Markofski 2015). Other evangelicals moved to urban neighborhoods and formed new congregations intended to address spiritual and physical needs (Bielo 2011a). Evangelicals continued to see cities as mission fields and places in need of church plants, even with the ongoing presence of many urban congregations (e.g., McRoberts 2003; Zelinsky and Matthews 2011). As one example, Manhattan pastor Tim Keller's work to engage the city could present an alternative approach to suburban evangelicalism: "His approach was especially popular with those who felt the culture wars—including a strong identification with the suburbs, the political mobilization of churches, and a strong strain of anti-intellectualism—had harmed their Christian witness" (Silliman 2023).

Beyond the United States, larger collectives emphasized the importance of cities for evangelical global engagement. For example, *The Cape Town Commitment* that emerged from the Third Lausanne Congress in 2010 included a section on cities:

> Cities are crucially important for the human future and for world mission. Half the world now lives in cities. Cities are where four major kinds of people are most to be found: (i) the next generation of young people; (ii) the most unreached peoples who have migrated; (iii) the culture shapers; (iv) the poorest of the poor.
>
> A) We discern the sovereign hand of God in the massive rise of urbanization in our time, and we urge Church and mission leaders worldwide to respond to this fact by giving urgent strategic attention to urban mission. We must love our cities as God does, with holy discernment and Christlike compassion, and obey his command to 'seek the welfare of the city', wherever that may be. We will seek to learn appropriate and flexible methods of mission that respond to urban realities. (Lausanne Movement 2022)

This text is in a section addressing world evangelization and on its own could be taken as another indicator of a willingness of evangelicals to emphasize cities as places for missions. However, the complete document discusses addressing physical, social, and cultural concerns of people and societies and the problems Christians and others face by perpetuating barriers.

Conclusion

In May 2022, the leaders of Gordon-Conwell Seminary in the suburb of Hamilton, Massachusetts announced plans to move the school to leased space in the city of Boston. The suburban evangelical school opened in 1969 with roots in two urban schools: the Boston Missionary Training Institute and the Conwell School of Theology in Philadelphia. Recent declines in the numbers of students, a majority of students commuting to the suburban campus, and long-term financial pressures prompted the school to pursue selling their 102-acre campus. The move would help the seminary get its finances in order for several decades. According to the institution's president, the move to leased urban space could help the seminary return to their roots: "'We're leaning into our heritage and our sense of calling,' he said. 'Our essential DNA has always been diverse and urban. We have this embedded-and-gathered model and we want to bring the education to where the people are'" (Silliman 2022).

In December 2023, the seminary announced they would remain in the suburb of Hamilton. The new plan emerged as the "Board of Trustees reaffirmed our commitment to residential theological education" and the school planned to sell its apartments (Gordon-Conwell Theological Seminary 2023).

This brief history of suburbanization and American evangelicalism provides context for locational decision-making at a leading evangelical seminary. Originally serving as ministry training institutes in big cities, Gordon-Conwell later sat alongside suburban Gordon College, a liberal arts college, and thrived for decades. Changes to students, finances, and education helped prompt a decision to head back to urban Boston for a new era of education and training. Even in a Catholic city and a slow-changing region (Bendroth 2005), leaders hoped they can again generate excitement and faith in the city. However, a later decision to remain on their suburban campus meant the school could continue to operate in familiar suburban settings.

By the early 2000s, evangelicals constituted over 20% of the American population and more than 50% of Americans lived in suburbs. These represent the largest groups percentage-wise in their respective categories; evangelicals are the largest religious tradition and roughly 20% more Americans live in suburbs than cities. These two phenomena present today required a series of policies, decisions, and circumstances over the course of multiple centuries. In other words, it was not ordained that evangelicals would embrace suburbia or that the United States would pursue suburban spaces more so than cities and rural areas.

Yet this shift to suburban life led to profound consequences for evangelicals. Reviewing this long history provides necessary context for the following chapters that consider specific locations and communities at certain points in time. The next chapter examines the white flight of Protestant denominations in the Chicago region. Now a leading global city, Chicago began as a Midwestern boom town after the removal of Indigenous populations to locations west of the Mississippi River, the coming of the railroad, and the development of the city as a transportation and commodities hub. In this context of a truly American city, perhaps even the paradigmatic one for the turn of the twentieth century, how did evangelical Protestant and other Protestant congregations respond to changing populations in the city? Did evangelicals move to the suburbs at similar rates as other Protestants?

3
Evangelicals (and Other Protestant Groups) Leave Chicago for the Suburbs

Fourth Presbyterian Church sits on bustling North Michigan Avenue, just across from the towering John Hancock Center. This congregation started as a merger of two earlier Presbyterian congregations that had initially been founded in 1848 and 1855, had a building destroyed by the Chicago Fire of 1871, and in the early 1900s eventually moved a little further north and east to its current location on a street that was not yet famous. It is a well-resourced congregation with a neo-Gothic structure, a history of social activism and aid, and regular support for the arts. As mainline Protestantism changed during the twentieth century, the congregation's pastors helped the church engage with social issues (Fourth Presbyterian Church 2023; Wellman 1999).

Contrast Fourth Presbyterian's history with that of Pilgrim Baptist on the city's south side. This congregation began in 1921 in the middle of Bronzeville, located at the center of the Black Belt where a growing population of Black residents was confined by white Chicagoans. The congregation met in a building constructed about 30 years earlier, designed by two famous architects, and built for a Jewish synagogue. The church was active for decades in gospel music and civil rights. A 2006 fire burned all but the skeleton of the structure and the congregation now meets across the street from the structure that is on the National Register of Historic Places. Recent grant money may help restore the religious building as a place to celebrate gospel music (Pilgrim Baptist Church 2011; Davis 2017; Reed 2022).

These two congregations have a long history in the city of Chicago amid decades of social, population, and religious change. They stayed in the city, met regularly, and engaged their communities among hundreds of other congregations. Following the flood of German, Irish, Polish, and other European immigrants into the city from the mid-nineteenth century into the early twentieth, the Black population increased quickly from the 1910s onward. In a state with a history of prestatehood slavery, poststatehood slavery

Sanctifying Suburbia. Brian J. Miller, Oxford University Press. © Oxford University Press 2025.
DOI: 10.1093/oso/9780197679623.003.0004

and Black Codes, and post-Reconstruction backlash including the establishment of sundown towns and whites committing violence, Black residents made up fewer than 5% of the city's population by the time of the Chicago Race Riot of 1919 (Kisiel and Miller 2023; Drake and Cayton 1945). Despite violence and limited housing opportunities that often forced new residents into the growing Black Belt (Meyer 2000), the Black population increased as hundreds of thousands of Black residents moved from the South to Chicago seeking jobs and opportunities (Hirsch 1983; Grossman 1989). With time, Black residents did move beyond the confines of the Black Belt and into neighborhoods on the South and West sides of the city, despite numerous efforts by white residents to keep Black residents out of their neighborhoods. And with growing Mexican and Latino populations throughout the twentieth century (Cruz 2007; Fernandez 2012), the population of Chicago looked very different in 2000 than it did in the first few decades of the 1900s.

As Fourth Presbyterian and Pilgrim Baptist matured, Chicago was an established center for religion. At the end of the nineteenth century, "Chicago was recognized for its concentration of religious leaders and reformers from a broad spectrum of religious traditions" (Mirola 1999, 398). The city hosted the World's Parliament of Religions in 1893. It was home to the mainline Protestant magazine *Christian Century* (Coffman 2013). Multiple religious schools and seminaries provided educations, including the Moody Bible Institute and seminaries at the University of Chicago and Northwestern University. Chicago had multiple notable religious buildings and congregations, particularly in the Catholic and Protestant traditions, woven into the fabric of the city (Bluestone 1991; McMahon 1995; McGreevy 1996). The city "was at one time a hub of dispensational organizations," a center for a popular subset of conservative Protestants who later established additional centers in "Dallas and Southern California" (Hummel 2023, 13).

While congregations formed and changed in Chicago, congregations also developed in the suburbs. In western Cook County, white settlers took up residence in the 1830s around the convergence of Salt Creek, the Des Plaines River, and the west end of Mud Lake because of the portage access between Lake Michigan and the Mississippi River. In 1869, the Riverside Improvement Company received a commissioned plan from Frederick Law Olmstead for what he called a "true suburb in which rural and urban advantages are agreeably combined" (Riverside 2023). The first congregation in the community started in 1869 as a union congregation where adherents of multiple Protestant traditions gathered in a stone chapel. Several years later, the union church split into multiple denominational congregations (Riverside Presbyterian Church 2023; Bassman 1995). Growth in this paradigmatic suburb, with the most growth happening in the 1920s, helped lead to the founding of more congregations. Postwar suburbanization also contributed to a changing religious landscape; one Lutheran congregation moved from Pilsen in Chicago to Riverside because of "population and industrial changes" (Bassman 1995). Growing suburban populations in Riverside and dozens of other suburbs spurred new buildings and congregations (Buggeln 2015).

Numerous suburban congregations developed as a result of white residents and congregations leaving Chicago amid demographic changes in the twentieth century. While Fourth Presbyterian and Pilgrim Baptist adapted to the changing city, many white residents and religious congregations moved to the suburbs in response. Multiple Chicago neighborhoods went from being over 90% white to have more than 90% Black residents in several decades. This affected not only residences and businesses, but also had significant effects on religious activity in the Chicago region.

This chapter examines the patterns in locations of Protestant religious congregations between 1925 and the late 1980s to show how they responded to changing racial patterns in Chicago. Set in a state with a long history of racial exclusion via property (Kisiel and Miller 2023), these responses had and continue to profoundly affect religion in Chicago and its suburbs. Religious buildings changed hands. New congregations and religious groups started meeting. The presence of religious traditions within neighborhoods and community areas changed rapidly. The moves to the suburbs included more than just a few congregations and included varied Protestant denominations, including groups now considered evangelicals such as the Christian Reformed Church (CRC) and Missouri Synod Lutherans (Steensland et al. 2000).

The new daily life in the growing Chicago suburbs was not just about cheap suburban homes accessible by newly constructed highways. It was also a rejection of changing racial demographics in the city and the problems whites felt this led to. The new suburban congregations opened one after another in largely white communities. These moving congregations joined the already-existing congregations in suburban communities. Within the Chicago region, religious congregations and traditions both reacted to and reinforced patterns regarding race, religion, and community. Religious change in the suburbs due to white flight and racial exclusion influenced suburban life and evangelical life in the Chicago area as well as in the suburbs in many metropolitan regions throughout the United States experiencing similar processes.

Studying Religious Denominations and Location Changes in the Chicago Region

Based on previous research regarding white flight and American cities (Sugrue 1996; Kruse 2005) and patterns in religious congregations moving to the suburbs discussed in the previous chapter (particularly Eiesland 2000; Mulder 2015; Numrich and Wedam 2015), I consider the evidence for five possible patterns in the locations of Protestant congregations in the Chicago region. First, did conservative Protestant denominations have higher percentages of suburban congregations and/or did they move to the suburbs more quickly than other Protestant groups? Second, were predominantly white churches in neighborhoods with increasing populations of Black residents more likely to leave for the suburbs? Third, did certain religious groups, particularly those with stronger white ethnic identities, cluster in certain suburban places? Fourth, were religious groups with more congregational-level polity more likely to move to the suburbs compared to churches with more top-down authority structures? Fifth, how does the number of congregations in suburban communities in 1925 compare to the number of congregations in these same communities in the postwar era of mass suburbanization?

To examine the patterns in the locations of churches in the Chicago region, I worked with addresses in a set of directories of churches in the Chicago metropolitan area published by the Chicago Church Federation, later known as the Church Federation of Greater Chicago. Directories cover a time span between 1925 and 1988–1990. They are not available for every year and the final directory spans multiple years as the group concluded its works around this time (Livezey 2000).

The directories provide a range of Protestant organizations from more liberal to more conservative as well as a variety of church polities. The directories included certain Protestant groups. Additionally, denominations changed quite a bit over this time period so it is difficult to group certain traditions such as Baptists (and they are not included in this analysis). With the data available, I analyzed the congregational locations of 10 Protestant denominations: African Methodist Episcopal (AME) (Black

Protestant), CRC (conservative Protestant), Congregational Christian (mainline Protestant), Disciples of Christ (mainline Protestant), Episcopal (mainline Protestant), Lutheran Church – Missouri Synod (LCMS) (conservative Protestant), Methodist Episcopal (mainline Protestant), Presbyterian (mainline Protestant), Reformed Church in America (RCA) (mainline Protestant), and Seventh-day Adventist (SDA) (conservative Protestant).

I mapped the church addresses in ArcGIS at increments spanning roughly 10 years: 1925, 1936, 1948, 1957, 1968–1969, and 1988–1990. In some maps, I also included Census data about the percentage of Black residents in Chicago community areas. The addresses did need to be cleaned up: some congregations had no addresses but had a community listed so the address was assigned to the downtown or central area of that municipality and some had an unrecognized address, often due to roads in Chicago changing names over time. While it is not clear that all congregations in a denomination are included in every directory, examining these years yielded hundreds of addresses.

I restricted addresses to the four Illinois counties that comprise the majority of the population in the Chicago region: Cook, Lake, DuPage, and Will counties. The directories include addresses in additional counties but listed relatively few locations in Kane, McHenry, Kendall, and Kankakee counties and counties in northwestern Indiana. While not mapped, the churches on the edges of the Chicago region are included in Table 3.1 comparing Chicago and suburban locations. The maps utilize 2014 municipality boundaries, including Chicago and its community areas, county boundaries, and current commuter railroad lines to help provide geographic references.

While this data source has limitations—it covers only certain Protestant groups so Catholics are not included, data on independent congregations is limited, denominations changed quite a bit over this time period so it is difficult to group certain traditions such as Baptists, and it is not clear that all congregations in a denomination are included in every directory— these data offer a unique opportunity to compare the changes in locations across multiple Protestant denominations in the same time period. As the number of Black residents in Chicago increased, the Chicago suburbs grew, and white flight occurred, what happened to the locations of Protestant congregations?

Table 3.1 Churches in the Chicago metropolitan region by denomination and location in the city or suburbs, 1925, 1936, 1948, 1957, 1968–1969, 1988–1990

Denomination	Year	Churches in Chicago	Churches in Suburbs	Total Churches	% in Chicago
African Methodist Episcopal (Black Protestant)	1925	12	1	13	92.31
	1936	25	9	34	73.53
	1948	24	13	37	64.86
	1957	25	10	35	71.43
	1968–1969	33	10	43	76.74
	1988–1990	31	18	49	63.27
Christian Reformed (Conservative Protestant)	1925	5	0	5	100
	1936	9	3	12	75
	1948	8	11	19	42.11
	1957	7	16	23	30.43
	1968–1969	6	22	28	21.43
	1988–1990	10	29	39	25.64
Congregational Christian (Mainline Protestant)	1925	66	36	103	64.08
	1936	53	34	87	60.92
	1948	50	38	88	56.82
	1957	48	42	90	53.33
	1968–1969			Not Available	
	1988–1990			Not Available	
Disciples of Christ (Mainline Protestant)	1925	17	10	27	62.96
	1936	14	16	30	46.67
	1948	13	13	26	50
	1957	12	14	26	46.15
	1968–1969	11	13	24	45.83
	1988–1990			Not Available	
Episcopal (Mainline Protestant)	1925	45	29	74	60.81
	1936	52	40	92	56.53
	1948	43	46	89	48.31
	1957	43	60	103	41.75
	1968–1969	36	71	107	33.64
	1988–1990	34	88	122	27.87
Lutheran Missouri Synod (Conservative Protestant)	1925			Not Available	
	1936	69	91	160	43.13
	1948	74	134	208	35.58
	1957	79	117	196	40.31
	1968–1969	79	140	219	36.07
	1988–1990	57	179	236	24.15

(*continued*)

Table 3.1 Continued

Denomination	Year	Churches in Chicago	Churches in Suburbs	Total Churches	% in Chicago
Methodist Episcopal (Mainline Protestant)	1925	97	72	169	57.40
	1936	92	88	180	51.11
	1948	106	102	208	50.96
	1957	103	106	209	49.28
	1968–1969	97	122	219	44.29
	1988–1990	84	185	269	31.23
Presbyterian (Mainline Protestant)	1925	65	36	101	64.36
	1936	67	50	117	57.26
	1948	63	56	119	52.94
	1957	65	79	144	45.14
	1968–1969	57	92	149	38.26
	1988–1990	47	91	138	34.06
Reformed Church in America (Mainline Protestant)	1925	8	2	10	80
	1936	9	3	12	75
	1948	9	8	17	52.94
	1957	9	7	16	56.25
	1968–1969	10	19	29	34.48
	1988–1990	5	18	23	21.74
Seventh-day Adventist (Conservative Protestant)	1925	13	11	24	54.17
	1936	13	10	23	56.52
	1948	14	12	26	53.85
	1957	14	15	29	48.28
	1968–1969	13	15	28	46.43
	1988–1990	13	8	21	61.90

Source: from directories of the Chicago Church Federation, later the Church Federation of Greater Chicago.

Patterns in White Flight and Locations in Chicago and the Suburbs

Between 1925 and 1990, Protestant denominations in the Chicago region differed in how many locations they had in the city or in the suburbs and the rate of change over this period (see Table 3.1). By 1988–1990, the one Black Protestant denomination studied, the AME, increased to 37% suburban locations from 8% suburban locations in 1925. The AME had the most Chicago congregations at the end of this study among the Protestant denominations studied.

Mainline Protestant denominations had variability in how many congregations were suburban in 1988–1990 and the percentage change between 1925 and 1988–1990. The percentage in the suburbs started with 47% of Congregational Christian (last data in 1957), 55% of Disciples of Christ, 66% of Presbyterian, 69% of Methodist, 73% of Episcopal, and 78% of RCA congregations. These percentages aligned with the percentage change over time (with a positive percentage indicating they became more suburban over time): 11% for Congregational Christian (last data in 1957), 17% for Disciples of Christ, 26% for Methodists, 30% for Presbyterians, 33% for Episcopalians, and 58% for the RCA.

Of the three conservative Protestant denominations analyzed here, two had some of the highest percentages of suburban locations and one had the highest rate of change over this period. The percentage of suburban congregations in 1988–1990 included 38% of SDA, 74% of CRC, and 76% of LCMS congregations. The rate of change included −8% SDA (the only group in this chapter with a higher percentage of Chicago locations in 1988–1990 compared to 1925), 19% LCMS, and 74% CRC. The CRC had the largest rate of change among the Protestant denominations, followed by the RCA, while the LCMS had the highest percentage of suburban churches at the starting point of the study.

The general pattern among the groups studied here is that traditions had more churches in suburban locations by the 1988–1990 directory. This process was underway prior to mass suburbia—already occurring in the 1930s and 1940s—and continued alongside the boom in suburban development and population in the postwar decades.

Multiple factors could be at work to explain how Protestant denominations ended up with more suburban locations. When considering Protestant churches in neighborhoods with growing numbers of Black residents, the patterns uncovered suggest the race of the neighborhood or community where the church was located is important for understanding the suburbanization of Protestant faith.

The locations of the AME in the Chicago region are instructive for understanding how race matters for the suburbanization of Protestant churches. Figure 3.1 shows the change in locations of AME churches between 1925 and 1988–1990. This denomination first started meeting in the late 1700s and officially began in 1816 (Dickerson 2020). The AME locations did become

Figure 3.1 The locations of African Methodist Episcopal Churches in 1925 and 1988–1990. (Community areas, based on 1930 and 1990 US Census data, with darker shades having higher percentages of Black residents. The categories: 0–9.99%, 10%–19.99%, 20%–39.99%, 40–99%.).

more suburban over the time in question, from 8% to 37%. Yet the locations are clearly linked to patterns of where Black residents could live in the Chicago region. These patterns reflect national patterns of residential segregation in the 20th century (Massey and Denton 1993). The number of Black residents in Chicago grew from 20,150 in 1900 to 109,458 in 1920 to 812,637 in 1960 (Hirsch 1998, 17). Originally confined to the community areas of Douglas, Grand Boulevard, and Washington, comprising the majority of the Black Belt and each community area containing over 90% Black residents, Black residents increasingly moved to South and West side neighborhoods plus suburbs after World War II.

These new communities often experienced quick demographic change (Wirth and Bernert 1949; Kitagawa and Taeuber 1963; The Chicago Fact Book Consortium 1984; The Chicago Fact Book Consortium 1995). Englewood, south of the traditional Black Belt, went from 2.2% Black in 1940 to 96.4% Black in 1970. North Lawndale, a Jewish population center, transitioned from 0.4% Black in 1940 to 91.1% Black in 1960 and Jews sold religious buildings to Black churches (Rosenthal 1960; Cutler 1996). Other areas transitioned even faster: Greater Grand Crossing went from 5.8% Black in 1950 to 85.8% Black in 1960. The change continued through the late twentieth century: Austin changed from 32.5% Black in 1970 to 87% Black in

1990 and West Pullman increased from 16.5% Black in 1970 to 94% Black in 1990. Sociologist Harvey Molotch (1969; 1972) discussed how this could affect religious congregations as church life outside of weekly worship services was segregated and white churches involved more Black children in Sunday School even as Black adults were not as welcome.

AME congregations accompanied Black residents to these new Chicago community areas. By 1968–1969, there were five AME churches in North Lawndale (none in 1925), two in East Garfield Park (none in 1925), and two in Morgan Park (none in 1925).

In 1925, the directory listed only one suburban AME congregation, located just north of the city in Evanston. By 1988–1990, 18 of the 49 churches were in the suburbs, mostly in communities with higher African-American populations such as the south suburbs, several satellite cities (Joliet, Aurora, Elgin, Waukegan), and several suburban Cook County locations. Whiter areas, such as DuPage County, had fewer AME churches: in 1970, there were no AME churches in a county of 491,882 residents (but only 0.03% Black) ("Racial Change" 1984), and in 1990 there was one AME church amongst 781,666 residents (1.98% Black) (US Department of Commerce 1990).

A second denomination, SDA, experienced locational changes at this same time. Today, this denomination is considered conservative Protestant but is also less white—54%—than numerous conservative or mainline Protestant groups (Pew 2015).

At the beginning of this period, SDA Churches tended to be in Chicago community areas that experienced growth in Black residents. By the end of the 1960s, no SDA congregations remained in the original Black Belt or in the Near West Side neighborhood. Some SDA congregations were in neighborhoods with more than 40% Black residents but these neighborhoods were further out from the center of the city to the south and west. The number of suburban SDA churches declined between 1968–1969 and 1988–1990 (see Figure 3.2).

Examining the locations of Presbyterian churches in Chicago and the region between 1925 and 1988–1990 shows larger moves. In 1925, Chicago neighborhoods with higher percentages of Black residents had some Presbyterian churches, including three in the Black Belt and five in the Near West Side. In 1988–1990, Presbyterian congregations were in multiple neighborhoods with high percentages of Black residents. But these locations had changed over time. Two of the three Presbyterian churches in the three Black Belt community areas were not present, the five churches in the

Figure 3.2 The locations of Seventh-day Adventist Churches in 1925 and 1988–1990. (Community areas, based on 1930 and 1990 US Census data, with darker shades having higher percentages of Black residents. The categories: 0–9.99%, 10%–19.99%, 20%–39.99%, 40–99%.)

Near West Side in 1925 were down to one by 1968–1969, and Presbyterian churches decreased in West Garfield Park, Humboldt Park, Austin, New City, West Englewood, Englewood, and Greater Grand Crossing. At the same time, suburban Cook County had more Presbyterian churches by 1988–1990 (see Figure 3.3).

Other Protestant denominations featured strong ethnic ties which might have affected their locations. Two such groups, the CRC and the RCA, involved a small but vibrant Dutch population in Chicago (Swierenga 2002). These denominations tended to cluster together in city and suburban locations, particularly to the south and west of Chicago's Loop (Mulder 2004; Mulder 2012; Mulder 2015; Zelinsky and Matthews 2011). Like other religious traditions, these denominations left increasingly community areas with growing Black populations, but they did not disperse evenly in the suburbs. Between 1925 and 1988–1990, the CRC added congregations and moved: they had four South Side locations and one Southwest side church early on and later were primarily suburban—28 in suburbs, 10 in Chicago. In the suburbs, they tended to be in two places: the southern suburbs or located near or between the Union Pacific and Burlington Northern train lines west of the city. The directories did not show any CRC congregations in the suburbs northwest or north of Chicago. See Figure 3.4 for the locations of the CRC in 1925 and 1988–1990.

EVANGELICALS LEAVE CHICAGO FOR THE SUBURBS 71

Figure 3.3 The locations of Presbyterian Churches in 1925 and 1988–1990. (Community areas, based on 1930 and 1990 US Census data, with darker shades having higher percentages of Black residents. The categories: 0–9.99%, 10%–19.99%, 20%–39.99%, 40–99%.)

Figure 3.4 The locations of Christian Reformed Churches in 1925 and 1988–1990. (Chicago and its community areas marked in crosshatch.)

Figure 3.5 The locations of Reformed Church in America congregations in 1925 and 1988–1990. (Chicago and its community areas marked in crosshatch.

RCA congregations followed a similar pattern. In comparison to the CRC congregations in 1925, the 10 RCA locations were more varied in Chicago on the south and west sides and only two congregations had suburban locations. After World War II, congregations became suburban with 18 of the 23 in 1988–1990 located outside the city. Most of the suburban congregations were located southwest and south of the city with just a handful north of the Union Pacific railroad line west of the city. Figure 3.5 shows the location of these congregations in 1925 and 1988–1990.

The patterns among these two Dutch Reformed denominations illustrate how the ethnic composition of the groups themselves—Dutch background—intersected with the changing demographics of Chicago neighborhoods. In 1936, Roseland on Chicago's South Side had seven CRC and RCA congregations. Roseland was 2.6% Black in 1930. In 1970, Roseland was 47.5% Black and there were still six CRC and RCA congregations. But the 1988–1990 directory listed only three CRC and RCA congregations in Roseland and the community area was 99% Black.

CRC and RCA congregations did not just disappear; new congregations sprang up in suburbs south of the city. In 1936, there were only two CRC and RCA congregations in Lansing, South Holland, Dolton, Riverdale, the eastern edge of Harvey, and Homewood. By 1968-1969, the directory listed 15 CRC and RCA congregations in these same suburbs.

Beyond these Dutch Reformed denominations, it can be difficult to track the immigrant and ethnic neighborhood patterns amongst other religious groups, particularly in a city known for immigrants and neighborhoods (e.g., Holli and Jones 1994). As one example, the Lutheran groups listed in the 1968-1969 directory are combinations of various smaller Lutheran groups that helped organize the lives of some immigrants (e.g., Gustafson 2003). The 1925 directory listed multiple Lutheran groups, including the Lutheran-Augustana Synod, United Lutheran Church of America, Wartburg Synod Churches, Norwegian Lutheran Church of America, and United Danish Evangelical Lutherans.

A fourth possible factor influencing the locations of congregations could be the organizational structure of denominations. Specifically, this involves the kind of church polity practiced and the ability of individual congregations to move on their own. Cantrell et al. (1983) pointed to differences in congregational autonomy across denominations. If they are correct, would denominations with more congregational autonomy—like the Evangelical Lutheran Church of America (ELCA)—have greater rates of suburbanization compared to denominations with less congregational autonomy—like Methodists?

Because the ELCA is not included in all five directories used in this study, see Figure 3.6, which compares the locations of ELCA and Methodist churches in 1988-1990. In this directory, 63.11% (154) of the 244 ELCA congregations are in the suburbs. For the Methodists, 68.77% of the 269 congregations are in the suburbs. The percentage in the suburbs is similar but there are some location differences within the suburbs: there are more Methodist congregations in the north and northwest suburbs while there are fewer congregations for both groups in the southwest suburbs.

Expanding beyond ELCA and Methodist congregations, Cantrell et al. (1983) provide an expanded list of congregational autonomy across denominations. Here is the percentage of suburban locations across denominations (listed from less autonomy to more autonomy) in the 1988-1990 directory: Methodist 68.77% suburban; Presbyterian 65.94% suburban; Episcopalian 72.13% suburban; Missouri Synod Lutheran 75.85% suburban; and the Evangelical Lutheran Church in America 63.11% suburban. These percentages do not go in one direction with the levels of congregational autonomy. Similarly, the locations of the congregations of the

74 SANCTIFYING SUBURBIA

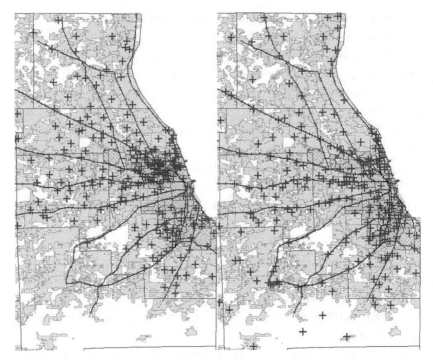

Figure 3.6 Locations of Evangelical Lutheran Church in America and Methodist congregations 1988–1990. (Chicago and its community areas marked in crosshatch.)

two Dutch Reformed traditions—groups with different polity and autonomy (Mulder 2015)—were both primarily suburban in the 1988–1990 directory.

The last portion of this analysis involves looking at congregations in older and newer suburbs. The addresses in these directories show expanding numbers of congregations in the suburbs as mass suburbanization occurred. At the same time, these suburban communities already had congregations and some suburbs had been settled for over 100 years prior to the postwar suburban boom. The locations of these older suburbs and congregations followed existing settlement patterns in the region with suburban populations first gathering alongside the region's railroad lines (Keating 2005) as Chicago became a recognized railroad center in the latter half of the 1800s (McLear 1980; Abbott 1980; Cutler 2006).

The locations of Lutheran-Missouri Synod congregations illustrate the patterns among suburban congregations across these conservative and mainline Protestant denominations. In 1936, most of the suburban LCMS congregations are in two locations: suburbs closer to Chicago where suburban development had already filled in between train lines, such as within Cook County, or communities along railroad lines connected to Chicago, such as in Lake, DuPage, and Will counties. In the 1988–1990 directory, the number of LCMS congregations near the railroad lines increased as did the number of congregations between railroad lines beyond suburbs close to Chicago. See Figure 3.7 for the locations of Lutheran-Missouri Synod churches in 1936 and 1988–1990.

Studying the locations of congregations within one county also shows the growth in suburban churches alongside the presence of existing congregations. Outside of suburban Cook County, DuPage County is the most populous suburban county. White settlers first arrived in the early 1830s (Pruter and Thompson 2022). Religious activity and congregations quickly followed; the first circuit rider operated in 1832, the first congregation was established in 1833, each of the nine townships had at least one

Figure 3.7 Location of Missouri Synod-Lutheran churches 1936 and 1988–1990. (Chicago and its community areas marked in crosshatch.)

congregation by the 1840s, and at least 115 congregations had existed by the early 1900s (Peters 1981).

The 1925 Church Federation of Great Chicago directory contains 20 Protestant churches in DuPage County. The county had a 1920 population of 42,120 while Chicago had over 2.7 million residents in that Census. All 20 churches are located in communities within a short distance of the three major east-west railroad lines. The church furthest from a railroad line was roughly one mile away but also just 0.1 miles from an interurban electric line to Chicago (that closed in the late 1950s). The churches tend to be located in communities settled in the 1800s like Elmhurst (4,594 residents in 1920), Hinsdale (4,042 residents in 1920), and Wheaton (4,137 residents in 1920). The number of congregations decreases as the distance from Chicago increases.

See Figure 3.8 for the churches in DuPage County in 1925, 1968–1969, and 1988–1990. These maps include a variety of Protestant churches not analyzed elsewhere in this study including all Baptist groups, Disciples of Christ, a variety of Lutheran groups, and Unitarian and Universalist congregations.

Four decades later, the 1968–1969 directory shows an increase in churches in both older communities and in communities and areas between the railroad lines. The county's population grew tenfold since 1920 to 491,882 in 1970, and new postwar suburbs like Carol Stream, Woodridge, and Glendale Heights now have churches. There are still parts of the county with relatively few churches; the southeastern, southwestern, and northwestern corners of the county are not as developed.

The county continued to grow and in the 1988–1990 directory churches had spread throughout the entire county. The 1990 population of the county was 781,666 and new congregations developed in expanding suburbs like

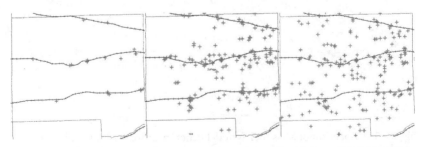

Figure 3.8 Churches in DuPage County in 1925, 1968–1969, and 1988–1990.

Naperville, in the southwest corner of the county, and Bartlett, in the northwest corner. More churches are listed in communities between the railroad lines in the central and eastern portions of the county, places that already had higher and denser populations.

Evangelicals, Protestants, and White Flight in the Chicago Region

Dozens of Protestant congregations changed locations during the twentieth century in the Chicago region. Some moved while others closed and others started. The Church Federation of Greater Chicago directories show congregations in nine of the 10 Protestant denominations studied became more suburban between 1925 and 1988–1990. This includes the one Black Protestant denomination, all six of the mainline Protestant denominations, and two of the three conservative Protestant denominations. Two of the evangelical denominations, the CRC and LCMS, were among the top three of 10 denominations with the percentage of congregations in the suburbs and the CRC had the greatest change from city to suburban congregations during this period.

All of this happened amid significant demographic change in the region. As Black migrants came to Chicago, numerous neighborhoods changed as Black residents moved in, and white residents and congregations left for growing suburbs. The religious landscape in these communities was altered, including the availability and use of religious buildings, the loss of some congregations and the start of others, and the presence of local ministries and services. These changes also occurred in suburban communities where growing populations contributed to new congregations, building projects, and an increased number of religious options for suburbanites.

While the Protestant denominations studied here primarily ended up in the suburbs, not all Protestant denominations moved to the suburbs at the same rate. The AME and SDA, two traditions with fewer white adherents than mainline and conservative Protestants overall, had more congregations in Chicago than the suburbs in 1988–1990. Additionally, not all of the Protestant groups moving to the suburbs in larger numbers ended up randomly distributed across the region. The two Dutch Reformed traditions, CRC and RCA, tended to locate near each other in suburbs south and southwest of Chicago. White flight and interactions between white residents and racial and ethnic minority residents continued to affect religious congregations in the Chicago region through the final decades of the twentieth century (Numrich and Wedam 2015).

Examining these denominations shows race and ethnicity in neighborhoods and congregations mattered for congregational locations, but church polity and congregational autonomy did not have a strong effect across the Protestant groups. This may be due to the groups compared here; previous work differentiated between polity differences between Catholics and Jews (e.g., Gamm 1999) in how much their locations became suburban and Mulder (2015) argued that the polity differences between the CRC and RCA slowed down the suburbanization of the RCA. Still, by the 1988-1990 directory, eight of the 10 Protestant denominations studied had a majority of their congregations in the suburbs.

As congregations moved to and/or opened in the growing suburbs, they joined an existing religious landscape. Older suburbs, often founded on railroad lines, had conservative Protestant and mainline Protestant congregations. The land developed between the railroad lines, including in newly founded municipalities, came to include numerous congregations across Protestant traditions. These land use patterns add to existing research stressing the ecological reasons congregations choose locations including finding a niche within a denomination (Doughtery and Mulder 2009), interactions with and competition between congregations within a community (Eiesland 2000), providing easy driving access to local and further-flung attendees (Form and Dubrow 2008; Sinha et al. 2007), and looking for cheaper land (Zelinsky and Matthews 2011, 54, 57).

Evangelical denominations were not alone in moving to the suburbs but two of them do so at higher levels. The LCMS had the most suburban congregations to start and then the number of suburban LCMS congregations almost doubled by 1988-1990. The CRC had only five congregations listed in 1925, all in Chicago, but the number of congregations in the region increased almost eight-fold and by then roughly three-quarters were in the suburbs in 1988-1990. These two denominations offered numerous options for suburbanites seeking churches in a region where Chicago's population between 1950 and 1990 but the population of the region continued to grow.

Conclusion

In the decades leading up to the end of the twentieth century, evangelicals were not the only ones moving to or operating in the suburbs. Writer and activist Bill McKibben (2022) describes the changes he saw regarding suburbanization and religion in his hometown of Lexington, Massachusetts. In a community with a long patriotic history and numerous religious congregations, McKibben observed two public issues in 1971 that split the social and religious consensus that community had experienced. One matter involved the Vietnam War; would Vietnam veterans protesting the war be welcomed? The local police arrested marching veterans for violating curfew and camping overnight on the Lexington Green, but the suburb shifted from a politically conservative to a politically liberal community. Responses to this war affected many communities in the United States. The second matter involved affordable housing in a wealthier suburb; would Lexington have housing for people of different backgrounds? Lexington voters turned this down despite support from multiple local leaders. Numerous suburbs with whiter and wealthier population have engaged with this question in recent decades with many residents striving to maintain a particular quality of life and demographics through land use and zoning decisions. According to the US Census Bureau (2023), Lexington is 60.1% white and 31.8% Asian with a median household income of over $202,000 and a poverty rate of 3.2%. Lexington, a suburb that stood for American freedom and values, chose a path that created a particular kind of community in which its religious congregations and adherents contributed to and operated.

In McKibben's experiences, the Chicago region, and suburbs across the United States, the suburban religious activity at the end of the twentieth century to today cannot be understood without accounting for white flight and racial and ethnic exclusion. Evangelicals left cities for the suburbs, alongside other Protestants, Catholics, and Jews, and took up residence within growing suburbs that were primarily white. As evangelicals embraced suburban life, they did not often have to reckon with neighbors with different backgrounds and experiences. Religious life in Chicago neighborhoods continued with numerous congregations and religious activity (e.g., McRoberts 2003; Zelinsky and Matthews 2011; Numrich and Wedam 2015) often without a significant presence of white evangelicals. In the suburbs, evangelicals could make direct appeals to embracing homogeneity in congregations (e.g., McGavran 1970) and to a suburban lifestyle. And with data showing middle-class whites leave some suburban Census tracts when middle-class Hispanic and Asian residents arrive and white suburbanites stay in or seek in mostly white neighborhoods, this dynamic continues to affect evangelical congregations and residents (Kye 2018; Rodkin 2018; Parisi, Lichter, and Taquino 2019).

The next three chapters examine additional factors that helped evangelicals embrace suburbs. Before considering the evangelical suburb of Wheaton, Illinois in Chapter 5 and four clusters of evangelical organizations and residents in Chapter 6, the next chapter takes up the locations of the developing National Association of Evangelicals (NAE). As a group purporting to advance the goals of American evangelicals, where did they choose to locate their headquarters in a rapidly suburbanizing nation?

4
United Evangelicals Across (Parts of) America

The Locations of the National Association of Evangelicals

Wooddale Church in the suburbs of Minneapolis is a megachurch with roughly 5,500 members (Hartford Institute 2021). The church now has four campus locations with a home base in the idyllic community of Eden Prairie, a community *Money* named a top place to live multiple times in recent decades. The brick and wood-clad home church is located at a busy intersection of a state highway and arterial local road. With a 200-foot spire topped with a cross on top of the roof, the church building features a sanctuary for 2,000, choir space for 125, a large pipe organ, and seating in wood pews almost 360 degrees around the pulpit (Bentz Thompson Rietow 2021). Founded in 1943 as a small congregation, the church became a megachurch in the final decades of the twentieth century under pastor Leith Anderson. Anderson served two stints as leader of the National Association of Evangelicals, first from 2002 to 2003 and then from 2009 to 2019 after scandal forced NAE leader and pastor Ted Haggard to step down.

The development and changes in Wooddale Church mirror the changes in both evangelicalism and metropolitan areas. According to a History Timeline on Wooddale's website (2021), the church, first called The Wayside Chapel, emerged out of a bible study in the inner-ring suburb of Richfield just south of Minneapolis. Six years later, the church became Wooddale Baptist Church. They affiliated with the Minnesota Baptist Conference. The picture on the church's website shows a modest church structure with a small parking lot next to a square brick tower attached to what appears to be a large house with steep pitched roof.

Leith Anderson became pastor in 1977 and served until 2011. The church timeline includes this description for 1977: "Planning for growth focused on a clear philosophy and direction of the church, building lay and professional staff for an equipping ministry, a major shift toward outreach, and relocation to provide adequate facilities for the future."

Moving further out from Minneapolis, the church bought land in Eden Prairie in 1981. The new facility opened in stages in 1984 and 1985 and then held services starting in 1990 in "a new 2,000-seat Worship Center to accommodate the growing congregation." Expanding beyond the church's Baptist roots, the church also affiliated with The Conservative Congregational Christian Conference in 2003. An Edina campus opened in 2008 followed by a 2016 campus in Minneapolis' Loring Park neighborhood.

A multicampus megachurch with a well-known lead pastor is not unusual today in American evangelicalism. Megachurch leaders contribute to the charismatic and emotional appeal of the congregation (Wellman, Corcoran, and Stockly 2020) and the growth of satellite locations began in the early 2000s (Thumma and Bird 2008). At the same time, few megachurch pastors serve as leader of an umbrella organization meant to bring together and represent American evangelicals within a pluralistic society. Anderson led the organization during a turbulent time and as one NAE director put it, Anderson hoped the National Association of Evangelicals would use "its influence for good—not for institutional power, or political gain, but for the good of people—especially the poor and the vulnerable and the immigrant and the persecuted" (Hopfensperger 2019).

The formation of a national organization to serve evangelicals in the middle of the twentieth century grew out of several impulses. Evangelicals desired to engage society, contrasting their interests to the more insular approach of fundamentalists (Henry 1947). Evangelicals also believed "the very antithesis of the Christian way of life" was "bring[ing] in the Kingdom of God by force or to impose the Christian ethic successfully upon an unregenerate society by the use of power politics" (Murch 1956, 44). The attempt to bring together evangelicals built on years of efforts by pastors and religious leaders, particularly in New England, to find common ground among fundamentalists (Carpenter 1997, 142–147).

After an exploratory October 1941 meeting in Chicago, 147 evangelical delegates met in April 1942 in St. Louis. At the 1942 meeting, the constitution for the new organization included a six-point doctrinal basis for membership:

(1) That we believe the Bible to be the inspired, the only infallible, authoritative word of God.

(2) That we believe that there is one God, eternally existent in three persons; Father, Son, and Holy Spirit.
(3) That we believe in the deity of Christ, in His virgin birth, in His sinless life, in His miracles, in His vicarious and atoning death, in His bodily resurrection, in His ascension to the right hand of the Father and in His personal return in power and glory.
(4) That because of the exceeding sinfulness of human nature we believe in the absolute necessity of regeneration by the Holy Spirit for salvation.
(5) That we believe in the resurrection of both the saved and the lost; they that are saved unto the resurrection of life and they that are lost unto the resurrection of damnation.
(6) That we believe in the spiritual unity of believers in Christ (National Association of Evangelicals 1942, 102–103).

Later in the constitution, they identified seven "fields of endeavor" for evangelicals to collectively address:

(1) Evangelism
(2) Relations with government
(3) National and local use of radio
(4) Public relations
(5) Preservation of separation between church and state
(6) Christian education
(7) Freedom for home and foreign missions (National Association of Evangelicals 1942, 104)

The new organization called themselves the National Association of Evangelicals for United Action. At a national convention the next year, the organization removed "for United Action" from their name and became known as the National Association of Evangelicals (National Association of Evangelicals 2021).

The new organization opened offices in cities throughout the United States and the national headquarters bounced between several locations for several years. By the early 1950s, the national headquarters were in Wheaton, Illinois with a key public affairs office remaining in Washington, DC. In 1962, the NAE moved its headquarters just north of Wheaton to the adjacent and new community of Carol Stream. The headquarters remained put until 1999 before relocation for several years to Azusa, California under NAE President Kevin Mannoia (Sellers 2002). The Washington office became more important with the connections to political leaders during the evangelical ascendance of the 1980s and became home to the NAE headquarters in 2002 (National Association of Evangelicals 2021).

The Location(s) of the NAE

This chapter considers the geography of the National Association of Evangelicals through examining the locations of the group's headquarters and the locations of the organization's delegates and board members at several time periods. The NAE purports to represent and speak for roughly one-quarter of the American population (Pew Research 2015). From the beginning, the group had both theological and political aims and a headquarters today in Washington, DC provides access to politicians and leaders.

The NAE serves a unique constituency and this could make its job more difficult. First, the members of the organization are a collection of denominations, congregations, and evangelical organizations. The conservative Protestant tradition is one with a history of independent and non-denominational churches as well as denominational splits and differences (Steensland et al. 2000). The largest Protestant denomination in the United States, Southern Baptists, have never officially been members of the NAE even as they theologically and culturally often fit with the emphases of the NAE. The first denominations to join the NAE in 1943 were mostly small ones: the Evangelical Free Church of America, Assemblies of God, Christian Reformed Church in North America, Open Bible Standard Churches, and the International Pentecostal Holiness Church.

Second, in a religious tradition marked by organizational fluidity and an emphasis on individualism, it can be difficult to speak for a group as varied as evangelicals. While certain NAE positions matched the interests of the group as a whole—as two examples: an early commitment to radio so that Americans could hear from evangelicals in addition to other Christian groups, and a coalescing around pro-life positions starting in the late 1970s—others, including some theological nuances, did not enjoy such consensus. The creative tension of maintaining a vibrant subculture by building internal cohesion and engaging society (Smith 1998) could lead to disagreements. For example, the National Association of Evangelicals (2021) describes a

NAE presidency in the early 2000s where an effort to develop a wider definition of evangelicals and welcome additional Christian groups met with resistance.

Third, and most important for this chapter, the geography of the National Association of Evangelicals matters as its works to represent a broad range of evangelical groups and members spread throughout the United States. How does the NAE represent the locations of evangelical organizations and members? Where do the Board of Administration members live and work? Why did the NAE choose the locations it did for its headquarters?

This chapter uses three data sources to examine the locations of the National Association of Evangelicals. The first two sources involve important leaders in the NAE: the addresses of the delegates to the key 1942 meeting in St. Louis and the addresses of the NAE Board of Administration Members from the early 1970s to the late 1990s. The third set of data involves the locations of the NAE headquarters: Wheaton and Carol Stream, Illinois for much of the NAE's history, a short sojourn in the suburbs of Los Angeles, and then Washington, DC.

The National Association of Evangelicals purports to represent the interests of American evangelicals. Yet through the location of its headquarters of the organization and the contexts of its board members, these collective interests are manifested in specific places, including suburbs. This chapter provides more details on how evangelicals writ large interact with suburbs and other locations in the United States.

The Locations of Delegates to the 1942 St. Louis Meeting

The first meeting in 1942 of the National Association of Evangelicals, then known as the National Association of Evangelicals for United Action, involved 149 delegates. Their names and addresses are listed in *Evangelical Action! A Report of the Organization of the National Association of Evangelicals for United Action* (National Association of Evangelicals 1942, 92–100). This information allows for studying patterns in the locations of the delegates.

According to the 1940 Census, fewer than 50% of Americans lived in metropolitan areas: 32.5% resided in central cities and 15.3% lived in suburbs (Hobbs and Stoops 2002, 33). In the same Census, 14 American cities had over 500,000 residents while five had populations over one million: New York

City, Chicago, Philadelphia, Detroit, and Los Angeles. Of the delegates, 64 of the 149 (43%) listed addresses in the 14 biggest cities. This included five delegates from New York, 14 from Chicago, eight from Philadelphia, one from Detroit, two from Cleveland, 22 from St. Louis (site of the meeting), five from Boston, one from Pittsburgh, and six from Buffalo. Some of these large cities had long legacies of evangelical and fundamentalist activity (e.g., Bendroth 2005; Roberts 2016). Several of the cities over 500,000 residents had no delegates: Los Angeles, Baltimore, Washington, DC, San Francisco, and Milwaukee.

Forty-four delegates hailed from cities with between 50,000 and 500,000 residents. These communities ranged from established cities like Minneapolis and Cincinnati (not much smaller than 500,000 residents) to smaller big cities like Memphis, Nashville, and Springfield, Missouri to six sizable suburbs (Long Beach, CA, Paterson, NJ, Gary, IN, East St. Louis, MO, and Cicero, IL).

The 39 remaining delegates hailed from communities of under 50,000 people. Thirteen of these locations were suburbs (among them Richmond Heights, MO and Quincy, MA) while many of the others were small towns and/or rural communities (among them Portsmouth, NH and Winona Lake, IN).

Compared to national figures, roughly 2% fewer delegates, 19 (13%), provided addresses in suburbs compared to the percentage of all Americans living in suburbs in 1940. In contrast, relatively few delegates lived outside central cities and suburbs: 26 (17%) lived in more rural areas.

There were also differences in which regions of the United States delegates hailed from compared to the American population at large. The most delegates came from the Midwest—just over half with 75 (50%). Next came 44 (29.5%) delegates from the Northeast, 23 (15.4%) from the South, and seven (4.7%) from the West. Both the Midwest and Northeast were overrepresented compared to the distribution of the American population by region in 1940 where 31.6% lived in the South, 30.5% in the Midwest, 27.3% in the Northeast, and 10.5% in the West (US Census Bureau 2002, 15). In the early years of the NAE, southerners expressed limited interest; they might theologically be considered analogous to evangelicals but also were often labeled as fundamentalists (Mathews 2006) who disliked connections to Northern religious groups (Matthews 1992, 85–86).

A closer look at the locations of several important attendees of the 1942 meetings illustrates how evangelicals involved in the 1942 meetings navigated urban and suburban settings. The life of Dr. Harold J. Ockenga shows the interplay of urban and suburban. Although associated with a historic urban church and connected to numerous evangelical institutions, he lived many of his adult years in the suburbs of Boston. Ockenga was a leader of the 1942 NAE meeting and continued as NAE leader (the first president from 1943 to 1956), as well as pastor, author, and board member for multiple evangelical organizations for several decades afterward. By the late 1940s, Ockenga called the evangelical activity exemplified by the NAE the "new evangelicalism," a term that later lost its modifier (Rosell 2008, 13).

Ockenga served as long-time pastor of Park Street Church, an influential independent evangelical congregation founded in 1809 just northeast of Boston Common in central Boston (Lindsell 1951, 53). Site of numerous famous sermons and speeches, Park Street grew, faced trouble at the turn of the twentieth century as the neighborhood changed and residents moved to the suburbs, and then revived again in the early decades of the twentieth century (Lindsell 1951, 54–55). This congregation continues to be influential within the NAE. In 2019, the NAE elected Rev. Dr. Walter Kim. When elected, Kim was pastor at a Presbyterian Church of America (PCA) congregation in Charlottesville, Virginia, but Kim had previously ministered at Park Street for 15 years (Shellnut 2019).

Ockenga was born in Chicago in 1905 and grew up in multiple west side churches (Lindsell 1951, 13). He attended Taylor University in rural Upland, Indiana, subsequently attended Princeton Theological Seminary with the goal of becoming a Methodist pastor, and finished his degree at Westminster in Philadelphia. He was ordained a Presbyterian minister in 1931 in Pittsburgh and then enrolled at the University of Pittsburgh to pursue a doctorate in philosophy. In 1936, Ockenga accepted a call to Park Street Church in Boston. He and his wife lived in suburban Belmont and suburban Hamilton. Ockenga was buried in Hamilton Cemetery (Lindsell 1951; Rosell 2008).

Another influential person present at the meetings lived in multiple settings before operating from suburban Philadelphia for decades. Listed as a delegate, Rev. Carl McIntire actually attended by invitation as the leader of a rival new evangelical organization: the American Council of Christian Churches (ACCC). McIntire had an established reputation as a fundamentalist who helped form the Bible Presbyterian Church. Negotiations regarding merging the two groups broke down as the larger group of evangelicals felt the ACCC was not the vehicle for evangelical goals due to disagreements over whether groups beyond denominations could join an umbrella organization, whether to admit Pentecostal denominations, and whether members needed to sever ties with the Federal Council of Churches (Matthews 1992, 32–37; Murch 1956, 53; Rosell 2008, 93–96).

Born in Michigan and raised in Oklahoma, McIntire attended college in Oklahoma and Missouri. Much of McIntire's adult life involved ministry in suburban New Jersey. As Finnish scholar Markku Ruotsila (2016, 9) put it, "The intertwined stories of Carl McIntire and American fundamentalism both begin at the same time, one in the rural American Midwest, the other in the halls of academe in big Northern cities." During his time at Princeton Theological Seminary, McIntire followed J. Gresham Machen, a conservative Presbyterian New Testament Professor, to Westminster Theological Seminary after controversy between liberal and conservative factions at Princeton (Ockenga also made this move). After completing seminary in 1931 and serving as pastor for several years in Atlantic City, McIntire settled in a pastor role in Collingswood, New Jersey. This borough founded by Quakers was just seven miles east of downtown Philadelphia and had a history as a dry community where alcohol could not be sold. From this suburban location, McIntire tenaciously pursued uncompromising fundamentalism while promoting his "view of America that was individualist, anticollectivist and capitalist" (Ruotsila 2016, 23) on both the national—such as close involvement in the National Bible Institute which later became Shelton College where McIntire served as president from 1965 to 1972—and international level.

Whereas McIntire served as a college leader decades after the 1942 meeting, Dr. J. O. Buswell and William Henry Houghton were two leaders of conservative Protestant institutions of higher education who served as delegates to the 1942 meeting. At the time of the meeting, both Buswell and Houghton presided over schools in major urban areas but both had life and leadership experience in suburban settings. Buswell led an institution, the National Bible Institute, founded in 1907 and located in midtown Manhattan. He had stepped into this role after the Trustees of suburban Wheaton College fired him as President in early 1940. Selected in 1926 as the Wheaton president for his defense of fundamentalism, Buswell increased the rigor of the academics and the size of the student body increased rapidly on his watch (even as under his watch the formerly abolitionist school enrolled no Black students; see Miller and Malone 2019). While at Wheaton, Buswell participated in and helped lead a split from the Presbyterian Church (USA) to form The Orthodox Presbyterian Church (The Orthodox Presbyterian Church 2021). Even though he was at the 1942 NAE meeting, Buswell soon sided with McIntire's separatist ACCC (Hamilton 1994).

While Buswell pursued a separatist path, Moody Bible Institute's president in 1942, William Henry Houghton, supported the National Association of Evangelicals. Born in Boston and saved at a suburban revival meeting, Houghton served as pastor of two churches in rural Pennsylvania, a suburban church outside Philadelphia, and churches in Atlanta and New York City before becoming Moody's president in late 1934. He was president for 12 years and then experienced a heart attack in 1946 and died the next year (Moody Bible Institute 2021).

The broad location patterns among the delegates and these brief locational biographies show how at the beginning the NAE was an organization whose leaders were marked by interactions with some of the biggest cities in the United States in the Midwest and Northeast and had familiarity with suburban life. Emerging from the 1940s with a collective mission to represent evangelicals and advance their interests in multiple domains, evangelicals approached a country headed toward a suburban majority with connections to particular metropolitan areas and regions as well as leaders who were less suburban and rural than the overall population of the United States.

The Locations of NAE Board Members 1973-1999

When evangelicals came to the forefront of American political and cultural life in the final decades of the twentieth century, the National Association of Evangelicals had played a role in helping develop this religious group. In this process, the NAE operated from particular locations in the United States. While multiple groups represented evangelical interests, including the Moral Majority, the Family Research Council, and the Christian Coalition, the National Association of Evangelicals had the longest history and experience in navigating collective activity and divergent opinions.

Directories of the Board of Directors from the National Association of Evangelicals found in the Special Collections of Wheaton College, available for the years 1973-1980 and 1985-1999, shed light on the locations of NAE Board members. These directories cover 23 classes of Board Members as a new group was appointed each year to serve a three-year term. Two hundred thirty-one different people served in these 21 years, more than half serving more than one term. These members had 306 different communities for which they listed an address.

I coded the addresses of the different Board Members for the size of the metropolitan region in which they were located and whether their address was in a city or suburb (US Census Bureau 2001). See Table 4.1.

On the whole, the percentage of Board Members in the suburbs was roughly equal to the percentage of Americans living in the suburbs: 146/306 (48%) compared to Americans overall at 45% in 1980, 46% in 1990, and 50% in 2000 (Hobbs and Stoops 2002, 33). At the same time, the percentage of suburban Board Members is particularly high in the biggest metropolitan areas in the United States of over five million residents. In these 9 metropolitan areas—New York City, Los Angeles, Chicago, Washington, DC, San Francisco, Philadelphia, Boston, Detroit, and Dallas –85% of the Board Members listed addresses in suburban communities. The largest cities in the United States had few NAE Board Members with addresses in those cities: one in New York City (compared to six in the NYC suburbs), two in Los Angeles (18 in the suburbs), and three in Chicago (37 in the suburbs). In metropolitan regions with smaller populations, evangelical Board Members were more likely to give an address in a city rather than a suburb.

What kind of metropolitan area Board Members hailed from differed most from the US population as a whole when it came to nonmetropolitan

Table 4.1 Locations of NAE Board Members, 1973–1980 and 1985–1999

	City	Suburb	Total	% Board Members in Metro type	% US in Metro type (2000)
Metropolitan area 5 million +	14	82	96	31%	30%
Metropolitan area 1–4.99 million	49	37	86	28%	28%
Metropolitan area 250–999k	46	27	73	24%	16%
Metropolitan area <250k	11	2	13	4%	7%
Non Metropolitan Area			38	12%	19.7%
Total	120	148	306	100%	100%

areas. While nearly 20% of the US population lived outside metropolitan regions, only 12% of the Board Members did so.

By 2000, the American population had shifted by region as had the regional locations of Board Members in the final decades of the twentieth century. Of the 306 Board addresses, 130 (42%) were in the Midwest, 70 (23%) were in the West, 66 (22%) were in the South, and 40 (13%) were in the Northeast. In the United States as a whole in 2000, 35.6% of residents lived in the South, 22.9% in the Midwest, 22.5% in the West, and 19.0% in the Northeast. Of the 38 addresses not in metropolitan areas, 33 were in the South or Midwest.

The locations of several members highlight the patterns among the NAE Board. In the membership directories to which I had access, Dr. David LeShana served in the Board of Directors class in 1974, 1977, 1980, 1987, 1990, 1993, and 1996. LeShana was the son of missionaries in India, attended Taylor University in rural Upland, Indiana, and then completed master's and doctorate degrees. For three of these directories, he provided his address as George Fox College where he served as president from 1969 to 1982. At this private Quaker institution in Newberg, Oregon, roughly 25 miles southwest of downtown Portland, LeShana's leadership was marked by fundraising, growth in the student body and academic programs, and the construction of new buildings on campus (Beebe 1991). Afterward, he had two additional addresses. One was at Seattle Pacific University, founded by Free Methodists, where LeShana served as president from 1982 to 1991. The second address was for a P.O. box in Portland, Oregon. Over the course of several decades as a Board Member of the NAE, LeShana served both suburban and urban locations in two metropolitan areas among the 25 largest in the United States.

Similar to LeShana, Reverend Juan Carlos Miranda provided multiple addresses while serving as a Board Member in multiple classes. Maria Miranda, his wife, also served in the 1993 class. The Mirandas had locations in Pasadena and LaVerne, California, two suburbs in the San Gabriel Valley east of Los Angeles, a suburb outside a Midwestern big city, and in a smaller city in the South. After being raised in the Brethren Church in Argentina (where he also met Maria), Miranda served as Director of Hispanic Ministries in the Fuller Evangelical Association, Director of the Charles Fuller Institute of Evangelism and Church Growth at Fuller Theological Seminary and was executive secretary of the Hispanic Congress on Evangelization held in 1986. Maria had a substantial ministry involving writing booklets, poetry, and thousands of programs for a successful radio show (Lausanne Committee for World Evangelization 1978; Plowman 1986; "Maria Miranda" 2017).

A third example, this time a particular address that showed up multiple times among Board Members, shows how a long-standing location in a smaller big city mattered in the National Association of Evangelicals. Among the Board Members analyzed here, ten different members reported their address as 1445 Boonville Avenue, Springfield, Missouri. This is the official headquarters of the Assemblies of God. The building, a several-story modernist structure with panels of glass windows ringing the building covers much of a city block roughly one mile north of downtown Springfield. The Springfield MSA has just over 325,000 residents in 2000 and is located in the southwest corner of the Midwest region.

In 1943, the Assemblies of God denomination was one of the first evangelical organizations to officially join the new National Association of Evangelicals. Building on Holy Spirit-filled and Pentecostal revivals in Topeka, Kansas, Missouri, Los Angeles (particularly important for the Holiness movement; see Conn 1984, 90), California, and additional locations, denominational leaders started meeting to form a new organization. After meeting in several locations, the denomination settled on Springfield, Missouri for multiple reasons: "Real estate prices were much lower than in the large cities; Springfield was the center of an excellent rail system for the distribution of mail throughout the country; its civic leaders were enthusiastically welcoming the move, and even offering financial assistance" (Brumback 1961, 212; Blumhofer 1985). Today, the denomination reports nearly 3.3 million adherents in the United States (Assemblies of God 2021).

The NAE Board Members approached their duties in the 1970s through the 1990s from a variety of locations, including the suburbs of the largest American cities and addresses in smaller big cities in the United States. Additionally, the Midwest was well represented, particularly compared to the percentage of Americans living there and the cultural strength of conservative Protestantism present in the South.

Headquarters in Suburban Illinois, Suburban California, and Washington, DC

After the emergence of the NAE in the early 1940s, the organization had headquarters in multiple locations. Following the October 1941 meeting that motivated subsequent activity, the Temporary Committee for United Action among Evangelicals started with an office in Brooklyn. After meeting in St. Louis in May 1942, the NAE offices moved to Park Street in Boston and then a nearby office. A Washington, DC office, best suited to consider legislation, interactions with politicians, and global missions, opened soon afterward (Matthews 1992, 59–62). The organization had staff in nine cities across the country by 1945. Under the third executive director of the NAE, Dr. Rutherford L. Decker of Kansas City, the NAE offices moved from Boston to Chicago in 1947. In 1954, the national offices moved from Chicago to Wheaton, Illinois. By 1956, the NAE had additional offices in Washington, DC, New York City, Boston, Cincinnati, Detroit, Chicago, Minneapolis, Wichita, Los Angeles, Portland, Oregon, and Williamsport, Pennsylvania (Murch 1956; Matthews 1992; National Association of Evangelicals 1992). However, changes in the 1960s prompted the NAE to close the regional offices and consolidate efforts in Wheaton (National Association of Evangelicals 2021).

When the NAE moved to Wheaton, the suburb was growing rapidly: it expanded from 11,638 residents in 1950 to 24,312 in 1960. Wheaton was the county seat of DuPage County, a county whose population also more than doubled between 1950 and 1960. Initially, the NAE had its headquarters in downtown Wheaton in a second story office on Main Street, very close to the downtown train station and the railroad tracks. By the 1960 local phone directory, the NAE offices had moved to East Willow several blocks southeast and across the railroad tracks.

But several years later the NAE moved to a new building just north of Wheaton on land in the growing adjacent suburb of Carol Stream. One delegate to the 1942 meeting helped the NAE relocate its headquarters. At the St. Louis gathering, Carl A. Gundersen represented the Chicago Business Men's Committee and the Scandinavian Alliance Mission. Additionally, Gundersen later served as NAE treasurer.

With his family, Gundersen came to the United States from Norway at age nine. Attending a Norwegian Evangelical Free Church from a young age, he started a successful career as a builder as a teenager and later also became a real estate broker. After going back to school at Moody Bible Institute, Gundersen combined his interests in development and ministry by serving Christian organizations. He served as general contractor and worked behind the scenes to ease the construction of a new Evangelical Free Church of America church in Wheaton that opened in 1954 (Gundersen 1966). As religion scholar Greg Chatterley (2018a) notes, this suburban congregation shed its ethnic and urban heritage with its founding in Wheaton, a largely white community with a significant number of evangelicals.

A few years later, Gundersen worked with Robert C. Van Kampen—a Christian publisher and bank executive in Wheaton, a cofounder of the Wheaton Evangelical Free Church, long-time associate of Billy Graham, and NAE Board Member in the Class of 1975 and 1978—to purchase land for residences in the new suburb of Carol Stream just north of Wheaton. When several evangelical groups said they hoped to expand, the businessmen donated land, helped fundraise and secure low-interest financing for the remaining funding, and facilitated construction of the new buildings. This included a new headquarters for the National Association of Evangelicals. This suburban development on behalf of evangelical organizations found the sympathetic ear of the developer and founder of Carol Stream, Jay Stream. Stream grew up in Wheaton and started Carol Stream in 1959 with the aim of mixing residences and industrial space to limit the need to commute to Chicago. At a cost of $100,000, the two story NAE headquarters "north of Wheaton" was dedicated on October 9, 1962. For his efforts, Gundersen was named by the NAE in 1962 as the second "Layman of the Year" ("Evangelicals Dedicate New Headquarters" 1962; Gundersen 1966; Moore 1984; Heise 1989; Matthews 1992; Chatterley 2018a; 2018b).

Within a decade, the NAE looked to expand their facilities to better serve its mission. A fundraising brochure from the mid-1970s (National Association of Evangelicals c. 1975) detailed the plans for and provided the rationale for a larger structure:

> The new Evangelical Center in Carol Stream (Wheaton), Illinois, will house several arms of NAE which previously have been located in as many as 10 separate offices. A common reception area and cooperative maintenance, printing, mailing and computer services will eliminate costly staff duplication. The present NAE headquarters, when sold, will supply some of the funds needed for the Center, a 23,280 square foot building to be located one block to the east. Because of its convenience to O'Hare airport, the Carol Stream location offers accessibility to any part of the country in a matter of hours.

An accompanying schematic of the proposed building and parking lots adds "The building will be so located on the site to leave ample room for future expansion."

Groundbreaking for the new headquarters took place on April 3, 1978 and the building opened in 1979. The new structure contained 24,000 square feet and cost $836,000. The contractor was listed as Gundersen Construction Co.—Carl had passed away in 1964 but his company continued—with the financing provided by Gary-Wheaton Bank, the institution where Robert Van Kampen worked. The new occupants of the building included: "the National Association of Evangelicals, World Relief Commission, National Association of Christian Schools, Evangelical Purchasing Service, National Christian Education Association, Universal Travel Service" (Matthews 1992; National Association of Evangelicals 1992).

The headquarters remained in Carol Stream until new NAE president Kevin Mannoia proposed in 1999 the organization move its headquarters from Carol Stream to Azusa, California. This was part of a larger vision to successfully engage society and culture. Mannoia said, "The motivation is to call the church to a new globalization mission that is culturally relevant, urban, and multiethnic." The NAE's Washington director, Richard Cizik, said Mannoia's larger vision for the organization would be easier to address in a "multicultural and ethnic community such as the L.A. base" ("Evangelical Association Will Relocate" 1999). The move would give the NAE offices near Los Angeles and in Washington, DC, providing a "bicoastal national image" (Kennedy 1999). As the NAE put it, such a move would lead to "offices on both coasts, at the governmental and cultural power centers" (National Association of Evangelicals 2021). In addition to the multicultural nature of the Los Angeles region, the location also offered access to Hollywood. Mannoia said, "The church has not had an advocacy presence in Hollywood since the mid-'60s. If we truly want to influence our culture, not through forcing our agenda, but rather by engaging and letting salt and light do its work, then we need to be present" (Rivera 2001). Scholar and pastor Peter Heltzel (2009, 143) described the physical location change as an indication of "missional engagement with culture as opposed to the cultural exclusion and separatism represented by the Wheaton, Illinois, location."

On September 13, 1999, a Special Meeting of the Board of Directors held in Washington, DC took up the proposed move. After some discussion for and against the relocation, the group voted on two items directly related to moving the office. On the item to "Sell the Wheaton Facility," the vote was 37 yes, 11 no, and 2 abstain and on the item "Relocation," the vote was 32 yes, 16 no, and 1 abstain (National Association of Evangelicals 1999).

The decision had immediate ramifications for employees and longer-term consequences for the NAE. The main Carol Stream headquarters only had six employees in 1999. At the same time, the building was also home to 52 employees of World Relief, an NAE organization first founded in the 1940s as the War Relief Commission. With the NAE selling the Carol Stream building, World Relief subsequently moved its operations to Baltimore (Murch 1956; Kennedy 1999; Pierce 2000). Looking back, the history of the NAE on the organization's website characterizes this decision to relocate as "costly" and contributing to significant financial difficulties for the organization (National Association of Evangelicals 2021). When Mannoia resigned as president of the NAE in June 2001, he listed reasons including an ongoing operating deficit plus organizational stresses that included the move of the organization to Azusa. The move to southern California was described as helping to have a "greater emphasis on urban ministry," "reaching out to growing ethnic groups in the United States," and "to have an influence on leaders of the entertainment industry" (Stammer 2001). The shift to southern California also built upon decades of evangelical growth in the region where migration from other parts of the United States, conservative politics, and the growth of megachurches and influential leaders and organizations created a home for evangelicals (McGirr 2001; Dochuk 2012; Wilford 2012; Mulder and Martí 2020).

With Mannoia no longer the president, the NAE board took up the question of the organization's headquarters in early 2002. The board voted in May 2002 to move the headquarters to Washington, DC. Not only did this offer an opportunity to interact more with the federal government and political leaders, the move enabled all of the NAE members to meet in a single location ("In Brief" 2002; Sellers 2002). The NAE Washington office had a long history; founded in 1943 as the public affairs office for the organization, the location allowed evangelicals to counter what they saw as political pressure from the more theologically liberal National Council of Churches (Cizik 2005). In addition to the move to Washington, DC, the organization opened a short-lived NAE Office of the President in the emerging evangelical center Colorado Springs with pastor Ted Haggard named as NAE president in 2003 (National Association of Evangelicals 2021).

Throughout much of its history, the NAE has had a central location in the Chicago suburbs and an important secondary office turned headquarters in Washington, DC. A short-lived sojourn to the Los Angeles suburbs intended to enhance the NAE's mission, particularly in regard to diversity and cultural influence, did not last long. Today, the former Carol Stream headquarters is occupied by Hope Publishing, an evangelical publishing house. Across the street is the headquarters for TEAM, The Evangelical Alliance Mission, and at the end of the short street is Tyndale House Publishers, another evangelical firm best known for the New Living Translation of the bible and popular *Left Behind* series. In the same time period, the National Council of Churches, an organization championed by country's largest mainline Protestant denominations, moved into the Interchurch Center near Columbia University in Manhattan (Billingsley 1990). (They also later relocated to Washington, DC in 2013 in order to save money and be close to "places of power"; see Markoe 2013.)

The Importance of the National Association of Evangelical in Multiple Locations

The official meetings in the early 1940s that helped launch the neo-evangelical project took place in major cities of the United States. In these crucial meetings, leaders and delegates of evangelical and fundamentalist organizations met in Chicago and St. Louis. At the foundational 1942 meeting, just over 40% of the delegates hailed from the biggest cities of the Northeast and Midwest including New York, Boston, Philadelphia, and Chicago. Many other delegates had locations in smaller big cities. Only 13% of the delegates listed addresses in suburbs.

By the final decades of the twentieth century, the NAE Board Members listed different locations compared to 1942. Many Board Members provided addresses in the largest metropolitan regions of the United States but those large metropolitan area Board Members listed suburban locations at much higher rates than Board Members as a whole. Overall, closer to the US population at large, nearly 50% of Board Members had suburban locations.

This data suggests over time the leaders of the NAE became more similar to the suburban composition of the entire United States. As I argue throughout this book, evangelicals, like Americans, adopted and embraced suburban life. This presents both opportunities and challenges for an evangelical organization intended to represent the broader interests of the religious group across a large country. If evangelical congregations, organizations, and laypeople are living in the suburbs, delegates and national leaders from similar locations know and can work within the spaces that reflect and shape evangelical sensibilities. From an ecological perspective, if evangelicals have found a niche in the suburbs, a national organization of evangelicals located in or familiar with the suburbs can serve them well.

On the other hand, from the beginning the NAE has desired to exert the influence of evangelicals as a collective in particular spheres. For example, NAE leaders raised concerns about radio airtime for conservative Protestants in the early 1940s. The Federal Communication Commission (FCC), legislators, lobbyists, and other actors in the Executive Branch who could influence the radio industry are located in Washington, DC. The early opening of a branch office amid the center of government and the eventual relocating of the headquarters there hint at the importance of being close to decision makers.

This interplay between suburban and urban locations highlights the tensions regarding place and cultural engagement within American evangelicalism. Suburban locations may make it more difficult to achieve evangelical goals of influencing society and government. As I argued with Benjamin Norquist in a study of the locations of evangelical colleges (Miller and Norquist 2021), suburban locations do not necessarily lead to involvement in networks and activities of the leading global cities of the United States. Locations in and the accompanying interactions with institutions and people in the biggest cities offers particular opportunities for creating change. Even in today's era of internet, social media, and global connectivity, proximity to and interactions with global centers matters. Evangelicals have some knowledge of this; from the beginning of the NAE, they have had a presence in Washington, DC and multiple leaders and board members in or near different big cities. When Billy Graham founded the evangelical counterpart to *Christian Century*, he wanted what became *Christianity Today* to be located in Washington, DC in order to have its best impact (Marsden 1987, 158). At the same time, the National Association of Evangelicals has been led in recent decades by multiple suburban pastors, not leaders from New York, Los Angeles, and Chicago, and for the majority of the group's existence its headquarters was in the suburbs of Chicago.

Another example of this tension involves the location of an important early neo-evangelical institution of higher learning. Strachan (2015) describes the academic shaping of the "Cambridge evangelicals" in the 1940s at Harvard.

The connections to and challenges from an elite institution just outside Boston sharpened the development of evangelical scholarship and theology. One of the group, Carl Henry, dreamed of an elite Christian research university. Other leaders provided feedback on a location, suggesting the Northeast with its academic prestige. More specifically, suggestions included a location in New York City with its influence or in nearby New Jersey.

Yet when fundamentalist pastor and popular radio host Charles Fuller worked with some of these Cambridge evangelicals to help found the first neo-evangelical institution of higher learning, Fuller Seminary, the school opened in suburban Pasadena, California in 1947. Fuller had lived in the suburbs of Los Angeles after graduating from Biola (Bible Institute of Los Angeles), an institution founded in the big city but that later moved to the suburbs in the late 1950s (Biola University 2007). The new evangelical school was first slated to open in a purchased mansion in a wealthier part of Pasadena. While Harold Ockenga wanted the seminary located in a city, others worried about the effects of being close to a big city and others advocated for moving further from Los Angeles. Fuller acquired a different property in Pasadena in 1951 and a new campus opened in 1953 (Marsden 1987, 58–60, 130–131).

This data also hints at regional shifts among evangelicals and the American population. Compared to the 1942 delegates, the Board Members from the 1970s through 1990s exhibit continuity with a high proportion of Midwest representatives. They also show change with more Board Members from the West and South and a significant decrease in Board Members from the Northeast, from a proportion higher than the percentage of Americans in the region to below the national distribution.

Missing from the NAE locations are places in the South. The traditional Bible Belt, stretching from Virginia to Texas, is underrepresented among delegates, board members, and the headquarters of the NAE. The identification of the South by the early 1900s as the region home to fundamentalists (Mathews 2006) and the discomfort Matthews (1992) describes among Southern evangelicals in working with a Northern organization or an evangelical label means that the NAE does not represent as many evangelicals as it could or in all the locations where evangelicals are present. Even as Southern cities and suburbs have boomed in population in the postwar era (Frey 2015), they remain underrepresented in the NAE.

While the Midwest provides a steady base for the NAE with evangelical denominations located there and heartland values, this again puts evangelicals at a disadvantage regarding locations in centers of power. While the NAE recognized a Washington office as a necessity, the coastal global cities of the United States—including New York City and Los Angeles—had a limited NAE presence.

Finally, the movement of the NAE headquarters—from Boston to Chicago to Wheaton to Carol Stream to Azusa to Washington—highlights a particular set of locations and one clear desired sphere of influence. Just over a decade after the founding of the NAE, the organization had their headquarters a small suburb with a strong evangelical reputation. From there and adjacent Carol Stream plus regional and department offices elsewhere, evangelicals sought to influence public policy and legislation over the next four decades. The NAE issued resolutions on many concerns and developed relationships with multiple powerful leaders, ranging from President Eisenhower, who was the first to welcome the group to the White House, to President Reagan, who delivered his "Evil Empire" speech to the NAE in 1983 (Cizik 2005).

The locations of the headquarters could be interpreted as ceding the cultural and financial power centers to others while solely focusing on political action. Without a significant presence in New York and Los Angeles, global cities and centers of influence, evangelicals have ignored certain kinds of power and influence in favor of others. For a religious tradition with a reputation of engaging in and fighting culture wars (e.g., Hunter 1991), locations outside the cultural centers of the United States means evangelicals may be at a disadvantage from the get go.

The short-lived efforts of NAE president Kevin Mannoia to connect the organization to Los Angeles and Hollywood—albeit from a suburban location—attempted to bring the NAE into big city conversations. The hard political power of Washington, DC is a known commodity but evangelicals are less effective at fostering and influencing soft cultural power in centers like Manhattan and Hollywood. Evangelicals may compete well in the suburbs, but feel less comfortable, whether as individuals or as a collective, in cultural centers. Even as evangelicals fought for radio time through national initiatives, they often centered their own separate media activities in locations like Nashville. Or, they had concentrations of organizations in places like Grand Rapids, Wheaton, and Colorado Springs (discussed further in Chapter 6).

Conclusion

Carl F. H. Henry was not a delegate to the 1942 NAE meeting in St. Louis but he was involved in the early days of the organization, including reporting on the first convention in 1943 and serving on the Commission on Educational Institutions while teaching and serving as the first academic dean at the newly created Fuller Seminary in the suburbs of Los Angeles (Murch 1956, 87–88; Matthews 1956, 52; Carl F. H. Henry Institute 2021). In 1947, he provided more fuel for the neo-evangelical fire with the publication of his book *The Uneasy Conscience of Modern Fundamentalism*. In responding to "the failure of the evangelical movement to react favorably on any widespread front to campaigns against social evils" (Henry 1947, 11), Henry twice refers to Augustine's influential work *City of God*. Here is one of the passages:

> Yet the early patriotic moralists attached pagan ethical standards—idolatry, sensuous luxury, sexual looseness, theatrical obscenity, gladiatorial cruelties, infanticide and abortion, commercial deceit; everywhere they pitched the Christian message against social immoralities. Augustine's *City of God* insisted that the temporal and eternal cities exist concurrently in history, as against the view that the kingdom of God is to be identified with super-history alone. (Henry 1947, 38)

Yet when calling evangelicals to action regarding "such admitted evils as aggressive warfare, racial hatred and intolerance, the liquor traffic, and exploitation or management" (Henry 1947, 3), Henry made little reference to place. The earthly cities referenced are more abstract than real cities in the United States. Prior to the Great Depression and World War II, suburbs across the United States started growing and soon after the publication of this book mass suburbanization began in earnest. How would evangelical locations affect their ability to address pressing social concerns? How did Henry's own position in suburban spaces, born and raised on Long Island and faculty member and administrator at multiple suburban Christian institutions of higher education, influence his perspective on the need for evangelicals to engage society as opposed to fundamentalist withdrawal? If Augustine had his vision of a *City of God*, what did a "suburb of God" in an increasingly suburban United States look like?

The next chapter examines a suburban community that has compelling reasons to be considered as much of a "suburb of God" as any in the United

States. Wheaton, considered with its neighbor just to the north Carol Stream, Illinois, was home to the National Association of Evangelicals, numerous evangelical parachurch organizations and businesses, Wheaton College, and many evangelical congregations and residents. How did Wheaton come to be known as "Christiantown, U.S.A.," according to one sociologist (Stellway 1990), out of the thousands of possible communities that could have developed such a reputation?

5
The Holy Suburb of Wheaton, Illinois

By the closing decades of the twentieth century, Wheaton, Illinois, a suburb 25 miles west of Chicago's central business district, was a large and high-status community. In the 1980 Census, it had the most residents of any suburb in DuPage County and had experienced four consecutive decades of population growth over 28%. It was the county seat of a wealthy and expanding county that included numerous jobs including in a burgeoning research corridor along I-88 (Edgerton 1983). It had a quaint downtown along the first railroad line built to and from Chicago as well as multiple historic buildings. It was a quiet bedroom suburb with numerous single-family home subdivisions, limited land devoted to industrial use, and prospects for a major new development on a former farm on the southern edge of the suburb.

Yet amid these suburban status symbols, Wheaton's most defining trait may have been the community's religious character. Two local history professors noted the presence of numerous evangelical organizations in the community (Maas and Weber 1976) as did an overview of DuPage County communities (Thompson 1985). Evangelical publishers, mission organizations, and ministry groups operated from Wheaton or adjacent Carol Stream. This concentration of organizations prompted a *New York Times* journalist to call Wheaton "the Vatican of evangelicals" (Vescey 1978). Alcohol could not be sold in Wheaton after the suburb voted in 1934 to enact a local prohibition after the passing of the Twenty-First Amendment (this was reversed by local vote in 1985). Wheaton College was emerging as a flagship college of evangelicals as the college itself moved out of a long fundamentalist period (Hamilton 1994) and the Billy Graham Center, named after the college's most famous alum, opened on the campus in 1980. A sociologist at Wheaton College dubbed the community "Christiantown, USA" (Stellway 1990). A congregational leader in a Jewish synagogue in a nearby suburb said they operated "within the 'Bible Belt' orbit of nearby Wheaton" (Numrich and Wedam 2015, 198). The city logo featured four buildings, including

Sanctifying Suburbia. Brian J. Miller, Oxford University Press. © Oxford University Press 2025.
DOI: 10.1093/oso/9780197679623.003.0006

Wheaton College's Blanchard Hall and a church steeple. This was no regular bedroom suburb; this was an evangelical center.

This status continues into the twenty-first century, even with the establishment of other evangelical centers in the United States (see Chapter 6) and change within Wheaton, nearby communities, and the Chicago region. Wheaton has been surpassed in population by neighboring Naperville, most new development is infill or redevelopment, and it is no longer the center of a Republican stronghold with an ascension of Democrats in local, state, and national offices. Wheaton is still home to Wheaton College, numerous evangelical organizations are based in the community and adjacent Carol Stream, and there are still dozens of churches. In interviews conducted in the late 2000s with leaders in Wheaton and nearby suburbs, they noted the community's reputation for being a dry community (even though this had ended over 20 years earlier in 1985 to help promote business and restaurant activity) and the dilution of the local evangelical presence with more new residents.

Given Wheaton's religiosity, what leads to the establishment of a suburb as a community with a religious character known to residents and outsiders? What factors prompted the concentration of evangelical residents, congregations, and organizations?

I argue that Wheaton presents a fitting case study to analyze how American evangelicals embraced the suburbs. I first studied the community in 2008–2009 as part of a larger project comparing the growth and development of Wheaton to two nearby suburbs: West Chicago and Naperville. For the larger project, I spent more than 60 days in local museums and historical societies and this included time at two institutions in downtown Wheaton: the DuPage County Historical Museum and the Center for History (no longer open). Additionally, I conducted semistructured interviews with 35 local leaders across the three suburbs. Eleven of these leaders were in Wheaton, including the city manager, the then current mayor, one past mayor, and several local business leaders. Even as Wheaton's actions over time regarding land and development led to different outcomes for the community compared to its neighbors (Miller 2013), the suburb's religious character recognized by insiders and outsiders stood out as a unique and influential feature of the city.

The case of Wheaton highlights the long-term concatenation of local decisions and regional and national patterns that can lead to an established evangelical presence in the midst of sprawling suburbia. Wheaton may be an outlier as relatively few researchers consider religion or religious character as a major organizing principle in thinking about suburbs. Few suburbs will likely follow a similar path; the Chicago region alone has hundreds of suburbs with few noted for religiosity. However, the evangelical convergence in Wheaton is not the only case of a community developing an evangelical reputation as the analysis of three additional communities in Chapter 6 illustrates. The case of Wheaton shows how responding to race and ethnicity in a changing region, a network of evangelical institutions, and a suburban lifestyle that overlapped with evangelical priorities contributed to the development of a suburb known for its evangelical activity.

The Character of Communities and Explaining the Convergence of Evangelicals

Wheaton is a suburb, a term widely used and understood (even if there is more complexity to this concept; see Chapter 1). Yet the common traits of suburbs that help differentiate them from cities or rural areas can also mask the different day-to-day experiences and local characters present in different suburbs. Two adjacent suburbs of the same type, edge cities or industrial suburbs or master-planned communities, may have very different internal and external understandings of who they are, how they arrived at their current state, and what their future might be.

Sociologists Harvey Molotch, William Freudenburg, and Krista Paulsen (2000) examined the idea of place character through comparing the growth and trajectories of Santa Barbara and Ventura, California. Both cities northwest of Los Angeles share important traits: located on the Pacific Ocean, they experienced the construction of interstates and expansion of the oil industry around the same time. However, how they responded to these common social forces differed: Santa Barbara did not want a highway along the waterfront, while Ventura's decision to allow this helped cut off the beach from the community's downtown. Ventura was more open to oil drilling so offshore sit drilling platforms while these cannot be seen from the Santa Barbara beach. These factors helped lead to two different cities, a Santa Barbara with stronger focus on arts and outdoor activity and a Ventura more focused on business.

Similar dynamics also play out in suburbs. The Chicago region has several hundred suburbs that differ in culturally meaningful ways. They all orbit the same global city and have experienced similar political and social pressures because of this. However, other factors and decisions push them down different trajectories that lead to significant differences today. For example, suburbs at their formation can have different purposes including being a center for agriculture, providing hundreds of thousands of square feet of office and retail space, or providing homes and property just outside the boundaries of the big city (e.g., Keating 2005; Garreau 1991; Hanlon 2010). The conditions at the formation of a community do not dictate all of the future outcomes. Local leaders and residents make subsequent decisions about growth, annexations, and the kind of development they desire to see (Miller 2013).

Often missing from these considerations of suburban character is the influence of religion. The majority of residents in the United States practice religion and/or cite a religious affiliation and the country has thousands of houses of worship. At the same time, relatively few suburban communities have an established reputation for being a religious community, let alone a community shaped by religious actors and organizations.

Studying the trajectory of Wheaton helps untangle the particular reasons for a suburb developing such a character and concentration. Describing religious suburbs is one matter; it is another to explain how they came to be communities marked by religion rather than other possible factors. I assess four explanations that could be helpful for understanding a convergence of religious adherents in one particular suburb. Each of these are complex in their own right and also possibly overlap with each other. The analysis of this chapter will consider which of the four best fits Wheaton's particular evangelical trajectory.

To start, issues of race and class pushed evangelicals, among many others, to the suburbs. In the process of white flight, middle- and upper-class whites left American cities in droves in the mid-twentieth century as more racial and ethnic minorities, immigrants, and lower-class residents moved to cities looking for opportunities (Massey and Denton 1993; Sugrue 1996; Lassiter 2006). Faced with changing demographics plus cities with growing problems, evangelicals and their churches fled to the suburbs where whiter, wealthier residents lived (e.g., Dochuk 2003; Doughtery and Mulder 2009; Mulder 2015). In the Chicago region, as churches in white denominations left neighborhoods changing in Chicago, they ended up in suburbs like Wheaton (see Chapter 3). Today, there is still a divide between white and Black congregations and religiously conservative whites tend to have individualistic views about racism works (Emerson and Smith 2000; Shelton and Emerson 2012). To apply this to Wheaton, evangelicals ended up in this suburb in large numbers because of a whiter and middle- to upper-class demographic profile.

A second possibility is that prominent evangelical leaders and institutions led the majority of evangelicalism to relocate in the suburbs. Social networks influence urban patterns as well as link different places (Neal 2013). This explanation emphasizes the importance of particular nodes or hubs within evangelicalism (Lindsey 2007). Influential pastors or heads of institution moved to the suburbs and encouraged others to join them or influential institutions or organizations operated as anchors around which others would gather. This could be considered a form of contagion where certain behaviors and values are passed through a network (Christakis and Fowler 2009) or migration patterns where pioneer leaders or influential groups and certain economic conditions help attract related people, in this case related by particular beliefs and a subculture, to a community (Haug 2008). Congregations may have been following the decisions made by other congregations or organizations—such as the National Association of Evangelicals (see Chapter 4)—and felt compelled to move to the suburbs. The mass movement of evangelicals to the suburbs then hinges on a small group of central evangelicals and institutions who persuaded others or provided a model to follow.

A third possible social force to explain Wheaton involves cultural meaning-making (Spillman 2020) of evangelicals matching those of suburban Wheaton. While definitions of evangelicals can emphasize theological distinctives (Bebbington 1989), evangelicals are also marked by a particular social history and a distinctive way of life (Smith 1998; Steensland et al. 2000; Larsen 2007). This is especially true for the evangelicals who emerged in the 1940s and coalesced around political and social positions starting in the late 1970s.

Evangelicals are known for particular cultural traits that both reflect and enact cultural meaning. Chaves (2004) argues that religious congregations and groups are notable for the cultural configurations in their services and communities with more conservative churches exhibiting relatively less ceremony and more enthusiasm than mainline Protestant denominations, Catholics, Eastern Orthodox, and Reformed groups. This informalism and emotional energy is present in numerous megachurches (Wellman, Corcoran, and Stockly 2020). The prevalence of "moral minimalism" in the suburbs (Baumgartner 1988), meaning that suburbs are relatively free of open strife and community members get along by not being highly engaged in the lives of others, leaves room for evangelicals to create a strong subculture by drawing strong boundaries and also developing alternative institutions (Smith 1998). Evangelicals are used to adapting their message and lifestyle to new contexts, including that of the more mobile, fragmented, and individualized suburbs (Wilford 2012; Mulder and Martí 2020).

One of the strongest cultural emphases in suburbs and evangelicalism is promoting families and raising children (Seeley, Sim, and Loosley 1956; Nash and Berger 1962; Nash 1968; Wilcox 2009). Luhr argues that this emphasis on family is closely linked to other values: "The valorization of the middle-class white family required that emotional themes such as nation, duty, authority, and tradition be linked with neoconservative economic themes such as competitive individualism and opposition to taxation and government" (2009, 11).

These links between evangelical and suburban culture fit Weber's (1930) classic argument about how theological and cultural understandings can develop and become intertwined with social practices and structures. As evangelicals looked at and then moved to the suburbs, their theology and view of the world melded with the suburban reality (Cavalcanti 2007).

The final possible reason for Wheaton's evangelicalism involves the religious economy or marketplace argument within the sociology of religion (e.g., Finke and Stark 2005; Iannaccone 1992). In this perspective, the separation of church and state (particularly compared to state endorsed churches and faith in other countries) and no state-sponsored religion leads to intense competition between religious groups. Conservative religious groups have thrived because they have been able to adapt to this competitive landscape, winning converts and members.

Have evangelicals competed better for adherents in Wheaton? As populations boomed in postwar suburbs, did evangelicals win this competition in these places? While mainline Protestants promoted ecumenism and comity, evangelicals and more independent churches adapted to the suburban landscape (Diamond 2003), leading to an increasing number of conservative Protestant congregations as well as innovations. In particular, megachurches have drawn a lot of attention (Thumma and Travis 2007; Karnes et al. 2007; Warf and Winsberg 2010; Elisha 2011a; Wellman, Corcoran, and Stockly 2020) as churches that promote a kind of spirituality amenable to suburban souls. Evangelicals have adopted the spatial logic of suburbia and that of places like Wheaton because it helped them gain an advantage compared to other religious groups.

Alternatively, evangelicals might have been bad at competing for religious goods in the suburbs. Evangelicals may have come to Wheaton and the suburbs late, assimilating after mass suburbanization began. Reluctantly or hesitantly, evangelicals realized that they had to engage the suburbs or they would become increasingly irrelevant. As one suburban megachurch founder says, "Suburban churches follow suburban development—not the other way around. Congregations always seem to be playing catch-up in new, shifting suburban communities" (DeKruyter and Schultze 2008, 6). Perhaps evangelicals did not discuss the implications of moving to the suburbs until long after other groups and were not aware of the advantages the suburbs might present. Or suburbanization swallowed up conservative Protestant churches that existed within once-rural communities (e.g., Eiesland 2000; Diamond 2003) and then congregations and evangelicals realized they needed to compete.

These four possible forces linking evangelicals and the character of Wheaton are not mutually exclusive. However, in order to not just describe how evangelicals and suburbs converged or provide data that show that this has happened, these explanations help aid the construction of causal arguments about how evangelicals came to Wheaton and suburbs more broadly. The movement of people, particularly evangelicals, to the suburbs simply did not just happen; social forces pushed people and institutions into particular spatial contexts and these new suburban residents had choices in how to respond and whether to fully adapt to the suburban context.

A Community and Religious History of Wheaton

The first white settlers arrived in the area in the early 1830s amid treaties between the US government and Native tribes opening the land to white settlement (Keating 2012). Erastus Gary arrived in 1831 from Pomfret, Connecticut and claimed the land that is now southwest of Wheaton. Gary helped prompt the brothers Warren and Jesse Wheaton to come to the same area from Pomfret; Warren started the journey in 1837 and settled on land in 1838, while Jesse arrived in 1838. The brothers officially received deeds for their land in the mid-1840s (League of Women Voters 1956; Moore 1974). As the first railroad in and out of Chicago, the Galena & Chicago Union, planned its route west of the city, the Wheaton brothers granted a right-of-way through their land (Blanchard 1882, 168; Moore and Bray 1989, 147). The community of Wheaton had its official start in the 1850s on this same rail line with the community platted in 1853 and incorporated in 1859 (Moore 1974, 43–44). The location of the community in the center of DuPage County plus its railroad access helped lead to a county election that resulted in the county seat moving to Wheaton from Naperville in 1867 ("Excitement in DuPage County" 1867; Buck 1992).

The community grew slowly and steadily between 1870 and 1940, increasing from 988 to 7,389 residents during that time. Via vote, Wheaton became a city in 1890 (City of Wheaton 1991). The first telephone lines arrived in the early 1890s and the Chicago Golf Course was founded in 1892 (Moore 1974, 68). In 1902, the first part of an electric interurban line opened up alongside the community's original railroad, giving residents multiple transit options for the next five decades ("Remember When Railroad Ran?" 1959b). As county seat, people from around the county came to the county courthouse and facilities to conduct business. Wheaton became a center of political conservatism; the county quickly turned Republican after the founding of the Republican Party in the mid-1850s (Buck 2019; Schmidt 1989) and Republican politicians dominated local, state, and national offices through the end of the twentieth century. First documented in the 1870 Census, Wheaton had a small Black population that lived on the eastern edge of the community. While residents resisted the construction of another Black neighborhood south of downtown near the prominent local golf course, Wheaton was unusual in DuPage County in having any Black residents (Miller and Malone 2019).

The community quickly acquired the reputation as a religious place. By the late 1800s, Wheaton had multiple congregations: a Wesleyan Methodist congregation (1843) that merged in 1860 with a Congregational Church; First Methodist Episcopal Church (1853), later renamed to honor the Gary family; a Universalist congregation (1862, later moved to neighboring Glen Ellyn); a second Wesleyan Methodist Congregation (1862, disbanded 1902); First Baptist Church (1864, moved from Stacy's Corners); St. John's Lutheran (1867); Trinity Episcopal (1875); and St. Michael's Catholic Church (1879) (Peters 1981; Moore 1974). The community became home to a religious school when Wesleyans in Illinois founded the Illinois Institute in 1853. The school was renamed Wheaton College in 1860 after a gift of land by Warren Wheaton (Bechtel 1984). The first president of the college and others noted the proximity to the railroad and Chicago (Willard 1950). An early history of DuPage County (Blanchard 1882) noted Wheaton's "tenacious religious connections, not only of its leading men, but of its every day sort of people." An 1897 guide (Pritchard 1897) said, "Wheaton is also pre-eminent as a religious center." Evangelist Billy Sunday spoke at Gary Methodist Episcopal Church in 1902 (Williams 1959).

Wheaton was not home just to evangelical or fundamentalist Christians. The suburb had a thriving Catholic parish, St. Michael's, just south of the downtown (Moore 1974, 251; Blanchard 1882, 183–184). The city had the county's only Black congregation, Second Baptist Church, for a period (Knoblauch 1951). The American Theosophical Society constructed its national headquarters in Wheaton in the late 1920s ("A Religious Headquarters" 1926).

In the postwar era, the suburb's religious and politically conservative reputation continued as the community expanded in population and size amid mass suburbanization. In the 1940 Census, Wheaton had 7,389 residents, 24,312 in 1960, 43,043 in 1980, and a peak of 55,416 in 2000. The number of Black residents grew slowly and residents helped lobby the city to pass Illinois's first fair housing ordinance in 1967 (Miller and Malone 2019). At the same time, Black residents did not necessarily feel welcome in Wheaton (Wheaton Public Library 2021). More recently, refugees experienced difficulties while they experienced support by local evangelical organizations and congregations plus the local school district (Asgedom 2002). Numerous new subdivisions of single-family homes added residents to the community. The suburb did not annex land at the rate of the most aggressive suburbs— nearby Naperville moved more quickly and decisively in expanding its municipal boundaries (Miller 2016)—but it added residences and land through the late 1980s. A brief attempt in the late 1960s to introduce more urban housing into the downtown led to the construction of two 20-story apartment buildings despite pushback from some residents. With limited greenfield space after the development of housing and retail space on the former Rice Farm, the city turned its efforts in the 1990s to developing downtown condos (Miller 2013).

The religious reputation of the community continued. An undated advertisement from Gary-Wheaton Bank (n.d.), itself founded by the founding families in the community, suggested that had the founders not been the same, there would be "No Wheaton College" and "Probably very few of the churches which give the town its character today." Several interviewed local leaders referred to how the Wheatons helped set the tone for the "moral fiber" of the community. Having expanded its student body during the Great Depression and with leading alum Billy Graham, Wheaton College emerged in this era as an important evangelical school (Hamilton 1994). A 1991 "City of Wheaton: Resident Information Guide" (City of Wheaton 1991) included Wheaton College as one of "the cornerstones laid by these founding fathers" that contributed to later growth. Some claimed that Wheaton had the most churches per capita in the United States (Community Profile 1994).

The concentration of religious organizations in and near Wheaton increased in the postwar era. Here is one list compiled early in the twenty-first century:

> Headquartered here, either formerly or currently, are such organizations as The Evangelical Alliance Mission (TEAM); Peter Deyneka Russian Ministries; *His* magazine; Harold Shaw Publishers; Tyndale House (publishers of the *Left Behind* series); Marianjoy Rehabilitation Clinic; Conservative Baptist International; *Christianity Today*; Van Kampen Press; Scripture Press, Creation House; Chapel of the Air; Hope Publishing (hymnals); Good News Publishers/Crossway Books; National Association of Evangelicals; Hitchcock Publishing (business magazines); Pioneer Clubs, Christian Working Woman; World Relief; Sword of the Lord; and the Evangelical Child and Family Agency. (Call 2006)

As discussed further in Chapter 6, Wheaton was one of the several communities in the United States evangelical organizations sought out and located in.

As Wheaton grew, a 1985 referendum to allow the sale of alcohol in the suburb demonstrated the intertwining of local regulations and local religious character. While Wheaton was not the only dry suburb in the Chicago region at the time—one article lists seven dry suburbs in early 1985 (Fegelman and Gibson 1985)—this referendum opened a conversation about local religion. Wheaton had initially banned the sale of alcohol in 1886 and after Federal Prohibition had been repealed, voted again in 1934 to ban alcohol sales (Lepillez 1981). A write-in candidate for mayor running in 1983 to allow liquor sales prompted the suburb's leader to decry the effort and say, "You have to understand the psychology of a town like Wheaton that has taken a certain amount of pride for not going in this direction" (Reardon 1983).

In an effort intended to help boost business in the community, help revive the downtown, and increase tax receipts ("Prohibition Information" n.d.; Letter n.d.; Fegelman and Gibson 1985), a more formal effort to repeal the local prohibition began in 1984. One of the primary supporters of repealing the ban suggested religious voters might be difficult to overcome: "I think that Wheaton College is taking a kind of neutral stand because they need motels and good restaurants... I think it's the 'born-again' Christians we can't do too much about" (Schwarze 1984). As the election neared, the opposition from religious groups in the community was not well organized: "Perhaps the greatest surprise was that despite Wheaton's long-standing reputation as a religious center, none of Wheaton's religious organizations took public views on the liquor issue, although at least one church counseled parishioners to vote against it" (Dungey 1985; Schwarze 1984).

Residents overturned the ban on liquor sales by a 4,247 to 3,353 vote on April 2, 1985 (Griffin and Barnum 1985). Decades beyond repeal of prohibition, it continues to be an enduring marker of the community. In interviews in the late 2000s, leaders in nearby suburbs still remembered Wheaton in these terms and Wheaton's leaders have heard or perceive that outsiders still think of Wheaton in such terms. The ban on alcohol sales was one of the most visible signs of Wheaton's religious character, notwithstanding the city's churches and religious college. The city's first "Ale Fest" in 2011 (Santana 2011), subsequent local events featuring alcohol, and that multiple establishments downtown feature alcohol counteract the long legacy of local prohibition. That liquor could be sold led to conclusions about the dilution of power and numerical strength of the evangelical population in Wheaton (Sullivan 1989). This idea was repeated in the late 2000s by multiple local leaders who also attributed this change to the growth of the city and the influx of new residents.

The liquor referendum was not the only area in which evangelical values or intentions clashed with others in the community. A local boycott of a 7-Eleven because of the sale of pornographic magazines successfully pushed the owner to close the location and the corporate parent took over (Kass 1985). Additional conflicts between religious members of the community and others included teaching evolution and using certain textbooks in elementary schools. This led a Wheaton City Council member and 30-year employee of Wheaton College to say, "The traditional evangelical character is still here, is still strong and it won't go away... the influx of new people as new housing develops may be diminishing that. We have a lot of people living in Wheaton who are not part of the traditional roots of the past" (Banas 1991).

Not all residents viewed the concentration of evangelicals positively. One resident said outsiders might "still only think of the churches" instead of all the other good qualities of the community (Wheaton Suburban Living 2003). Residents could see those connected to the college as "righteous overmuch" at times (Willard 1950, 143). In interviews, more recent leaders said the concentration could lead to a "holier-than-thou" attitude, and a perception that nonevangelicals may not fit in. Conflict emerged over the proposed expansion of several churches near downtown into more historic neighborhoods in the community (Stewart 1989; Mehler 1990). Finally, with a large county complex in the community plus lots of churches and Wheaton College within the suburb, there have been consistent complaints about the loss of this property from the tax rolls (Willard 1950, 141–142; Moore 1984).

With growth limited in the early decades of the twenty-first century to infill development, whether through teardowns in desirable neighborhoods or office space and apartments on desirable downtown properties (Mann 2008), or redevelopment, Wheaton is largely established and mature. The religious character of the community continues. An entry for the community in the *Encyclopedia of Chicago* notes, "it is a metropolitan religious center" (Grossman, Keating, and Reiff 2004). The suburb has over 40 churches plus other religious centers, including a Sikh congregation, a mosque that opened in a former Assemblies of God building, Wheaton College, numerous evangelical businesses or organizations, and The Theosophical Society in America, that continue to operate in the suburb or in adjacent Carol Stream.

Compelling Reasons for Wheaton Becoming an Evangelical Center

Explaining Wheaton's enduring religious character and concentration of evangelicals involves considering multiple social forces. Why did Wheaton's evangelical and religious character emerge in a way that stands out from other suburbs in the Chicago region and across the United States?

Of the four reasons discussed above regarding the development of an evangelical character, three are more compelling after considering Wheaton's history. First, Wheaton today continues to be a majority white and wealthy community. Like many Chicago suburbs, Wheaton gained white residents who left Chicago and those who did not want to live in more diverse cities or communities. Wheaton was unusual among DuPage County communities in having any Black residents and was the first community in Illinois to pass a fair housing ordinance, but the Black population was small, Black and other residents of color were not always welcome, and the vast majority of Wheaton leaders have been white (Miller and Malone 2019; Kisiel and Miller 2023). According to 2022 American Community Survey estimates, Wheaton is 78.4% white alone, the median household income is $108,737, and the poverty rate is 5.3%. Just 3.5% of residents are Black alone, 7.1% are Hispanic or Latino, and 6.6% are Asian alone. Numerous suburbs within DuPage County and the Chicago region are more diverse and DuPage County itself is 65% white alone, 15% Hispanic or Latino, 13.2% Asian, and 5.4% Black. The county's median household income is $100,292 with a poverty rate of 6.9%. Development in Wheaton in recent decades has tended to emphasize single-family homes or condos with limited construction of apartments or cheaper homes.

The boom in church construction in the Chicago suburbs highlighted in the discussion in Chapter 3 on the white flight of Protestants from Chicago also occurred in Wheaton. Even as the community had several important long-standing congregations, the suburb witnessed the founding of dozens of new congregations since the end of World War II. Twelve churches were built in Wheaton from 1947 to 1959 ("Decades of Progress" n.d.). Listings in the Yellow Pages in local phone books show an increase from 10 congregations in July 1951 to 19 in November 1960 to 27 in June 1970 and 37 in October 1980 (these are not comprehensive sources; I know of at least a few congregations who were active in the community and are not listed in earlier years). Many of the congregations founded in the postwar era were white and at least middle-class.

A Wheaton congregation founded right before the Great Depression helps illustrate these patterns. Wheaton Bible Church began in 1929 with a group of residents initially meeting on the campus of Wheaton College. They opened their first building two blocks north of downtown Wheaton and several blocks west of the college in 1936. The church building grew, the congregation added services, and members of the church founded multiple nearby congregations over the next few decades. The congregation "started a Hispanic Sunday School class that evolved into Iglesia del Pueblo" that meets in the church's building. In 2008, the congregation moved to a larger facility and more land several miles northwest in West Chicago (Wheaton Bible Church 2022).

This congregation has expanded, constructed multiple sizable buildings, and aimed to reach new people and non-Christians in the region. The growth of the church has echoed the suburbanization pressure of the area. At the same time, the congregation is careful to note on its history page that "our faith and practice stand on the foundation of the Bible, which is the inspired, infallible, and inviolable Word of God" and in describing a new social service ministry in West Chicago, a community that is majority Latino, the church says it was motivated by "Understanding that the Gospel we embrace is *not* a social gospel, but it *is* a Gospel with social implications" (Wheaton Bible Church 2022). Although the church is now located in West Chicago and has a significant service presence in that community, continuing with the name Wheaton Bible Church connects it to its starting place and a community with a religious reputation.

Just as race and ethnicity played a role in growing suburbs across the United States, so too has it affected evangelicals concentrated in Wheaton. Compared to numerous other Chicago suburbs, Wheaton was more inclusive through the late 1960s, but the community is not known for its racial and ethnic diversity today. In a community that is majority white and well-off, evangelicals have found a home.

Related to the composition of the community is the daily life evangelicals can live in Wheaton. How does meaning-making in Wheaton line up with that of evangelicals? Wheaton is a stable suburban community with numerous amenities, the kind of quiet, conservative, and family-oriented bedroom suburb that could prove attractive to evangelicals. In 2008 interviews, several leaders noted the stability of the suburb. The suburb has received multiple awards over the years. *Look* magazine named Wheaton an "All-American City" in 1968. As the magazine noted positive change in the community, such as the recently passed fair housing ordinance, it also acknowledged the role of local evangelicals:

> Change came slowly, hesitantly at first, as might be expected in a town that prides itself accurately on being "churchgoing, conservative and dry." Wheaton is still under the lingering, rectifying influence of Wheaton College, a fundamentalist institution that produced Billy Graham and still forbids its students to dance or see a movie. (Look 1968)

The library in the community is top-rated, the suburb has low levels of crime, local schools receive positive ratings, the park district offers numerous activities for all ages, and local congregations offer numerous programs and weekend services. A 1993 book *50 Fabulous Places to Raise Your Family* included Wheaton (Rosenberg and Rosenberg 1993). Niche (2022) gives Wheaton an "A+" grade and it is listed as "#6 in Best Places to Live in DuPage County." In other words, Wheaton is a stable, upper-middle-class, whiter suburb with numerous opportunities for families.

The allure of life in Wheaton was also clear to Billy Graham. Graham graduated from Wheaton College in 1943. Before leading a crusade in Chicago, Graham hosted an eight-day event in Wheaton in late September and early October 1959 as the college started celebrations for its 100th anniversary. Before the event started, one journalist said, "At first glance, carrying the Gospel to Wheaton would seem as superfluous as carrying holy water to the Vatican" (Gould 1959). Even in "a city known worldwide for its churches, as headquarters for many religious organizations, and the site of Wheaton College" ("Feel Greatest Impact" 1959a) at his opening press conference Graham himself described how the Crusade could contribute to the suburb:

> The city of Wheaton is very much like most towns, he explains. "While it may have certain virtues that are above the average for a city of its size, it also has its share of sin and social problems.
>
> One of the problems that the church faces in a city like Wheaton is lethargy and indifference. There are hundreds of people within a few miles of the college who rarely, if ever, darken the door of a church. It is hoped that many of these may be reached for Christ and His kingdom.
>
> In addition, these special services could provide a new spiritual link between the college and the community, and bring a new spiritual unity among the churches and religious leaders of the area. (Gould 1959)

Graham spoke to a little more than 100,000 people who gathered in fields and buildings of the suburban college ("Statistics on Crusade" 1959c). After finishing in Wheaton, Graham announced a larger Crusade in Chicago and in 1962, this Crusade attracted over 700,000 visitors and the final meeting drew 116,000 to Soldier Field (Philbrick 1962).

Nearly two decades later, Graham chose Wheaton College as the institution to house a new center devoted to evangelism. Speaking at the 1977 groundbreaking for the Billy Graham Center, Graham provided multiple reasons why Wheaton was chosen over other places including Charlotte, North Carolina, Baylor University, and the University of North Carolina–Chapel Hill:

> There are at least four reasons why we felt Wheaton was the right place for this Center. First was Wheaton College's long record of complete loyalty to the Scriptures and its history of financial integrity ... and today probably more than ever stands "For Christ and His Kingdom." The second factor is the favorable location. You are standing not only at the crossroads of America but in a way at the crossroads of the world here ... Another factor is the city of Wheaton itself... How happy I am that this Center can be built in this lovely suburban city which has always represented to me a city of families ... of homes ... stability ... character, a city that stands for those virtues and qualities of the heartland of America that have made our country great. A final reason is that Wheaton and its environs is probably one of the world's centers of evangelical Protestantism. We will be able to draw on this vast reservoir of talent and inspiration. (Bechtel 1984)

In addition to the presence of Wheaton College in an advantageous location outside of Chicago, Graham praises the virtues of the suburb and the concentration of evangelical actors.

Graham started his explanation with Wheaton College, home to the then new Billy Graham Center, a long-standing institution in the suburb. Wheaton College can be viewed as an anchor that helped draw students, faculty, staff, and additional residents and organizations to the community (Schmeltzer 1986). Tied initially to the abolitionist leanings in the community and later to the growing neo-evangelical movement that emerged from pre–World War II fundamentalism (Hamilton 1994), Wheaton College is a visible and persistent evangelical symbol.

The evangelical organizations that came to Wheaton in the postwar era had some connections to Wheaton College. Ken Taylor, creator of the paraphrase bible The Living Bible, was a graduate of Wheaton College who later founded Tyndale House Publishers in Carol Stream. At the formation and early years of the National Association of Evangelicals, Wheaton College was an important institution but just one of numerous evangelical institutions represented. Carl Gunderson, the businessman who helped build the Wheaton Evangelical Free Church and donated land to evangelical organizations in adjacent Carol Stream, was not a graduate of Wheaton College and was more involved in his denomination and the NAE.

As discussed further in Chapter 6, a network and inertia developed among all of these evangelical organizations, congregations, and Wheaton College. Churches provided homes for worship and possible partners for organizations, organizations provided means by which others interested in particular areas or businesses could work or volunteer, and Wheaton College trained future workers and provided a stable institution.

The period from the late 1940s to the late 1970s was particularly crucial to the development of this network and evangelical character in Wheaton. Prior to World War II, the claims about the community's religious character were more local. By the early 1950s, the National Association of Evangelicals locating in Wheaton plus their partner and Wheaton College alum, Billy Graham, helped give Wheaton more recognition as a religious center. By the late 1970s Wheaton's evangelical character had expanded to businesses and parachurch organizations and this was recognized throughout the United States.

There is less evidence that evangelicals in Wheaton were more successful in attracting evangelicals to their communities compared to other suburbs or that evangelicals in Wheaton lagged behind other places in attracting evangelicals. Wheaton's population growth was tied to the pressure of suburban growth from Chicago in DuPage County which first spread to the eastern side of the county, involving suburbs like Elmhurst (which became home to a small Christian Reformed Church population centered around church and school; see Mulder 2015), before spreading along transportation corridors away from the city. With two railroad lines and growing housing options from the late 1940s onward, Wheaton attracted residents. All the suburbs in DuPage County grew and new communities were founded, even as decisions made by each suburb helped ultimately determine how much land they acquired and how they used that land.

With evangelicals often emphasizing evangelism, congregations and organizations in and near Wheaton have promoted this. Sometimes, this focus has been at a larger scale: Billy Graham preached to millions in the United States and abroad and evangelicals emphasized global missions. Other times, evangelicals in Wheaton have targeted their own community and neighbors for evangelism and outreach. Whether they have reached suburbia better than others is hard to assess. In a history of Wheaton College, Willard (1950, 141–143) shares a local anecdote and sentiments regarding what community members viewed as aggressive evangelism. At the same time, Willard (1950, 178–179) spoke positively of Wheaton College students sharing the gospel far and wide. Regarding congregations, numerous Wheaton churches have decades of history in the community even as two long-time Wheaton churches are now satellite congregations of Naperville megachurches: the former Wheaton Evangelical Free Church is now part of Compass Church and the former First Baptist Church is now part of Highpoint Church. Evangelical organizations promote local evangelism; for example, YoungLife and its members work with local middle school and high school students.

Conclusion

During the 2020 Super Bowl, Walmart ran a minute-long advertisement titled "United Towns." The commercial featured images of small towns across America and a voiceover extolling the virtues of their residents and the presence of Walmart down the street.

About 10 seconds into the commercial is a two second video looking down a street lined with brick buildings toward a freight train moving right to left through a downtown. Though not announced in the ad, this is a view of Wheaton. The video looks south on Main Street toward the railroad tracks that helped give rise to the community over 150 years before. On this same block now featuring Starbucks, numerous hair salons, and other small businesses, the National Association of Evangelicals once had its headquarters.

The Walmart ad starts with, "If you looked at America like a bird, and that was all you knew, would you really understand it with just that point of view?" From a 10,000-foot view, is Wheaton just like all other similar whiter and wealthier bedroom suburbs? The commercial does not feature any imagery of a religious building nor is Wheaton associated with any religious character. In Walmart's view of America, summed up at the end with the written words "Live Better. Together.," religion plays little visible role. Similarly, when *Money* magazine selected its best place to live in each state in 2018 (Mishkin, Akhtar, and Bhardwaj 2018), the description for Wheaton, the winner for Illinois, made reference to the city's abolitionist founders and local amenities like the DuPage County Historical Society, the Popcorn Shop, and Cosley Zoo but did not note anything about religiosity.

But Wheaton's religious character is regularly noted by residents and outsiders who attest to the concentration of evangelical activity and groups. The abolitionist founders were motivated in part by religious convictions. Numerous important churches were and are located right outside the quaint downtown and throughout the community. Dozens of evangelical organizations and businesses operated from Wheaton and adjacent Carol Stream.

I argue that the development of an evangelical character in Wheaton came about because of three important forces: race and exclusion operating amid suburbanization pressures in the Chicago region, a developing network of evangelical congregations and organizations with Wheaton College serving as an anchor, and a stable and family-friendly community with values that aligned with those of the emerging evangelicals of the postwar era. These factors helped create a bedroom suburb uniquely known for a concentration of evangelical residents, congregations, and organizations. Amid hundreds of suburbs in the Chicago region and thousands in the United States, Wheaton developed a reputation as an evangelical place.

This case study shows how Wheaton as an evangelical suburban center came about, but what happened in other locations that also became home to clusters of evangelical organizations and residents? The next chapter adds three communities to the case of Wheaton—Orange County and suburbs east of Los Angeles, Colorado Springs, and Grand Rapids—by looking at why evangelical nonprofit organizations with a national or international focus chose to locate in communities with concentrations of evangelicals.

6

"Evangelical Meccas"

Clusters of Evangelical Organizations in Suburbs and Cities

with Benjamin E. Norquist

In 1990, evangelical parachurch organization Focus on the Family announced plans to move from Pomona, California to Colorado Springs, Colorado. Focus on the Family, under the leadership of Dr. James Dobson, began in 1977. Dobson formed the organization and rose to prominence as a Christian psychologist after working at the University of Southern California as an associate clinical professor of pediatrics. Dobson acquired fame and power through multiple spheres including through a regular presence on Christian radio throughout the country on a daily show, authoring several successful books on family life and parenting, and exerting influence on the national conservative political scene (Du Mez 2020). Focus on the Family had been rapidly growing in Arcadia first, roughly 16 miles northeast of downtown Los Angeles, before relocating to Pomona, roughly 30 miles east of downtown Los Angeles (Schultz 2017, 60–61).

Focus on the Family had pragmatic reasons for the move to Colorado. The cost of living, specifically housing, plus overhead in California was too high. In addition to reduced costs in Colorado Springs, Focus on the Family could take advantage of a $4 million grant from the El Pomar Foundation to relocate ("Focus on Family" 1990).

Many organizations might move for financial reasons. A new location could offer tax breaks or access to new resources. The cost of doing business might be lower. Yet a move across states or regions is still not easy as it impacts local relationships and employees. Is the story of Focus on the Family moving from the second largest metropolitan area in the country to the second largest metropolitan area in Colorado as simple as an effort to save money?

Further investigation into the history of Colorado Springs hints at more reasons for why an evangelical organization would make such a move. For decades, two evangelical organizations had been located near Colorado Springs: Young Life was founded in Texas and moved to the city in 1946, and The Navigators was founded in Southern California and moved to the city in 1953 (Atkins 2019, 127–140). Both organizations ministered to young people, an important group of emphasis for evangelicals in the postwar baby boom era (Bergler 2012).

Decades later, the city sought to attract more evangelical organizations in response to local economic malaise. In 1989, one staff member in the Colorado Springs' Economic Development Corporation started to use her connections to evangelical organizations. By the time her efforts ended in 1994, dozens of evangelical organizations had relocated to Colorado Springs (Sahagun 1994; Schultz 2017; Scheitle et al. 2017, 519). The city was also home to the Air Force Academy in an era of merging of military and evangelical values (Du Mez 2020); at the opening of Focus on the Family's new building in 1993, a parachute team delivered Dobson "the Keys of Heaven" (Weinstein and Seay 2006, 9).

In other words, Colorado Springs provided not only a cheaper place to do business: the city had several important evangelical organizations for decades, intentionally sought more evangelical organizations toward the end of the twentieth century and developed a reputation as an evangelical center. The case of Colorado Springs helps provide answers to a larger question beyond this one city and the unusually evangelical suburb of Wheaton, Illinois discussed in the previous chapter: How do clusters of evangelical organizations and residents develop and continue? Why would evangelical organizations choose to locate near other like-minded organizations when they could be competing with each other or reaching other populations elsewhere? What difference might it make that these clusters occur in suburbs, such as outside Los Angeles, or sprawling cities, such as Colorado Springs? Interviews with employees in 55 evangelical organizations in four evangelical clusters shows they have particular reasons for locating in these places.

Agglomerations, Evangelical Organizations, and Explaining Clusters

The United States is an unusually religious and pluralistic country among WEIRD nations (Putnam and Campbell 2010) even with a growing religiously unaffiliated population (Pew Research 2015). Religious groups reside throughout the vast United States and there are patterns to where they are located. Religious people and organizations in the United States, ranging from hundreds of thousands of religious houses of worship (Zelinsky 2001) to religious corporations (e.g., Lindsay 2007) to religious nonprofits (e.g., Scheitle 2010), are not randomly dispersed throughout the country or metropolitan regions. Geographers have studied religious diversity through the analysis of religious groups at the county or regional level (e.g., Zelinsky 1961; Warf and Winsberg 2010; Bauer 2012). Among looks at clusters of Americans or American "tribes," writers include religion as part of the analysis of clustering and highlight evangelical or Mormon areas, explore how evangelical Protestants targeted homogeneous lifestyle groups, and discuss how the values of initial settlers can affect areas for decades (Garreau 1991; Bishop 2008; Woodard 2011; Chinni and Gimpel 2010). In this context, is there an advantage for a community or organizations within it to build and maintain a religious identity, particularly a conservative Protestant one?

Sociologist Christopher Scheitle has studied the locations of evangelical parachurch organizations. In the comprehensive 2010 book *Beyond the Congregation: The World of Christian Nonprofits*, Scheitle (2010, 63) highlighted the locations of Christian nonprofits per capita by state. Washington, DC and Colorado led the way followed by four Sun Belt states.

Later, Scheitle, Dollhopf, and McCarthy (2017) examined four "spiritual districts," urban locations with high concentrations of evangelical parachurch organizations. These locations included Tulsa, Colorado Springs, Nashville, and Washington, DC. They found several commonalities across the clusters: a central catalyst helped give rise to the cluster and provided spillover effects; the cluster of parachurch group provided positives for the community; organizations found niches in their operations and missions as they oriented themselves toward competing with organizations beyond their local proximity; the cluster prompted the founding of additional organizations to support and benefit from the cluster; and the clusters provided benefits both for the community and the religious organizations.

Scheitle et al. (2017) developed the concept of a "spiritual district" based on the idea of "industrial districts" developed by Alfred Marshall (1895). Economists describe the development of agglomeration economies to better understand groups of like-minded firms in particular locations (Hoover 1948). Clusters in certain regions develop due to "concentrations of highly specialized knowledge, inputs, and institutions; the motivational benefits of local competition; and often the presence of sophisticated local demand for a product or service" (Porter 1996, 87). Similarly, concentrations in cities provide benefits in terms of "labor market pooling, input sharing, and knowledge spillovers" (Rosenthal and Strange 2004) as well as heterogeneity of employees and organizations and ways to share gains and match resources (Duranton and Puga 2004).

Certain industries or business sectors are associated with certain places, whether it is auto companies in Detroit, the steel industry in Pittsburgh, or finance firms in major cities. Two additional examples highlight this kind of research. First is the rise of the tech industry in certain locations like Silicon Valley or Route 128 outside of Boston (e.g., Saxenian 1996; Kenney and Von Burg 1999). Today, numerous cities and regions would love to develop their own tech agglomerations that generate jobs, revenues, and status even as the existing locations try to maintain their advantages. A second example involves studies of the locations of business associations that work on the behalf of particular sectors or industries. Warner and Martin (1967) found that nearly 70% of business associations were located in New York, Chicago, and Los Angeles. Several decades later, Spillman (2012) showed that the percentage of these organizations in the three largest cities was reduced to just under half and an increase in business associations located in Washington, DC.

To explain the location decisions made by religious organizations, scholars have often turned to ecological arguments. In this perspective, groups seek resource-rich niches and interact with other social groups within a community (Eiesland and Warner 1997). Studies established how religious groups seek resources or competitive advantages in similar ways to other organizations (Demerath, Hall, Schmitt, and Williams 1998; Miller 2002; Scheitle and Dougherty 2008). For instance, Ammerman (1997) details how dozens of congregations in multiple locations acquired needed resources while adapting (or not) to changing local conditions.

Often the most vital resource for religious congregations are people (Ammerman 1997, 347; Dougherty and Mulder 2009, 336). New as well as existing congregations need attendees. White churches that moved from cities to suburbs after World War II often followed their members. While congregations generally spread throughout suburbanizing areas (e.g., Diamond 2003; Miller 2017b), not all religious groups dispersed evenly across the new suburban settings as they sought different resources. Orthodox Jews clustered in the Toronto suburbs due to their religious and lifestyle requirements (Diamond 2000) while members of the Christian

Reformed Church (CRC) continued a life structured around their churches and religious schools even as they moved to the suburbs (Mulder 2015). In more recent years, members of religious groups new to the suburbs—such as Hindus, Buddhists, and Muslims—can continue to cluster in order to pool resources and gather together (e.g., Numrich and Wedam 2015; Howe 2018).

Another example of competing for attendees and resources comes from evangelicals utilizing marketing approaches through megachurches and "seeker-sensitive churches" such as at Willow Creek outside of Chicago (Shibley 1998, 75) or Radiant Church in Surprise, Arizona (Mahler 2005). This competition for attendees occurs in multiple geographic settings: congregations old and new competed for members within a growing Atlanta exurb (Eiesland 2000), churches tended to locate near their members within the Columbus metropolitan region (Form and Dubrow 2008), and Grand Rapids area churches within the same denomination competed to occupy particular niches (Dougherty and Mulder 2009). These approaches may fit the tendency of evangelical congregations to target and hold onto people of similar social groups (Emerson and Smith 2000; Cadge 2008).

One study shows how the population mix of counties can affect the creation of new evangelical parachurch groups. Looking at county level data across the United States, Scheitle and McCarthy (2018) found more organizations located in places with larger populations of evangelicals. At the same time, too many evangelicals lowered the number of parachurch groups as did a larger presence of other Christian traditions. The research suggests there is a sweet spot in which a critical mass of evangelicals—roughly 50% of the population of the county—leads to the highest number of evangelical parachurch groups.

While religious groups seek resources present in particular locations, they also have agency to alter conditions in particular places as well as move to new locations. Sociologist Omar McRoberts (2003) argues that both a more passive or active approach to local interaction can influence neighborhoods and institutional arrangements. Numrich and Wedam (2015) place congregations in the Chicago region on a weak to strong scale on their engagement with and impact on their community. Of course, religious organizations operate in communities alongside other actors, such as political and business leaders (Logan and Molotch 1987), as the community responds to local change, potential development, and outside forces (Molotch, Freudenburg, and Paulsen 2000; Miller 2013; Ammerman 1997; Eiesland 2000). This existing research hints at the ability of religious groups to both be shaped by and shape communities. When clusters of religious groups form, this can create momentum that establishes a particular reputation for the community and attracts additional actors (Scheitle et al. 2017).

Organizations and Clusters in Four Locations

The four evangelical clusters studied in this chapter became known as evangelical centers in the second half of the twentieth century. News stories and local historians noted the cluster of evangelical organizations in Wheaton in the late 1970s, calling it the "Vatican of evangelicals" and "Christiantown" (Maas and Weber 1976; Vescey 1978; Stellway 1990), and in Colorado Springs, also called "Jesus Springs" (Schultz 2017, 29) and "the "evangelical Vatican," in the 1990s and 2000s (Gottleib and Culver 1992; Johnson 1993; Heath 1994; Sahagun 1994; Brady 2005; Dunn 2014). The Orange County area was the subject of several studies involving evangelical Protestants (McGirr 2001; Luhr 2009; Dochuk 2011; Luhr 2012; Mulder and Martí 2020) and Grand Rapids is the largest city in the region of West Michigan that contains a concentration of Dutch Reformed churches and organizations (Vanderstel 1983; Swierenga 2004). We followed municipal boundaries for two clusters (the cities of Grand Rapids and Colorado Springs), paired the suburbs of Wheaton and Carol Stream outside Chicago as numerous local sources noted the presence of evangelical Protestant organizations in the adjacent communities, and included all Orange County communities and Los Angeles County communities east of I-710.

We limited our analysis to nonprofit organizations with a national or international scope within these clusters among the August 2018 members of the Evangelical Council for Financial Accountability (ECFA), a group that provides accreditation to evangelical Protestant groups that apply. A master list of Christian nonprofit organizations is difficult to assemble (see Scheitle 2010) and we compared the number of ECFA accredited organizations in these clusters versus other communities in their state. In late 2017, the membership of ECFA yielded 45 organizations with a national or international scope in Colorado Springs (we randomly selected 17—for comparison, there were five such organizations in Denver and five in Littleton), 22 in Grand Rapids (17 randomly selected—three were in Holland, none in Detroit), 43 in East Los Angeles County and Orange County suburbs (21 randomly selected—the rest of Los Angeles County had 22 organizations,

San Diego County 17, and Riverside County 10), and 28 in Wheaton and Carol Stream (18 randomly selected and then another five randomly selected after we found multiple organizations used a Wheaton firm for back office operations—five such organizations in Chicago).

We contacted each organization in our sample at least three times. We conducted 57 interviews with 55 organizations (for a response rate of just over 70%): 12 in Colorado Springs, 15 in Grand Rapids, 15 in Orange County/East LA suburbs, and 13 in Wheaton. The vast majority of these organizations are ministries of various kinds—38 of 55—with smaller clusters of organizations in education, humanitarian, missions, and publishing sectors.

When we called each organization, we asked who would be best to talk to understand the location of the organization. Receptionists or operators often routed us to either well-positioned employees (such as administrators or historians/archivists) or long-tenured employees (which might include the receptionist themselves). Overall, 27 interviewees were in administrative positions (directors or vice presidents and above), six were in public relations, communication, or human resources departments, and 23 were in other positions (one did not provide this information). Given the different positions of the respondents as well as the varying sizes of organizations, they may have had varied levels of participation in location decisions. We promised anonymity to the interviewees.

We carried out the interviews between October 2016 and April 2018. Interviews typically took 10 to 20 minutes. We used a template of three questions (with several follow-up prompts to obtain information): (1) Why is your organization located where it is?; (2) Why does your organization stay in its current location?; and (3) Does your organization find it advantageous to be located near other Christian organizations? We coded the responses separately, looking for emergent themes and patterns across organizations. We then discussed case by case which codes best matched what respondents said before settling on our final codes for the responses.

Colorado Springs

Founded in 1871 as part of an effort to develop land around the planned Denver & Rio Grande Railway, Colorado Springs gained a reputation as a refined resort community where alcohol was not sold, manufacturing was not allowed in city limits, and agriculture was limited in scale (Sprague 1971; Berwanger 2007, 95–97; Wyckoff 1999, 133–143; Foote 1918, 163–164). After significant population increases following World War II, the city today is known for mining and tourism industries near the Rocky Mountains, strong military and defense connections (Camp Carson, later Fort Carson, started in late 1941 and the Air Force Academy opened in the 1950s), and the presence of evangelical organizations, anchored by the Focus on the Family campus (Sprague 1971; Heath 1994; Wallace 2003; Swint 2010; Dunn 2014; Schultz 2017).

Amid poor local economic conditions in the 1980s, intentional efforts by the city at the end of the twentieth century added evangelical organizations to the community's existing economic base. In 1989, one staff member in the city's economic development department started to use her connections to evangelical organizations. This brought roughly 25 national evangelical organizations to the city before the efforts ended in 1994 (Sahagun 1994; Schultz 2017). These efforts added evangelical groups to two long-present young adult ministries: Young Life, founded in Texas and in Colorado Springs since 1946, and The Navigators, founded in Southern California and in Colorado Springs since 1953. However, these two groups did not attract other evangelical organizations or significantly impact the local community (Scheitle et al. 2017, 519). Focus on the Family, which moved from southern California in 1991 with the city "offering cheap land, and a local foundation ponied up $4 million in grant money to help it relocate" (Kelly 2004), became emblematic of the changes and tensions occurring in the city with the influx of evangelical organizations (Rabey 1991; Gottleib and Culver 1992; Johnson 1993; Heath 1994; Brady 2005; Religion & Ethics Newsweekly 2013). The Chamber of Commerce offered "cheap land, cheap labor, and low taxes" (Schultz 2017, 30). Two interviewees cited the warm welcome from the city: one said, "They made us feel welcome and hosted us well" and another said the welcome was accompanied by no competition between the groups or no pushback from new people. Focus on the Family also benefitted from different local and state tax structures as Colorado had recently passed a law expanding what kinds of religious properties were exempt from taxes (Lee 2006; Schultz 2017). Furthermore, megachurch pastor Ted Haggard led the National Association of Evangelicals into the 2000s from his Colorado Springs church (e.g., Sharlet 2005). The city's efforts appear to have been a success, particularly compared to the other clusters: 10 of the 12 organizations we interviewed started elsewhere.

In our interviews, multiple reasons garnered four mentions each from interviewees as to why their organization located in Colorado Springs. These reasons included that the founder or leader lived there (with two mentions each), a community incentive/invite, the cost of living, proximity to partners, and quality of life. Regarding community incentives, two interviewees referenced the city's efforts to attract certain kinds of organizations while two others discussed the role of local foundations and private actors. One group said they experienced a high cost of living in California while another two noted the higher taxes and living costs in California. Further, one organization noted the high cost of housing in Miami. Four interviewees said having other Christian organizations nearby was a draw and more interviewees in Colorado Springs than any other cluster cited the quality of life (with references to it being a nice place and having natural beauty).

When asked why their organization stays in Colorado Springs, respondents provided 11 different reasons. By far, the top reason (cited by five interviewees) was that their organization's leader and employees live there. One interviewee explained that all their employees are settled while another stated that it would be costly to uproot their staff. With three organizations noting the positive quality of life, two of these three answers involved natural beauty. The majority of organizations (seven of 13 with two no answers) agreed it was advantageous to be near Christian organizations with the clear leading answer involving networking opportunities across Christian organizations. For example, interviewees described exchanging ideas, sharing software systems, and the presence of a synergy among Christian groups.

Grand Rapids

Whites engaged in the fur industry took interest in the Grand Rapids area in the late 1700s. A Baptist mission to Indigenous residents was built on the Grand River and Louis Campau established a homestead on the opposite bank in the 1820s (Lydens 1966; Mapes and Travis 1976). White settlers began arriving in earnest in the 1830s (Tuttle 1874; Baxter 1891). The city grew around a number of industries, particularly lumber and furniture (Olson 1989), and became part of the largest center of Dutch residents in the United States (Bratt 1984, 238).

Among other early residents, Grand Rapids and southwestern Michigan attracted Dutch Reformed migrants. Dutch immigrants fleeing European religious persecution arrived in western Michigan in the late 1840s with a concentration settling in Grand Rapids (Vanderstel 1983). Initially interested in land in Wisconsin, the residents of Grand Rapids impressed them during a winter delay and the Dutch immigrants stayed (Swierenga 2004). Dutch residents from New York constructed the First Reformed Church of Grand Rapids in 1842 and Dutch immigrants started the Second Reformed Church within a few years (Mapes and Travis 1976). The two major Dutch Reformed denominations in the United States—the Reformed Church in America, founded in New Amsterdam in 1628 and bolstered by the immigration of 1847, and the Christian Reformed Church which split off in 1857 (Reformed Church in America 2017; Swierenga 1980; Swierenga and Bruins 1999)—have major offices in Grand Rapids.

Even as not all of the organizations we interviewed in Grand Rapids emerged from the Dutch Reformed tradition, the leading reasons for why organizations located in the city hinted at the Dutch Reformed roots in the region. Across the 15 organizations we interviewed, a clear leading answer emerged as to why they located where they did: their founder or leader lives there. Only a few other categories were mentioned by more than one organization: they came out of a church (four mentions), they were incubated or spun-off from a local organization (three mentions), or land or a building was available (two mentions). The three leading answers for why these organizations stay in Grand Rapids are related to the reasons for locating in Grand Rapids: the leaders and employees live there (eight mentions), proximity to other ministries (seven mentions), and customers and donors are there (six mentions). One interviewee said Grand Rapids is one of the centers of Christian thought in the United States with organizations like Calvin College and Christian publishers. A second interviewee described how all but one of the organization's employees lives in the area and the organization likes the accessibility to Christian publishing and Christian colleges and seminaries. Thirteen of 15 organizations said it is advantageous to be near other Christian groups with multiple reasons cited by four or five organizations: networking opportunities, partnerships with other organizations, the publishing industry, and nearby colleges.

The members of the Christian Reformed Church and the Reformed Church in America make up under 10% of the Kent County population that includes Grand Rapids and an additional 400,000 residents (Grammich et al. 2023), yet the Dutch Reformed roots in West Michigan and Grand Rapids helped give rise to multiple institutions mentioned by interviewees.

Dutch immigrants started four major evangelical publishing companies in Grand Rapids: Baker, Eerdmans, Kregel, and Zondervan. Three evangelical Protestant colleges in the city also had their start among local religious groups. Calvin College was founded by the Christian Reformed Church denomination (the college began in locations closer to downtown Grand Rapids before purchasing 166 acres further from downtown and moving all operations to the quieter and safer location by the early 1970s; see Timmerman 1975, 114–117, 148–149), Kuyper College had its start as a Bible institute when founded by a local CRC pastor, and Cornerstone University also began as a Bible institute founded by members of the General Association of Regular Baptist Churches.

Only two organizations we interviewed moved to Grand Rapids from another location; one started in Kalamazoo and soon moved to Grand Rapids while another moved from Detroit as the founder of the ministry already had a home in Grand Rapids.

Orange County/East Los Angeles County Suburbs

The Spanish first settled the area in and around Orange County in the late 1700s and they constructed the first mission in 1776. Orange County was formed in 1889 and had relatively few residents with land devoted to large ranches and agriculture, particularly oranges (Armor 1921; Orange County Board of Supervisors 1975). The suburbanization of the Los Angeles region transformed Orange County and surrounding areas; the county grew from 34,000 residents in 1910 to just over three million residents in 2010 and the explosion of residents brought about new opportunities and challenges (Baldassare and Katz 1991; Kling, Olin, and Poster 1991; Baldassare 1998; Starr 2009). Similarly, the suburbs just to the east of Los Angeles within Los Angeles County expanded greatly in the era of mass suburbanization (Starr 2009).

Postwar suburban growth helped cement the area as more politically and religiously conservative (McGirr 1991; Luhr 2009; Dochuk 2011; Luhr 2012). Numerous new institutions served conservative residents and influenced evangelical Protestants across the country. A noted evangelist and pastor founded Fuller Seminary in Pasadena in 1947, joining Azusa Pacific University in the suburbs while Biola later moved from Los Angeles to the suburbs. Orange County has several influential evangelical churches: Garden Grove Community Church, which moved from a drive-in to the Crystal Cathedral; Calvary Chapel influenced the charismatic movement; and Saddleback Community Church first met in a high school before establishing their own campus (Mulder and Martí 2020; Wilford 2012; Lee and Sinitiere 2009).

The organizations we interviewed in this cluster tended to have their start in the area. Only one of 15 began outside the region though several mentioned moving within the region. The average founding year for the organizations in the cluster was the oldest of any of the four clusters with five organizations founded before 1945. Similar to Colorado Springs and Grand Rapids, the leading reason cited by Orange County organizations for being in their current location (nine noted this) was the founder lived there. Yet the second most common reason given—a mission focus (six total)—connects to the population growth of the area in the twentieth century. These organizations saw particular opportunities to reach people in southern California. One interviewee said they were founded by a missionary who after returning from overseas saw Orange County as a mission field, another described a particular gap in knowledge among Christians that the founder wanted to address, and a third explained how the organization wanted to reach the people of Los Angeles at the founding and moved to the suburbs with much of the region in the 1950s.

Asking why the organizations stayed in Orange County and the East Los Angeles County suburbs prompted three leading answers: leaders and employees live there (six mentions), customers and donors are there (six mentions), and missional values (four mentions). Regarding the first two reasons, one interviewee said the founder was from the area and their reputation and support base developed around this person. In terms of seeing these suburbs as a mission field, one interviewee said they serve both international communities as well as their own.

More than any other cluster we studied, four organizations said there were no advantages to being located near other Christian organizations. One organization went so far as to say that their current location in a building among non-Christian organizations is preferable to their former site near Christian groups. The three categories larger than this and involving advantages included churches (six mentions), networking opportunities (six mentions), and partnerships with other organizations (six mentions). One interviewee discussed multiple partnership opportunities available for members of their organization (particularly highlighting the benefits of personal fellowship between organizations) while another interviewee described how networking and partnerships with churches and Christian organizations helped further their mission.

Wheaton

With the history of Wheaton and clustering of evangelicals there and in adjacent Carol Stream addressed in the previous chapter, we summarize the interview responses here. Typical explanations for the clustering in Wheaton involve Wheaton College (Schmeltzer 1986) and the community's longstanding reputation as a religious community. Interviewees echoed these themes as two of the leading reasons for their organization's presence in Wheaton were the founder lived there (eight organizations) and Wheaton College alumni (three mentions). Additionally, three organizations noted land or a building was available and three discussed the proximity to partners. For example, one organization started as a ministry run by Wheaton College students and later returned to Wheaton. Three others described how the founder or founders worked for Wheaton College while another noted the founder stayed in the area after attending Moody College in Chicago.

Five interviewees said their organization stayed in Chicago because of regional infrastructure while five explained that their leaders and employees live there. Regional infrastructure involved the ease of travel to and from Chicago with one mention of the railroad (for an organization founded in the mid-1800s) while several others explicitly mentioned O'Hare Airport. The only mention outside of Grand Rapids about Wheaton being a Christian center occurred with one interviewee who said the former president saw Wheaton as the Mecca of evangelicalism with its intellectual resources and churches.

According to interviewees, the primary advantages of being located near other Christian organizations involves networking generally and specific references to individual interactions received five mentions each, churches (four mentions), and colleges (four mentions). Two interviewees cited both general and individual networking: one said networking happens on both official and personal levels while another said small Christian organizations in the area have meetings regarding best practices and they find support in friendships with leaders of other small Christian groups. Regarding churches and colleges, one interviewee said they love Wheaton College and have good relationships with local churches and another interviewee described how the Wheaton area is a catalyst of encouragement to effective ministry with multiple church partners, easier donor acquisition, and interns, volunteers, and staff with backgrounds with Wheaton College.

Only two of the organizations we interviewed had their start prior to 1945 with the rest emerging in the postwar era. Most (10) had their roots in the Chicago region and seven started in Wheaton or Carol Stream.

Comparisons Across the Four Clusters

These clusters had varied historical paths toward later hosting numerous evangelical organizations. Colorado Springs made the most explicit moves to seek out such organizations, businessmen Carl Gunderson and Robert C. Van Kampen gifted land to evangelical organizations just north of Wheaton (Chatterley 2018a), and the other locations presented attractive settings or resources for evangelical Protestant groups. Colorado Springs was the latest developing cluster as it became widely known as an evangelical center at the end of the twentieth century due to organizations relocating from other clusters. In contrast, Grand Rapids and Wheaton have deeper roots with white settlers arriving in larger numbers in the Midwest in the mid-1800s. The coming of Dutch immigrants to Grand Rapids in the late 1840s started a Dutch settlement point while Wheaton's founding in the mid-nineteenth century helped lead to the location of Wheaton College (officially established as such in 1860). Like Grand Rapids and Wheaton, a majority of the organizations we interviewed in Orange County and the East Los Angeles County suburbs started in the region. The organizations there were the most explicit about serving and evangelizing the region. The movement of organizations into and out of these clusters also hints at their development at different times: groups moved to Wheaton from the 1930s to the 1970s, to Colorado Springs starting in the 1980s, and out of southern California starting in the 1980s.

By far, the leading reason interviewees provided for locating in one of these clusters was that the founder lived there (28 organizations) plus four more noted moving because of a leader living in that location. The next leading reasons involved a building or land (15 mentions across three categories), organizational history (15 mentions across three categories), and proximity to clients, partners, and supporters (13 mentions across three categories).

Multiple organizations, almost all located in Colorado Springs, mentioned cost of living or operating and quality of life factors.

The reasons given for staying in one of these clusters followed several patterns. The most common reason given—over 40%—said that their leaders or employees lived there. Personnel is an important concern for any organization as a move may require hiring many new employees. The next two reasons—customers and donors also located there (14 mentions—only one in Colorado Springs) as well as proximity to other ministries (12 mentions—more than half of these were in Grand Rapids)—are important resources for any nonprofit organizations. Other commonly cited reasons for staying put included buildings (nine mentions in two categories), moving could be costly (eight mentions) and quality of life (seven mentions).

When asked whether organizations found it advantageous to be located near other Christian organizations, the vast majority said yes. Only a few in each location—nine total—said there was no advantage or a negative effect from a location near other Christian organizations. Three interviewees said a location near other Christian organizations could lead to a competitive disadvantage. For those who saw benefits to clustering, the largest reasons involved networking (25 mentions of broader networking while 11 mentioned specific individuals in their organizations networking) and partnering with other Christian organizations (15 mentions). Relationships with churches (14 mentions) and local Christian colleges (10 total—though none in Colorado Springs) also received double-digit mentions. The advantage of connections with Christian publishers—seven mentions—only applied in Grand Rapids and Wheaton. Overall, interviewees described the benefits of proximity in various ways including synergy within sectors as well as helpful partnerships across sectors and with supporting industries, proximity to institutions of higher education that provide employees and academic expertise, and formal and informal interactions between religious nonprofits, among organizational leaders, and ongoing relationships with local congregations.

These patterns across the clusters also highlight both the influence organizations can have on clusters and the agency of these nonprofit organizations to make decisions regarding locations. Forty of the 55 organizations began in the metropolitan region of the cluster, such as a founding in Chicago before moving to Wheaton or in West Michigan before locating in Grand Rapids. This suggests many of these organizations could have deep roots in these regions based on the personal networks of founders as well as a long-term presence in the community. Numerous interviewees mentioned the importance of network connections, indicating interpersonal and organizational ties within the cluster and with a variety of social actors including nonprofits in similar and different spheres, congregations, and supporters and donors. One interviewee in Orange County said, "We are central now to the community we serve locally." A respondent in Colorado Springs mentioned their organization's participation in "the Community Table nonprofit to contribute to the needs of Colorado Springs," an effort the respondent said the city appreciates.

Fifteen of the organizations we interviewed moved across regions. This was most common in Colorado Springs: 11 of the 13 we interviewed moved there. While these Colorado Springs organizations may have focused their efforts on a national or international scale more than on the city (Dunn 2014), media stories highlighted local and state clashes over culture war concerns (Heath 1994; Religion & Ethics Newsweekly 2013). In the three other clusters where more organizations had their beginnings within the region, numerous interviewees discussed moving within their cluster or region. Organizations do occasionally decide to switch locations even though eight noted the cost of moving and four said no discussions regarding moving had taken place. A shorter-distance move could limit the costs of moving and find a better property or building without sacrificing the ties of the founder or leader as well as retain valued employees and supporters.

Explaining Clusters and Their Influence

These four cases show how suburbs and metropolitan areas influence the clustering of evangelical organizations. In four sprawling locations, two sets of suburbs outside major cities and two small big cities, numerous evangelical organizations found resources and communities amenable to their goals. Even within the metropolitan regions represented here, these organizations could have located elsewhere with dozens and maybe hundreds of other choices in the larger regions. Parachurch organizations with a national or international focus could locate in the biggest American cities—Scheitle, Dollhopf, and McCarthy (2017) highlight the presence of such organizations in Washington, DC alongside more sprawling locations like Nashville, Colorado Springs, and Tulsa—but smaller big cities and suburban areas offer particular advantages.

In both the Los Angeles and Chicago regions, sprawling suburban areas offered new opportunities for evangelicals among more conservative populations. Colorado Springs is a rapidly growing and a more sprawling city; the population density is roughly 2,500 people per square mile, a density significantly less than Wheaton. And while Grand Rapids might be a Rust Belt city, its population density is roughly the same as Wheaton. Three of these four clusters emerged in a particular time period—Grand Rapids as a cluster built around a long-established ethno-religious constituency—and in locations where sprawl and suburbanization offered opportunities and resources.

The cases studied here suggest clusters can form in smaller big cities as well as suburban areas. Clusters likely need some baseline level of population density for there to be conditions conducive to synergy across organizations, a common labor pool, and access to local institutions and resources. The four cases selected and studied by Scheitle et al. (2017) contains a similar mix; outside of Washington, DC, the other regions include smaller big cities and more sprawling regions. There is little reason to suspect from their study or this study that clusters of evangelicals are possible in more of the biggest cities on the coasts such as New York City, Boston, Miami, San Francisco and the Bay Area, and Seattle. Instead, clusters of evangelicals are more likely to be found in suburbs of some of the biggest cities or in and around smaller big cities between the coasts.

An ecological perspective focusing on the needs of organizations and competition between them can help explain these four clusters, their formation, and their persistence over decades. Nonprofits have their own resources to pursue compared to religious congregations (e.g., Ammerman 1997; Dougherty and Mulder 2009) and locating in proximity to similar organizations enhances this. Interviewees did not provide one sole reason for the clustering of religious nonprofit organizations; while ecological studies of congregations often emphasize acquiring members, the evangelical nonprofit organizations across these four clusters pursued resources including the residences of leaders and personnel, buildings and property, and proximity to donors, partners, and other evangelical nonprofits.

At the same time, communities do not just emerge as places where conservative religious organizations want to locate or where parachurch resources are available. How such clusters start and go on to provide benefits to both organizations and communities involves decisions made by municipalities, developers, key organizations, and residents. A particular milieu or character is the result of dozens of choices involving development, growth, zoning, and local infrastructure as well as major turning points. These help shape landscapes that could develop into clusters with certain resources. Even if there are broad patterns to where evangelical clusters are located—more likely between the coasts, in counties with a certain number of evangelical residents—this does not mean that every location with these traits develops a concentration of evangelicals. All of the clusters had certain favorable conditions for religious nonprofits such as the early growth in west Michigan that proved attractive to Dutch immigrants and the rapid twentieth-century growth of the Los Angeles region that presented opportunities for evangelical Protestants. Evangelicals did not start the four communities studied here but they benefitted from existing conditions and then helped shape subsequent outcomes.

The interviews with organizations also highlight the ways religious parachurch groups understand their own positions, interact with the development of and ongoing status of clusters, and exercise agency regarding where they want to locate (McRoberts 2003; Cimino, Mian, and Huang 2013). In other words, these organizations could be located in many different places, but they have reasons for staying. If optimizing access to resources is indeed critical for the ongoing operation of parachurch groups, this could lead them to regular analysis of their location and how other places might provide new opportunities and efficiencies. They can move and many of the ones we interviewed had done so, whether within the same metropolitan region or a significant distance. The moves often involved seeking a particular advantage such as retaining valuable leaders or acquiring a better property. But staying and not actively considering moving might often be easier.

The choices these organizations can make to move have consequences for these clusters. Even if the organization had a limited presence in their community (such as having few network ties or limited participation in local activities), organizations leaving for another location would eliminate local jobs and decrease the size of the cluster of conservative Protestant nonprofits. Focus on the Family presents a good example: in moving from southern California, the organization left behind jobs and a social impact in an evangelical cluster while also helping to create a new energy in Colorado Springs. This agency of organizations plus the actions of local communities means these clusters are not permanent or inevitable. The four locations in this study are largely twentieth-century creations and they can form within the span of a few decades. However, it would take time for their status to change or for other locations to develop a similar reputation.

The connections between these four clusters are also worth considering. While they have independent histories and organizations exercise agency, there are several notable links between the clusters. Focus on the Family moved from one cluster and anchored another. The growth of Colorado Springs led local convention planners to dub the city the "Wheaton of the West" (Rabey 1991). The example of an influential southern California congregation further illustrates the links. Sociologists Mark Mulder and Gerado Martí (2020) detail the rise and fall of Robert Schuller's Garden Grove Community Church, which later became The Crystal Cathedral, and their study highlights the long-lasting connections between clusters. Schuller was born in Iowa but had connections to the Dutch Reformed of west Michigan through his Reformed Church in America (RCA) background, spending his college years at Hope College in Holland, Michigan, and obtaining his seminary degree in Holland at Western Theological Seminary. Schuller started Garden Grove Community Church in 1955 in Orange County as an RCA congregation. Nominally tied to the larger denomination, Schuller brought innovation, charisma, and an emphasis on hope to the Dutch Reformed tradition. Mulder and Martí discuss some of the back and forth between Schuller and RCA leaders: Schuller leaned on the tradition and gravitas of the denomination when he received criticism while the denomination benefitted from Schuller's success even if Schuller operated outside RCA cultural norms. In other words, Schuller translated the Dutch Reformed tradition so familiar in Grand Rapids and West Michigan into the new car-loving suburban sprawl of southern California with repercussions for both locations and all the actors involved.

Conclusion

The four clusters of evangelical organizations studied here demonstrate how particular clusters, sprawling suburbs and small big cities, start and continue. Clusters form in specific communities with certain conditions and resources, organizations utilize local resources, and organizations make choices about whether they begin in a cluster, move to a cluster, and engage with the cluster. In the four locations studied in this chapter, evangelical organizations contribute to a particular reputation, local resources and possibilities, and the religious, economic, and social landscape.

These local processes also occurred within a broader national context. Three larger patterns within Christianity in the United States after World War II contributed to the development and persistence of these clusters. First, the rise of the nondenominational parachurch organization (Wuthnow 1988) parallels the development of several of these clusters. The majority of the organizations studied here, 43 of 55 (78%), had their start after 1945. Only one of the clusters examined here owes much to denominations: Grand Rapids is a spiritual center for two small Protestant denominations. In 2010, the Christian Reformed Church had around 180,000 members and the Reformed Church in America had around 246,000 members (TheArda 2017). Second, the move of evangelical Protestant institutions from big cities in the Northeast and Midwest like Boston, New York, Philadelphia, and Chicago (Executive Committee 1942) to the suburbs, the South, and the West is reflected in the rise of these four clusters. Early in the twentieth century, predicting these four locations as centers of evangelical Protestant groups (or Nashville and Tulsa; see Scheitle, Dollhopf, and McCarthy 2017) may have proved difficult. Third, the evangelical shift from fundamentalist retreat to neo-evangelical societal engagement (Executive Committee 1942; Henry 1947; Smith 1998; Hunter 2010) may have affected when and where evangelical Protestant organizations locate. Two of these clusters are close to global cities and centers of influence: Chicago and Los Angeles. Yet remaining in these four clusters or consistently locating near like-minded organizations could limit the influence of evangelical Protestants through comparative deficits in the Northeast (Boston, New York, Philadelphia) or West Coast (Bay Area, Seattle) or in central cities.

The next chapter broadens the analysis beyond patterns in four evangelical clusters and uses General Social Survey data to look at how American evangelicals and adherents of other religious traditions are distributed across urban, suburban, and rural areas in the United States. In what kinds of communities do higher proportions of evangelicals live and how has this changed since the early 1970s?

7
Where Evangelicals and Other Religious Traditions Live, 1972–2016

In early 2017, pastor Tim Keller announced to Redeemer Presbyterian Church, the Presbyterian Church in America (PCA) congregation in Manhattan he founded in 1989, that he planned to step down as pastor. In the announcement made "at all eight Sunday services" for the megachurch of roughly 5,000 members, Keller said, "New York is our home, and you are our people." Reporting on this news, an article in *Christianity Today* called Keller "Manhattan's most popular evangelical pastor and apologist" (Shellnut 2017).

For decades, Keller stood out as an evangelical leader in an unusual place: Manhattan, the center of the global city of New York City with all of its money making, culture, and diversity. Even with New York's vibrant religious past and current religious dynamism (Butler 2020), few would think of Manhattan as a hotbed of evangelicalism. Keller's church grew from a small gathering in a Manhattan apartment to a multisite congregation holding numerous services every weekend (Redeemer Churches & Ministries 2022). Additionally, Keller helped lead a national Reformed evangelicalism marked by calls to biblical orthodoxy and traditional families and did so with a more sophisticated approach that promoted engagement with the people and culture of New York City (Vermurlen 2020).

In his book *Serving a Movement: Doing Balanced, Gospel-Centered Ministry in Your City*, Keller (2016, 10) says his church's ministry did not present an urban model for evangelical church success that could easily be copied. Rather, Keller suggests a Gospel-centered doctrinal foundation leads to a theological vision and then a particular ministry expression. Within the city, Keller (2016, 17) promotes "the need to be sensitive to culture" through "adopting city-loving ways of ministry rather than approaches that are hostile or indifferent to the city." To reach the city, Keller suggests evangelicals need to embrace a catholicity of church models and approaches.

Sanctifying Suburbia. Brian J. Miller, Oxford University Press. © Oxford University Press 2025.
DOI: 10.1093/oso/9780197679623.003.0008

As one reviewer notes, Keller highlighted the ways in which cities exemplify the best and worst of humanity and cities offer the culminating locations for spreading the gospel (Myatt 2016). As another example of this approach, Keller (2012b) provided "A Theology of Cities" in five pages for CRU Press, the publishing arm of the widespread campus ministry. Starting with the idea that cities are "God's invention" and that God intended cities to be diverse and produce culture, Keller recommends Christians should "reach the city to reach the culture," Christians in the city should engage those who "seem 'hopeless' spiritually" and "people of other religions or no religion and of deeply non-Christian lifestyles that are wiser, kinder, and deeper than you," and that "the poor and the broken are often much, much more open to the idea of gospel grace and much more dedicated to its practical outworking than you are."

Keller's location and approach stands in contrast to the kinds of communities where some might expect to find evangelicals. In studying the alienation of the American political right and the Tea Party over several years leading up to 2016 elections, sociologist Arlie Hochschild talked with and observed life among conservatives in Louisiana. At several points, she notes the ways in which conservative religious beliefs and practices mixed with support for the political right. For example, in describing the purposes and outcomes of presidential candidate Donald Trump's rallies, Hochschild (2016, 226) uses sociologist Emile Durkheim's concept of a totem: "Seen through Durkheim's eyes, the real function of the excited gathering around Donald Trump is to unify all the white, evangelical enthusiasts who fear that those 'cutting ahead in line' are about to become a terribly, strange, new America."

This image of a more rural or small-town evangelicalism is the inverse of sociologist Anna Strhan's study of a large, white, middle-class, evangelical Anglican congregation in London. Her exploration of the ways in which evangelicals navigate the tensions of urban life—particularly navigating secularity while holding to traditional religious views—echoes similar work in the United States (e.g., Bielo 2011a; Bielo 2011b; Elisha 2011b). Strhan's (2016, 33) claim that "In contemporary British evangelicalism, cities are imagined as both sites of disorder and as presenting opportunities for the spread of faith" would sound familiar to American evangelicals across decades of decisions about where to live and direct ministries.

This chapter shifts the analytical focus away from communities with many evangelicals—Wheaton in Chapter 5 and concentrations of evangelical organizations in Wheaton, Grand Rapids, Colorado Springs, and Orange

County and the East LA suburbs in Chapter 6—to the kinds or types of American communities in which evangelicals live. When examining longitudinal data from the General Social Survey (GSS), started in 1972, are evangelicals more likely to live in large cities, smaller big cities, suburbs of big cities, or smaller towns or more rural areas? Or, to return to the example at the beginning of this chapter, does national survey data over more than 40 years suggest Tim Keller's ministry and congregation was an anomaly?

Examining this question with the General Social Survey data also allows for comparisons to other religious traditions. Are Catholics, often linked to major cities during significant waves of immigration to the United States, more likely to be found in big cities today? Given the rise of "religious nones" in recent years, where are they most likely to reside? The analysis in this chapter makes use of the concept Reltrad developed by scholars in 2000 (Steensland et al. 2000). They argued that the prior measure of religious affiliation in the General Social Survey inaccurately used a continuum of religious liberalism to conservatism. In practice, this meant religious adherents of different denominations or backgrounds might be grouped together even if they did not see themselves as joined together. As initially proposed, Reltrad uses six categories based on the historical, religious, and political markers of distinct religious traditions: "mainline Protestant, evangelical Protestant, black Protestant, Roman Catholic, Jewish, and other (e.g., Mormon, Jehovah's Witness, Muslim, Hindu, and Unitarian)" (Steensland et al. 2000, 297). In this chapter, I use a Reltrad measure with seven categories—including an Unaffiliated or No Religiontradition—developed by political scientist Ryan Burge that is applied to the waves of the General Social Survey from 1972 through 2016 (Stetzer and Burge 2015; Burge 2018).

With Reltrad applied to GSS data, I compare the kinds of communities in which different religious traditions reside across three different ways of conceptualizing community. All three variables are included in all waves of the General Social Survey. In comparison to an urban-suburban-rural continuum often utilized in surveys measuring religion (Miller 2016a), the three variables provide different details about the kind of place identified (Okulicz-Kozaryn 2017). XNORCSIZ has six categories for respondents within a Standard Metropolitan Statistical Area (SMSA)—from residing in cities of more than 250,000 residents to suburbs to unincorporated areas—and four categories for those outside SMSAs. SRCBELT differentiates between those in cities or suburbs of the 12 largest SMSAs, cities or suburbs of the 13–100th largest SMSAs, and those living in other urban counties or rural counties. SIZE rounds the population of the respondent's community to the nearest thousand. For this analysis, I divided the populations of communities into quintiles to roughly match the 20% of Americans who live in each quintile: 0–4,000 residents, 5,000–14,000 residents, 15,000–41,000 residents, 42,000–192,000 residents, and 193,000 residents and greater. Using all three of these location variables helps get at multiple dimensions of places: their location within or outside a metropolitan area, the size or kind of the community within a metropolitan area or not, and the absolute number of residents in the community.

The analysis in this chapter follows two approaches to take advantage of applying Reltrad to the GSS data over time and adjust for the lower Ns for some religious traditions in each wave (such as Jewish adherents who are clearly recognized as part of a distinct and important religious tradition in the United States—e.g., Herberg 1955—but are relatively small in number). First, I examine the locations of the adherents of each religious tradition involving all the waves of the General Social Survey. Analyzing community types by religious tradition with cases from all the waves together provides larger Ns for each group. Second, I examine the slopes of the percentage of each religious tradition living in each location from 1972 to 2016. Even as singular waves of the GSS may have smaller number of adherents in certain traditions, looking at trends over time helps adjust for variation. Using both approaches allows for comparing religious traditions as a whole and also considering change in locations over more than three decades.

Before discussing the patterns in the General Social Survey data, two questions need to be addressed first. In previous research, do researchers find evangelicals in particular kinds of communities? Additionally, are they unique in residing in these locations compared to adherents of other religious traditions?

Evangelicals and Other Religious Traditions Across Community Types

Starting with big cities, urban neighborhoods have high concentrations of religious congregations overall (Zelinsky and Matthews 2011), and American cities contain numerous traditions and adherents (e.g., Orsi 1999; Livezey 2000). For example, New York City and its neighborhoods have been and continue to be home to religious variety, cooperation, and conflict (Hansen 2016; Miller 2020; Butler 2020). Similarly, the cities of Chicago and Indianapolis and their suburbs have histories and current realities full of religious activity and pluralism (Zelinsky and Matthews 2011; Numrich and Wedam 2015; Diamond 2003).

In addition to big cities, other communities can be home to religious competition and change. Sociologist Nancy Eiesland (2000) described the religious change in the Atlanta exurb of Dacula where existing congregations quickly found new religious actors and institutions at work in the developing community. Rural areas have numerous long-standing, usually Christian, congregations that are part of the close-knit fabric of the community (Salamon 2003; Wuthnow 2015, 217–261). Certain regions are known for certain religious traditions, whether the South and conservative Protestants and the Pacific Northwest for the religiously unaffiliated (e.g., Wellman and Corcoran 2013; Silk and Walsh 2008). Particularly in the South, rural areas contain higher percentages of Americans who attend church weekly and who have had a born-again experience (Dillon and Savage 2006). Even though evangelicals constitute a higher percentage of residents in rural areas, because more Americans live in suburbs, more evangelicals (34%) live in suburbs according to one national survey and those evangelicals go to church more frequently than rural evangelicals (Burge 2019).

Certain communities and regions are known for concentrations of particular religious traditions. Two examples involving concentrations of Catholics highlights such research. Dugandzic (2022) examines the concentration of conservative Catholics in a Washington, DC suburb. Due to the availability of local resources and particular affordances, a group of Catholics have been able to establish a social sphere built around their understanding of a traditional Catholic life. In contrast to Catholic life in the suburbs, McMahon (1995) analyzes the importance of race and ethnicity, place, and religion in Irish Chicago Catholic parishes. By looking closely at the racial change in the St. Sabina parish in the city's Auburn-Gresham neighborhood, McMahon illustrates how concentrations can change as white Catholics left for the suburbs and the parish became home to Black Catholics.

In one analysis of types of American communities based on counties, Chinni and Gimpel (2011) identified 12 types of counties. Two of them had religious connections in their titles. "Evangelical Epicenters" tend to be whiter, have more Walmarts, and nearly half of the residents of the community are evangelical Protestants. Another community type was "Mormon Outposts" found out West. While religion could be influential in other county types, this religiosity did not rise to the level of the title of the type (with other examples of types including "Monied Burbs," "Minority Central," "Tractor Country," and "Boom Towns").

As discussed in previous chapters of this book, multiple scholars suggest evangelicals cluster in particular places. Scheitle, Dollhopf, and McCarthy (2017) find high concentrations of evangelical parachurch groups in Colorado Springs, Tulsa, Nashville, and Washington, DC, while Chapters 5 and 6 add Wheaton, Grand Rapids, and Orange County and the East LA suburbs to this mix. As noted in Chapter 3, some of this clustering depends on the larger process of white flight (Sugrue 1996; Kruse 2005) as evangelicals and numerous other white religious adherents, evangelical, mainline, Catholic, and Jewish, left cities for suburbs (McGreevy 1996; Cutler 1996; Gamm 1999; Diamond 2000; Diamond 2003; Dochuk 2003; Mulder 2015; Miller 2017b).

Yet while evangelicals have drawn significant research interest in recent decades alongside their emergence as a collective in social and political life by the 1980s, relatively little analysis considers where evangelicals are located and how they are shaped by and shape particular kinds of communities. From the postwar era onward (e.g., Hudnut-Beumler 1994), religious leaders and scholars (Greeley 1959; Winter 1961; Shippey 1964) and evangelical themselves have written about the challenges and opportunities of living in suburbs (explored further in Chapter 8).

Even as Americans as a whole developed anti-urban sentiments through the twentieth century (Conn 2014), evangelicals have anti-urban biases built up over decades and tied to concerns about cities and their residents, desires to protect families and children, and interests in more homogeneous small town and private lives (Conn 1994; Mulder and Smith 2009).

Scholars have found a small number of evangelicals engaging with big cities in recent decades. Anthropologist James Bielo (2011a; 2011b) studied evangelicals living in and engaging with Cincinnati, Ohio and surrounding communities. Pastors and attendees found motivation through a dislike for suburban megachurches and an interest in reclaiming cities for God's kingdom. In examining suburban evangelicals engaging in cities, anthropologist Omri Elisha (2011b) studied evangelicals outside Knoxville, Tennessee who wanted to engage with Black churches in poorer urban neighborhoods. Through a lens that prioritized evangelism first, these evangelicals could keep the city at a physical and theological distance even as they engaged with urban communities.

Sociologist Wes Markofski detailed life in a monastery-like evangelical community intentionally located in and engaging with urban life. Markofski (2015, 2) summarizes their approach: "Rather than remaining isolated in safe, suburban pockets of evangelical subculture, neo-monastic communities like the Urban Monastery intentionally establish themselves in places where social needs are evident and the practice of Christian spirituality less common." These often younger Christians addressing social issues and doing so from the big city position themselves in contrast to the suburban megachurches exemplifying the evangelical right of the 1980s. One participant described the differences between the physical and social spaces of the city and the suburbs, the place more familiar to and embraced by evangelicals: "In a suburb, either you are a stranger passing through the street, or you are welcome into the most intimate space of the family. I enjoy how Urban Monasteries organize their life to create that sort of gray, middle social space, which creates room for strengthening relationships and a different kind of social progression" (Markofski 2015, 8).

If certain religious traditions—such as evangelicals—are more likely to be in some locations and not to be found in others, this affects both religious traditions and communities. As religious groups compete for resources (e.g., Iannaconne 1992; Finke and Stark 2005), their location influences what resources are available and with whom they compete. Where people and groups are located is connected to residential patterns determined by race, ethnicity, and social class, access to capital and local resources, presence in and engagement with social networks, and political representation and activity. Religious adherents, congregations, and organizations adapt to particular locations, and they can shape places and communities (Numrich and Wedam 2015). At the same time, the concentration of a religious tradition in particular kinds of communities can help build synergy, solidarity, and identity within the tradition.

Existing research suggests evangelicals are less likely to be found in big cities. The next section considers the patterns in the General Social Survey data that detail where evangelical adherents and adherents of other religious traditions are more and less likely to be found.

Religious Traditions in Different Kinds of Communities Over Time

I first look at religious traditions across community types for all three variables with the full number of GSS respondents from 1972 to 2016 and then discuss trends over time for the religious traditions across community types.

Religious Traditions and Community Types with All GSS Cases

When looking at XNORCSIZ community types (see Table 7.1), four categories contain the most residents: 20.1% in suburbs of large cities, 17.7% in cities of greater than 250,000 residents, 13.4% in cities of 50,000 to 250,000 residents, and 10.1% in suburbs of medium cities.

Starting the analysis with the largest religious tradition by number of adherents (Pew Research Center 2015), in these four locations, evangelicals are less likely to live in two of the four while they are even with Americans overall in the others. In large cities, evangelicals are found at 6.2% lower rates than Americans as a whole and 4% lower in suburbs of large cities. In contrast, evangelicals are more likely to be found in smaller areas—2% more—and in open country—5.5% more. Mainline Protestants are similar to evangelicals in all categories with at most a 3% difference.

Other religious traditions are more likely to live in different kinds of places compared to evangelicals. Black Protestants are much more likely than Americans as a whole to be located to large cities, more likely to be in cities of 50,000–250,000 residents, and less likely to be in all other locations. Similarly, Jews are 20.3% above the US population living in large cities and 11.8% higher in suburbs of large cities while being less represented in other locations. Catholics are less likely to be in rural areas (smaller areas, open country) and more likely to be in large cities and suburbs. Overall, the Unaffiliated are more likely to be in cities and suburbs of large cities while 0%–2% lower in all other locations.

In the GSS results from 1972 to 2016, according to SRCBELT the largest percentage of Americans live in "Other Urban" contexts followed by the suburbs of the 13–100th largest metropolitan areas and the 13–100th largest cities. In comparison to Americans as a whole, the percentage of evangelicals in the largest cities are 5.1% lower, 4.3% lower in the suburbs of the largest cities, and 6.3% more in Other Urban and 6.7% more in Other Rural (see Table 7.2).

Mainline Protestants again have similar population distributions compared to evangelicals across the SRCBELT location categories. Black Protestant and Jewish adherents are much more likely to be in the 12 largest cities (9.8% and 20.8% more, respectively), Black Protestants are more likely to be in the 13–100th largest cities (10.7% more) and Jews are more likely to be in the suburbs of the 12 largest cities (11.7% more), and both groups are

Table 7.1 The difference between the percentage of adherents in religious traditions in each community type versus the percentage of all residents in that community type, XNORCSIZ

XNORCSIZ categories	Evangel.	Mainline Prot.	Black Prot.	Catholic	Jewish	Other	Unaffiliated	Total %
City gt 250,000	-6.2	-6.3	16.6	1.0	20.3	3.1	4.3	17.7
City, 50,000–250,000	-1.1	-1.5	4.3	-0.7	-3.4	2.7	2.5	13.4
Suburb, large city	-4.0	-1.2	-6.7	5.5	11.8	2.2	1.4	20.1
Suburb, medium city	-0.1	0.6	-4.9	1.5	-3.1	1.0	0.0	10.1
Uninc, large city	-0.5	0.6	-2.1	1.1	0.0	-0.1	-0.4	6.2
Uninc, medium city	1.6	1.8	-3.5	-0.6	-4.4	0.2	-1.4	7.0
City, 10,000–49,999	2.2	0.9	-0.5	-1.6	-5.1	-0.8	-1.3	6.4
Town gt 2500	0.9	1.6	-0.8	-0.8	-4.7	-0.5	-1.2	5.3
Smaller areas	2.0	1.6	-0.8	-1.3	-3.9	-2.7	-1.8	4.5
Open country	5.5	2.1	-1.5	-3.9	-7.4	-5.0	-2.1	9.2

Source: General Social Survey cumulative cases 1972–2016.

Table 7.2 The difference between the percentage of adherents in religious traditions in each community type versus the percentage of all residents in that community type, SRCBELT variable

SRCBELT categories	Evangel.	Main Prot.	Black Prot.	Catholic	Jewish	Other	Unaffiliated	Total %
City 12 largest SMSAs	-5.1	-4.6	9.8	1.9	20.8	2.2	2.2	9
City SMSAs 13–100	-1.6	-2.9	10.7	-1.5	-0.2	1.1	2.7	13.9
Suburb, 12 largest	-4.3	-1.9	-2.7	5	11.7	2.3	0.8	11.4
Suburb, 13–100	-2.1	-0.4	-5.6	3.1	3.6	2.1	0.9	14.9
Other Urban	6.3	5.5	-11.2	-3	-24.3	-1	-3.2	37.7
Other Rural	6.7	4.1	-1.2	-5.5	-11.7	-6.8	-3.7	13.2

Source: General Social Survey cumulative cases 1972–2016.

found in lower proportions in Other Urban and Other Rural areas. Catholics are represented more in suburbs (5% more in suburbs of the 12 largest cities, 3.1% more in suburbs of the 13–100th largest cities) and less likely to be in Other Urban and Other Rural areas. Other religious traditions are slightly more represented in the cities and suburbs of the 100 largest SMSAs and less likely to be in Other Rural locations. Similarly, the Unaffiliated are slightly more likely to be in the 100 largest SMSAs and roughly 3% less in Other Urban and Other Rural areas.

Examining the quintiles of the SIZE variable reveals differences in the population size of communities where adherents of different religious traditions are located (see Table 7.3). Evangelicals are more likely to be in the smallest communities—up to 14,000 residents—as are mainline Protestants. However, Catholics, Jews, Others, and the Unaffiliated are less likely than Americans as a whole to be in smaller towns. While evangelicals are then found in smaller proportions in larger communities (topping out at a 6.7% difference in the largest quintile of communities), other groups are more likely to be in larger communities including Black Protestants (only in communities of 193,000 residents and more), Jews (in the last three quintiles), Others (in the last two quintiles), and the Unaffiliated (the last two quintiles).

Across more than four decades and in three measures of community types, evangelicals are found more than Americans as a whole in smaller communities outside of the largest metropolitan regions. Mainline Protestants roughly follow the patterns of evangelicals. Catholics are more often found in suburbs and less likely to be in rural areas. Black Protestants are more often found in large cities and Jews are more likely to be in the largest cities and their suburbs. Religious Others and the Unaffiliated are more often in bigger cities and their suburbs and less likely to be in smaller communities outside metropolitan regions.

Religious Traditions and Community Types Over Time

Examining the best-fit slopes of the percentage of adherents living in different community types across the three variables over time shows changes in where adherents of religious traditions were located between 1972 and 2016. A slope of greater than 0.10 (absolute value) suggests the religious tradition

Table 7.3 The difference between the percentage of adherents in religious traditions in each community type versus the percentage of all residents in that community type, SIZE variable.

SIZE categories	Evangel.	Main Prot.	Black Prot.	Catholic	Jewish	Other	Unaffiliated	Total %
0–4k residents	8.52	7.17	−6.83	−6.70	−16.87	−6.58	−4.94	21.5
5k–14k residents	3.00	2.27	−7.36	−0.13	−7.52	−1.30	−2.35	18.7
15k–41k residents	−1.79	0.01	−4.24	3.88	1.75	−0.94	−1.02	19.8
42k–192k residents	−3.02	−2.92	−0.48	2.33	3.59	5.76	3.59	19.9
193k–8175k residents	−6.72	−6.53	18.91	0.61	19.06	3.07	4.73	20.0

Source: General Social Survey cumulative cases 1972–2016.

Table 7.4 Slopes of the percentage of adherents in religious tradition by community type (XNORCSIZE) over time, 1972–2016

XNORCSIZ categories	Evangel.	Main Prot.	Black Prot.	Catholic	Jewish	Other	Unaffiliated
City gt 250,000	−0.0379	−0.0414	−0.5433	−0.1045	−0.4762	−0.0651	−0.3561
City, 50,000–250,000	0.1520	−0.2373	0.2108	0.1472	0.2895	0.1711	0.2349
Suburb, large city	0.1183	0.0623	0.2157	0.1094	0.3025	0.0241	0.1543
Suburb, medium city	0.1745	0.2466	0.1452	0.1349	0.1302	0.1910	0.1110
Uninc, large city	0.0786	0.0302	0.0823	0.0034	−0.1502	−0.0291	−0.0251
Uninc, medium city	0.0000	−0.0250	−0.0127	0.0189	0.0203	−0.1877	−0.0178
City, 10,000–49,999	−0.0536	−0.0385	−0.1006	−0.0593	−0.0313	−0.0075	0.0338
Town gt 2,500	−0.0160	−0.1142	0.1182	−0.1047	−0.0122	−0.0407	0.0329
Smaller areas	−0.1090	−0.0767	−0.0598	−0.0218	0.0308	0.0162	0.0246
Open country	−0.3071	−0.2806	−0.0559	−0.1235	−0.1034	−0.0723	−0.1924

Source: General Social Survey cumulative cases 1972–2016.

experienced more than a 2% change (31 waves) among their adherents in that category between 1972 and 2016.

Using XNORCSIZ categories (see Table 7.4), multiple groups had significant shifts away from the biggest cities: Black Protestants, Catholics, Jews, and the Nonaffiliated. These four same traditions had significant increases elsewhere including in smaller big cities and suburbs of cities. At the opposite end of community types, multiple traditions had declining percentages in open country including evangelicals, mainline Protestants, Catholics, Jews, and the Unaffiliated. Across religious traditions, the biggest growth in percentages over time took place in three categories (only mainline Protestants had a decline in one of these locations): city, 50,000–250,000 residents; suburb, large city; and suburb, medium city. For evangelicals, the slopes for community types were negative for all four rural categories,

Table 7.5 Slopes of the percentage of adherents in religious tradition by community type (SRCBELT) over time, 1972–2016

SRCBELT categories	Evangel.	Main Prot.	Black Prot.	Catholic	Jewish	Other	Unaffiliated
City 12 largest SMSAs	0.0574	0.0133	−0.2203	−0.0775	−0.4345	−0.0484	−0.2527
City SMSAs 13–100	−0.0941	−0.0190	−0.2790	−0.0101	0.0807	0.0279	−0.0655
Suburb, 12 largest	0.1055	0.0277	0.2379	0.0409	0.3794	0.1058	0.0533
Suburb, 13–100	0.1308	0.1160	0.0975	0.1710	0.0140	−0.0392	0.1507
Other Urban	0.0636	0.0945	0.0765	0.0116	−0.0534	−0.0839	0.1493
Other Rural	−0.2637	−0.2320	0.0875	−0.1358	0.0137	0.0278	−0.0351

Source: General Social Survey cumulative cases 1972–2016.

sharply so for smaller areas and open country, and positive for smaller big cities and suburbs of large and medium cities.

Looking at the slopes of religious traditions across SRCBELT categories shows similar patterns (see Table 7.5). Black Protestants, Jews, and the Nonaffiliated experienced sizable decreasing percentages in the largest cities in the United States. Evangelicals, mainline Protestants, and Catholics experienced decreasing percentages in Other Rural locations. In between, almost all groups, including evangelicals, experienced increases in the suburbs of the 100 largest cities with Black Protestants and Jews experiencing larger positive increases in suburbs of the largest cities.

Table 7.6 shows the slopes of traditions across the SIZE categories over multiple decades. While almost all traditions decreased in the percentage of their adherents in the communities with the biggest populations, particularly Black Protestant and Jewish adherents, results were mixed in other sized communities. All groups increased their percentages in communities of 42,000–192,000 residents and all but one increased in communities sized 15,000–41,000 residents. Evangelicals had a larger percentage decrease in

156 SANCTIFYING SUBURBIA

Table 7.6 Slopes of the percentage of adherents in religious tradition by community type (SIZE) over time, 1972–2016

SIZE categories	Evangel.	Main Prot.	Black Prot.	Catholic	Jewish	Other	Unaffiliated
0–4k residents	−0.3002	−0.2403	0.0356	−0.0887	0.1027	0.0667	−0.0121
5k–14k residents	0.0161	−0.0598	0.0942	0.0166	0.0694	−0.2241	−0.0103
15k–41k residents	0.1192	0.1115	0.1441	0.0448	0.0651	−0.0012	0.1111
42k–192k residents	0.1730	0.1940	0.1962	0.0639	0.1842	0.1493	0.2028
193k–8175k residents	−0.0081	−0.0054	−0.4700	−0.0467	−0.4213	0.0093	−0.2916

Source: General Social Survey cumulative cases 1972–2016.

residents in the smallest communities while the percentage in the third and fourth quintiles covering 15,000 residents to 192,000 residents increased.

The slopes across the three location variables show several patterns over more than four decades. The percentage of adherents in the largest cities decreased for most groups, especially for some religious traditions like Black Protestants and Jews. Similarly, the percentage of adherents in more rural areas and the smallest communities decreased, particularly among evangelicals and mainline Protestants. However, results were more mixed in smaller big cities, suburbs, and medium-sized communities.

Moving from Cities and Rural Areas to the Suburbs

Looking at the religious traditions as a whole across 45 years and 31 waves of the General Social Survey, different religious traditions are more likely to be in different kinds of communities compared to Americans as a whole. Four areas for further discussion arise from these patterns.

Of most interest in this book are the community types in which evangelicals are more likely to reside and the changes in where evangelicals lived during these decades. Considering all cases between 1972 and 2016, evangelicals were less likely to be in the biggest cities—either defined as places with more than 193,000 residents or 250,000 residents or the cities at the center of the 12 largest metropolitan regions—and more likely to be found in rural areas and communities with few residents—defined as open country, other rural, and communities with 4,000 residents or fewer. For communities in between larger population centers and places with small populations, evangelicals lived there in similar percentages to Americans as a whole.

These percentages did not remain static between 1972 and 2016. The percentage of evangelicals declined noticeably in open country, other rural, and the smallest communities. At the same time, the percentage of evangelicals increased in suburbs of cities between 50,000 and 250,000 residents, in suburbs of large and medium-sized cities, in suburbs of the 100 largest metropolitan regions, and in communities between 15,000 and 192,000 residents.

Over this time, other religious traditions lived in different locations and experienced different patterns of mobility. Across all of these decades, Black Protestants were more likely to be in large cities, Jews were more likely to be in the largest cities and their suburbs, Catholics were more often found in suburbs and not in rural areas and smaller communities, and religious Others and the Unaffiliated were in larger cities and suburbs in higher percentages. In terms of change over these decades, the percentage of Black Protestant and Jewish adherents in the largest cities declined. The percentage of Jews in suburbs of the largest cities increased. Evangelicals and mainline Protestants, two groups roughly found in similar percentages in many community types, had larger declines among their traditions in rural areas. Almost all religious groups increased their proportions of adherents in suburbs.

All of this suggests that evangelicals are both firmly found in particular community types and these concentrations are shifting slowly over time. The findings in this chapter echo that of sociologist Robert Wuthnow (2007, 80) who found younger evangelicals are more mobile and more likely to live in suburbs than older evangelicals. Like other religious traditions, more evangelicals moved to the suburbs. Like mainline Protestants, the evangelicals moved from rural areas to suburbs. Unlike Black Protestants and Jews, the percentage of evangelicals living in cities did not decrease appreciably in the move to the suburbs.

The types of places in which evangelicals reside are connected to a second significant area to consider regarding communities: the intersection of race and ethnicity in the United States with place and communities. As discussed in Chapter 3, research documents the impact of religious white flight involving evangelicals, mainline Protestants, Catholics, and Jews after

World War II (e.g., McGreevy 1995; Cutler 1996; Gamm 1999; Diamond 2000; Diamond 2003; Mulder 2015; Miller 2017b). Much of that research ends with experiences and data in the final decades of the twentieth century. The findings here suggest the proportion of certain primarily white religious traditions in the suburbs increased even after the clear period of postwar white flight ended. American Jews left the biggest cities for suburbs of big cities. Evangelicals and mainline Protestants did not necessarily leave the biggest cities over this period as their percentages there were lower to start but more adherents did end up in the suburbs.

Suburban areas now have larger populations of racial and ethnic minorities and poorer residents (Frey 2022; Kneebone and Berube 2013). More immigrants and minority religious groups are found in suburban communities (e.g., Numrich and Wedam 2015; Howe 2018; Miller 2020). The ongoing spatialization of race and ethnicity in the United States, particularly with more groups now residing in the suburbs, includes ongoing religious change across communities.

As the percentage of suburban adherents grew, rural populations—typically whiter populations—shrunk in recent decades: the percentage of Americans living in rural areas declined from 31% to 19.7% between 1970 and 2000 (Hobbs and Stoops 2002, 38). The percentage of rural religious adherents in certain traditions declined. Some traditions—evangelicals and mainline Protestants—are still more represented than others in rural areas by the end of this period. The loss of rural or small town populations and life is also the loss of rural religion. Even as denominations and religious groups have attempted to address this, certain religious traditions lost adherents in rural areas while other traditions lost adherents in big cities.

These two trends—fewer adherents in big cities and rural areas—are connected to an increase in religious adherents in suburbs across religious traditions. The suburbs themselves are growing: in 1970, over 37% of Americans lived in suburbs, while by the early 2000s more than 50% did so (Hobbs an Stoops 2002; Mather, Pollard, and Jacobsen 2011; Bucholtz 2020). Much of this suburban growth took place in two regions: the population in the South and West grew at 25.97% and 24.35%, respectively, between 2000 and 2020, while the Northeast and Midwest grew at 7.49% and 7.13%, respectively, over the same period.

These spatial changes hint at the continuing influence of racial and ethnic residential patterns, including where immigrants live, on religious traditions. Spatial and segmented assimilation patterns (e.g., Massey and Mullen

1984; Portes and Zhou 1993) intersect with religious beliefs, behaviors, and belonging (e.g., Warner 2007). Even as Black Protestants and Jews continued to maintain higher proportions in big cities and their suburbs, they and other traditions continued to increase in number in suburbs. Catholics were spread throughout a number of community types, hinting at older waves of Catholic immigration and the movement of those residents (e.g., Alba, Logan, and Crowder 1997; McMahon 1995; Gamm 1999) as well as more recent Catholic and Protestant immigrants in the post-1965 era (e.g., Mulder, Ramos, and Martí 2017; Calvillo 2020). The suburbanization of religion is an evolving process that also did not end in the immediate postwar decades as religion continues to be shaped by suburban patterns and landscapes (e.g., Eisland 2000; Wilford 2012; Howe 2018) and religious congregations and traditions can shape communities (Clark 2011; Numrich and Wedam 2015).

A third significant implication of these findings involves the fastest growing religious tradition over this period: the Unaffiliated (Pew Research Center 2015). This growing group has a particular spatial distribution. Across the time period in this study, the Unaffiliated are more likely than Americans as a whole to be in larger cities. This fits with images of cities providing space for free thinkers and a variety of religious and nonreligious practices.

Yet the Unaffiliated were not that much more likely than Americans as a whole to be in large cities—4.3% more according to XNORCSIZ and over 4.7% according to SIZE—and the percentage of them in large cities declined over this period. Their percentages increased in smaller big cities and suburbs. The Unaffiliated were not as commonly found in rural areas and smaller communities but their percentages are not far off (2%–5%) from Americans as a whole.

The willingness of more Americans to not affiliate with a religious tradition is not just a religious and cultural shift in particular places; it involves community types across the United States (Thiessen and Wilkins-Laflamme 2020). While scholars have examined religious denominations and congregations in particular communities and regions, also examining the presence and influence of Unaffiliated people and groups across community types will contribute to our understanding of religiosity in different contexts, including the suburbs.

Finally, these results add to the findings of the last two chapters that religious traditions can influence communities in terms of their character and their developmental trajectories. With religious traditions found in certain kinds of communities more than others, how does this shape communities more broadly? In addition to other factors that shape types of communities—including economic and political leadership (Logan and Molotch 1987) and demographics—what role might the presence of particular religious traditions in larger numbers than others mean for not just religious activity but also social organization, decisions about development, and character?

The changes uncovered here suggest an increasing religious change and dynamism in suburban areas. Adherents of different religious traditions, including evangelicals, have moved to the suburbs in the decades before and after the turn of the twenty-first century. This adds to the significant shift of evangelicals and other religious groups to the suburbs after World War II. As one quick example from this data, how does the ongoing presence of Black Protestant and Jewish adherents in the biggest cities affect local social, cultural, and political life? And when adherents of these traditions move in sizable numbers to the suburbs over more than four decades, what is the impact on big cities and the new kinds of communities they call home? All together, with the increasing diversification of the suburbs in terms of race and ethnicity and social class, the suburbs could be a new center of religious pluralism and/or conflict.

Conclusion

By the early 2000s, at least a few evangelical actors were trying to reinvigorate evangelical life in and engagement with the city. They did not always go the route of the erudite Redeemer Presbyterian congregation in Manhattan. For example, evangelical activist Shane Claiborne (2006) helped found The Simple Way, a Christian commune, in Philadelphia. Claiborne described growing up in the Bible Belt, visiting inner-city Philadelphia while a student at a Christian college in the suburbs, and spending a summer in Calcutta and admiring the work of Mother Theresa. In his final year of college, Claiborne took classes at Wheaton College while interning at suburban megachurch Willow Creek half an hour away. According to Claiborne (2006, 95, 101), being in Wheaton "wasn't the easiest place to be" and while God was "alive at Willow Creek," "there still seemed such a chasm between the good folks of the suburbs and the suffering masses in Calcutta or Lower Wacker." In his life and work, Claiborne followed in a line of evangelicals engaging difficult social issues in what now are often considered as liberal or progressive ways

(Schwartz 2012), but Claiborne's work in the city stood out in a religious tradition that had come to embrace the suburbs.

The patterns discussed in this chapter suggest there is much that would need to change so that evangelicals move in large numbers to the biggest cities in the United States or adopt a different ethos in order to live in and engage with cities. Tim Keller and Shane Claiborne are notable exceptions for their long presences in major cities and ministries aimed at addressing urban realities, not the norm among American evangelicals. Two decades into the twenty-first century, evangelicals are more likely to be found in suburbs than in largest cities.

Following multiple chapters considering data on where evangelicals live, the next chapter considers the cultural toolkits evangelicals employed when considering changing suburbs and places. To do this, I look at how the popular evangelist Billy Graham discussed suburbs, cities, and rural areas in 29 books written across his career. How did places fit within his toolkit aimed at helping individuals obtain salvation?

8
Evangelical Cultural Toolkits and Changing Suburbs

How do American evangelicals think about and act within the American suburbs and other types of settings? Theologian Willie James Jennings provides a story that illustrates the evangelical cultural toolkit and what fits and does not fit in their conception of faith and place. A lover of working with soil and plants, Jennings's mother was approached by two white men one day while in her garden in Michigan. Twelve-year old Jennings was nearby. After asking his mother's name, the men issued an invitation to worship at their church down the street. Here is how Jennings recalls the scene:

> The strangeness of this event lay not only in their appearance in our backyard but also in the obliviousness of these men as to whom they were addressing—Mary Jennings, one of the pillars of New Hope Missionary Baptist Church. I thought it incredibly odd that they never once asked her if she went to church, if she was a Christian, or even if she believed in God. Mary and her twin sister, Martha, were about as close to their scriptural counterparts as you could get. Without fail they were in their customary seats in church every Sunday, and you could calibrate almost every activity of the church by and around them or us, their children . . .
>
> My mother finally interrupted the speech of this would-be neighborhood missionary with the words, "I am already a Christian. I believe in Jesus and I attend New Hope Missionary Baptist church, where Rev. J. V. Williams is the pastor." I don't remember his exact reply to my mother's declaration of identity, but he kept talking for quite a few more wasted minutes. Finally they gave her some literature and left. I remember this event because it underscored an inexplicable strangeness embedded in the Christianity I lived and observed. Experiences like these fueled a question that has grown in hermeneutic force for me: Why did they not know us? They should have known us very well. (Jennings 2010, 3)

In this example, the two white men had difficulty knowing Jennings's mother, even as she described her church home and connections to the place.

This chapter considers the evangelical toolkit regarding suburbs. Sociologist Ann Swidler (1986, 277) described culture as "more like a toolkit" or repertoire from which actors select differing pieces for constructing lines of action." These are particularly visible in "unsettled lives" or "periods of social transformation" where "ideologies—explicit, articulated, highly organized meaning systems (both political and religious—*establish* new styles or strategies of action" (Swidler 1986, 278). Individuals and groups have "strategies of action" which are "ways actors routinely go about attaining their goals" (Swidler 2001, 82). They provide people "a cultural repertoire" that "allows people to move among situations, finding terms in which to orient action within each situation" (Swidler 2001, 30). These conventions for approaching the world around them shape activity and beliefs as well as groups and structures.

These influential ideas in the sociology of culture form the basis for this chapter: as the United States transformed from a rural to suburban nation between roughly 1900 and 2000 (among other significant changes during this time; see Fischer and Hout 2006), how did evangelicals approach suburbs? What cultural toolkits did they bring to these unsettled times of changing places and settings? To examine this, I look at how evangelist Billy Graham approached suburbs, cities, and rural areas in 29 books Graham wrote between 1947 and 2015. While Graham is one evangelical leader among many in a movement that emerged in the second half of the twentieth century, his reputation, reach, and ability to help evangelicals coalesce mean his writings are worth examining as the United States became majority suburban and Graham's listeners interacted daily with places. I argue that the unsettled nature of rapid suburban growth provided space for evangelicals to exercise and reify their cultural toolkits regarding places by the early twenty-first century. Specifically, Billy Graham commented on suburbs, cities, and rural life, discussed the lessons from biblical cities for cities today (including heaven as the ultimate city); and expressed a specific interest in New York City.

Evangelical Cultural Toolkits

As evangelicals emerged as a constant and potentially powerful force in American society, scholars examined not just the outcomes evangelicals contributed to but the repertoires and means—the cultural toolkits—evangelicals employed in pursuit of their goals. While these previous works show how evangelicals operated in regard to race, social class, gender, history, and more, few works address how evangelicals applied their cultural toolkits to places, and specifically, suburbs.

In studying how white evangelicals approach race in the United States, Emerson and Smith (2000, 74) found tendencies to see "the race problem" as an issue among individuals and downplay race as a problem (and blame Black people and others for raising the issue). They depend on a three-fold toolkit: "'accountable freewill individualism, 'relationalism' (attaching central importance to interpersonal relationships), and antistructuralism (inability to perceive or unwillingness to accept social structural influences)." (Emerson and Smith 2000, 76) This approach limited evangelical support for the Civil Rights Movement, a response influenced by Billy Graham, and prompted calls that political activism was not the answer (e.g., Emerson and Smith 2000, 46–48; Evans 2017; Curtis 2021). These tools regarding race could change if white evangelicals engaged in "extensive cross-race networks" (Emerson and Smith 2000, 132). But these tools are firmly embedded in the evangelical world and may not apply just to race. Evangelicals long applied individualistic approaches to social problems, including race, with suburban churches furthering privatistic approaches (Moberg 2007 [1972], 91–92). Emerson and Smith (2000, 89) suggest confronting the individual approach to race is also getting at larger concerns as it "would challenge the very basis of their world, both their faith and the American way of life." In other words, the evangelical individualism tool applies to more situations than just race.

Earlier, Smith (1998) argued that evangelicals have developed a particular subcultural identity. Smith does not utilize the language of toolkits but he discusses the ongoing social and narrative negotiations inherent with engaging with the world while working to maintain group cohesion. This involves a highly individualistic and interpersonal approach: "The only truly effective way to change the world is one-individual-at-a-time through the influence of interpersonal relationships" (Smith 1998, 187). This leads to a simplistic approach to complex social problems.

Similarly, sociologist James Hunter (2010) argues that evangelicals often take an individualistic approach to transforming society. Whether through saving souls, having the right values in politics and political leaders, or reformed civic institutions, evangelicals pursue a ground-up approach. He sums this up as an evangelical belief that "cultures are shaped from the cumulative values and beliefs that reside in the hearts and minds of ordinary people" (Hunter 2010, 273). Hunter suggests this is unlikely to influence society and culture significantly and long-term as "cultural change at its most profound level occurs through dense networks of elites operating in common purpose within institutions at the high-prestige centers of cultural production" (Hunter 2010, 274).

Other scholars question whether a toolkit emphasizing individualism fully explains the ways evangelicals address race and ethnicity. Tranby and Hartman (2008) argue that the individualism and anti-Blackness in white evangelical toolkits is also the result of white culture and a racialized society. A continued emphasis on colorblindness allowed white evangelicals to uphold white influence and leadership while dismissing calls to address structural inequalities by race and ethnicity (Curtis 2021). Oyakawa (2019) considers the influence of both individualistic toolkits and promoting whiteness by showing how pursuing racial reconciliation in congregations limits social change and allows a white hierarchy to persist. The racial reconciliation frame purports to represent both sides but continues an individualistic approach to addressing sin and promotes a solution of a unified congregation with strong relationships (and does not emphasize structural inequalities). Even when presidential candidate Donald Trump did not express evangelical faith or practice, Martí (2020, 251) found evangelicals supported Trump as they continued to hold to ideas that "the intervention of God works through individuals" and pursued political control and the dominance of white influence and structures. Looking at the broad sweep of evangelical history in the United States and noting Graham's contribution to their cause, Butler (2021, 138) argues that evangelicals are less about religion and rather are "a nationalistic political movement whose purpose is to support the hegemony of white Christian men over and against the flourishing of others."

Additional work also highlights the white evangelical toolkit applied in other social spheres. Within a changing economic and social landscape, evangelicals utilize a particular toolkit regarding family life drawing on both gender-essentialist and egalitarian perspectives as many promote a more traditional form of nuclear family life—husband working, wife staying at home—yet many evangelical women work (Gallagher 2004; Swartz 2023). Particular narratives about men, women, and family values developed in interaction with social change (Du Mez 2020). Prayer is a strategy of action with complex means of practicing it and understanding its purpose (Luhrmann 2012; Winchester and Guhin 2019).

Billy Graham as Evangelical Exemplar

Starting in the late 1940s and into the early twenty-first century, Billy Graham spoke to millions and received numerous public accolades. Graham stated in a 1992 book that he "had the privilege of preaching to more than 100 million people in eighty-four countries" between 1949 and 1992 (Graham 1992, 9). Summary figures of his whole career suggest he spoke to over 200 million people in person and 61 times he was named one of the "Ten Most Admired Men" in a Gallup poll (Wacker 2019, 1). He also reached many others through additional means, including a weekly radio show, numerous appearances in the press, live satellite broadcasts available in multiple countries and continents (Graham 1992, 186; Wacker 2019, 1–2), and numerous books (selling in the millions; see Wacker 2019, 2).

Graham was one of numerous evangelical leaders who emerged in the twentieth century. He prayed with presidents, met with important political and religious leaders, and was regularly in the media. One historian said, "he belonged on the Mount Rushmore of American religious history," others suggested he "was the closest thing to a pope that Protestants had," and he became at his peak "like a Hollywood star" (Wacker 2019, 4, 161). His story and influence—from a small town in North Carolina, graduate of a Christian college in the Midwest after earlier semesters elsewhere, development as a dynamic and admired evangelist relatively free of public scandal, and globally known—suggest he is an important representative of white evangelicalism as it emerged in a rapidly suburbanizing country. Graham was not necessarily the most influential actor—considering institutions as well as individuals—among evangelicals, yet at the same time, his words and actions were observed by many.

I examined 29 books Graham wrote (see the list in Grossman 2018 and a mostly complete list at the beginning of Graham 2005) to see what he said about suburbs and places. I previously studied portions of his public messages (Miller 2022) with that analysis focusing on portions of his speeches that explicitly referenced cities and suburbs. The work in this chapter expands this previous analysis to additional sources and situates Graham's discussions of suburbs and places in the broader context of his broader themes.

Graham wrote a range of books, involving everything from messages from his Crusades (Graham 1947; 1969; 2005) to his answers to questions he regularly received (Graham 1960; 1988) to devotional treasuries (Graham 1988; 2002) to addressing issues of interest to him and the general public including angels (Graham 1975), the apocalypse (Graham 1981; 1983; 1992), and finding peace or happiness or hope (Graham 1953b; 1955b; 2003). Graham had a variety of publishers: he published his first two books with Zondervan, a Christian publisher; his own ministry association, the Billy Graham Evangelistic Association, published several; Doubleday and Company published books early in his career; and Word Books published him starting in 1977 and became home to almost all of his books from that point on (including W Publishing Group and Thomas Nelson as Christian publishers merged and evolved; see Vaca 2019).

During his public career starting in the late 1940s and going into the early decades of the twenty-first century, much happened with cities and suburbs in the United States. By the early 1960s, more Americans lived in suburbs than in cities the country was majority-suburban by 2000 (Hobbs and Stoops 2002). As suburbs grew, numerous cities experienced change. New metropolitan regions, such as in the Sun Belt and West, grew rapidly. Additionally, Americans faced multiple social challenges involving suburbs and cities including experiences and perceptions regarding poverty, crime, unrest, and racial discrimination.

Billy Graham and Evangelical Cultural Toolkits

In books published in eight decades, Graham had much to say about American society and changes within. He discussed places even as they were not his primary focus. More often, he wrote about social problems and he had a particular approach he recommended readers adopt—secure personal salvation—to find peace and joy within turbulent times (Wacker 2014, 58–59). As Evans (2017, 157) argues, "Graham's consistent call for a transformed heart, his clear and urgent preaching that sought to get to the root causes of problems, and his skepticism about any grand or utopian schemes for social transformation made his message appealing and convincing to many Christians."

This focus on personal salvation is evident in Graham's books. This typically involved discussing the true human problem within a society that had lost its moral bearings. For Graham, humans did not suffer from lack of resources or disordered societies or changing social norms. Rather, humans are sinful. The true cause of the world's problems, even amid prosperity and technological success, is a sinful heart in rebellion against God. Despite what experts might say about how social and environmental factors push people to immorality ("Today many of our leaders are blaming environmental, social inequality, lack of material benefits"; Graham n.d., 122), Graham said, "we are never going to change until we look into the mirror of our own soul and face with candor what we really are inside" (Graham 1971, 166). In a message delivered in New York City in 1969, Graham (1969, 97) said,

> We're suffering from only one disease in the world. Our basic problem is not a race problem. Our basic problem is not a poverty problem. Our basic problem is not a war problem. Our basic problem is a heart problem. We need to get the heart changed, the heart transformed. That's why Jesus said you must be born again. You must have a new nature, a new heart, that will be dominated by love.

Graham described this approach as "the social policy of Jesus": "If only we in the church would begin at the root of our problems, which is the disease of human nature. However, we have become blundering social physicians, giving medicine here and putting ointment there on the sores of the world, but the sores break out again somewhere else. The great need is for the church to call in the great Physician who alone can properly diagnose the case. He will look beneath the mere skin eruptions and pronounce on the cause of it all—sin" (Graham 1965, 184). Regardless of the setting, knowing Jesus would lead to peace: "It's possible to live in a rich man's home and be happy. It's possible to live in a ghetto and be happy with Christ in your heart. It's possible to live in a prison, to live in a mental institution, and have Christ in your heart and find peace and happiness" (Graham 1969, 41).

But Graham did not often start his books with the disease of sin. Rather, he often started with the problems of the world. Multiple times, he wrote a version of this idea: "To one who accepts the Biblical account, it is exciting to pick up a newspaper in one hand and the Bible in the other hand and to watch the almost daily fulfillment of prophetic events" (Graham 1965, xv). Graham acted as if times were always unsettled for society and for individuals. In his first book, consisting of sermons, he said, "Socially and spiritually America reached a high point immediately preceding the First World War" (Graham 1947, 19). By the early 1950s and for decades, he decried communism and secularism taking place under the threat that cities and people could be vaporized by powerful nuclear weapons. In the 1960s, Graham considered the unrest in the United States, involving race and college campuses and political action and war (Graham 1965). In the early 1980s (Graham 1981; 1983), he emphasized a coming apocalypse and signs of the end times. Even after the fall of the Berlin Wall, Graham suggested the future was not rosy (Graham 1992) and that even "Compared with the 1990s, the 1960s, for all of their rebellion and turmoil, seem almost quaint and placid" (Graham 1991, 13). After the shock of 9/11, toward the end of his life in the late 2000s and into the 2010s he decried increasing assaults on the family and wayward morality (Graham 2013; 2015).

Here is one example of a list of issues Graham said the world faces—and cannot solve on its own:

> Other columns, editorials, news stories and letters to the editors were permeated by the common fears: nuclear war, economic chaos, the misuse and drying up of the earth's nonrenewable resources, runaway crime, violence in the streets, mysterious new killer viruses, terrorism, radically changing weather patterns, earthquakes, floods, famines, destruction and death. Everywhere I go I find people, both leaders and ordinary individuals, asking one basic question: 'Is there any hope?' And the answer comes roaring back from the world's press: 'There is no hope for planet earth!' (Graham 1983, 29)

He wrote about these themes over and over again with goal of pushing readers to Graham's source of hope and salvation.

Graham regularly described human advancement and technological progress, and then suggested these improvements would not lead to lasting change. For example, "Science is learning to control everything but man. We have not yet solved the problems of hate, lust, greed, and prejudice, which produce social injustice, racial strife, and ultimately war. Our future is threatened by many dangers, such as the nuclear destruction that hangs over our heads. However, the greatest danger is from within" (Graham 1986, 128).

At other points, Graham would lament how far he perceived the United States had fallen from an earlier mission. From one of his final books (Graham 2013, 163), Graham described how "our nation has wandered further down the moral ladder" due to abortion, glorifying violence, and trying not to offend each other. And just after this passage, he suggested this is not the way it had always been: "It wasn't prosperity and living the American dream that made America great but reverence for God and living according to His Word. The results were untold blessings. God used America to spread the Gospel to the world. Now we see many of its citizens shaking their fists in the face of Almighty God" (Graham 2013, 163). The answer to this distressing news? The book ends, like many of the others, with an invitation to pray, repent, and accept salvation (Graham 2013, 83).

Throughout these writings, Graham told readers that the world was in turmoil. Life was not secure. The United States was under threat. Individuals, millions of them, were living life apart from God. Whether in 1965 or 1981 or 2013, Graham told of society falling apart. He said, "It is only the strong Christian family unit that can survive the coming world holocaust" (Graham 1981, 179). While Graham did write about how readers could and should live as Christians (e.g., Graham 1955b; 1978; 2003), he worked to show readers that amid chaos and sin they needed stability and true change that could only come from God.

What was constant or could bring lasting peace? Unchanging were God, the human condition where people suffered from the consequences of sin brought into the world by the actions of Adam and Eve, and the opportunity to obtain salvation and life in heaven. Graham told of God sending Jesus, whose shed blood atoned for sin and whose resurrection overcame death. Graham tended to end his books by inviting readers to consider praying to repent and asking for salvation. This invitation often came with a vision of perfect life with God in heaven as described in the Bible.

Throughout his books, Graham suggested Christians should address social concerns. He stated over and over again that Christians have a responsibility to care for and love others. For example, he said, "We can show mercy by *caring for the social needs* of our fellow men" (Graham 1955b, 61, emphasis in original).

Yet the first priority was always on the spiritual needs. Jesus healed sickness but he, more importantly, transformed hearts. Christians should demonstrate their Christlikeness by serving others but they can only do so out of hearts filled by the Holy Spirit. Graham said, "Many people have criticized the so-called 'social gospel,' but Jesus taught that we are to take regeneration in one hand and a cup of cold water in the other" (Graham 1953b, 190). When asked about whether he should emphasize the social gospel when speaking, Graham said, "In other words, as a Christian minister, my first responsibility is to win men to Christ, then, and only then, can and will they live as Christians in the world. There have been Christians who have neglected their social responsibilities, but let us remember that almost all great social reforms have come through the application of Christian principles"

(Graham n.d., 157). Without God's love in their hearts, people could split apart "the social gospel" and "the redemptive gospel" when "The truth is: There is only one gospel" (Graham 1986, 178).

Billy Graham on Suburbs and Other Places in His Books

In Graham's discussions of social issues and problems, he referenced suburbs, cities, and other kinds of places occasionally. There are patterns in the ways Graham approached suburbs and places. I discuss three themes here: comments about life in suburbs, cities, and rural areas, including his preference for the last setting; lessons from biblical cities for cities today (including heaven as the ultimate city); and a specific interest in New York City. With a broader audience for his books, there are far fewer mentions of specific cities and their good qualities, as could be found in his messages delivered in particular locations (Miller 2022).

Across these themes and places, Graham was consistent about what communities needed: "The greatest need of our great cities at this moment is evangelism" (Graham 1986, 145). Additionally, cities might be centers of innovation and corporate activity; he once highlighted Pittsburgh as having "solved some great human problems through technology" (Graham 1986, 273). But he quickly followed by writing, "there's one problem none of our great cities has solved—the problem of human iniquity: lying, hate, lust, greed. When Christ comes back He's going to solve that problem" (Graham 1986, 273).

Two passages that clearly discuss suburbs and cities together come from Graham's 1965 book *World Aflame*. In the introduction, Graham (1965, xiv) suggests sociologists assume "bad environment, in the form of poor living conditions such as urban slums and rural poverty areas, is the breeding ground of evil and trouble." But a few sentences later, he argues that it is not about environments but people: "Indeed, some of the greater social problems we now face are found in the more affluent areas of suburbia" (Graham 1965, xv). It matters less whether people are in cities or suburbs; what is important is that "we must determine which way God is moving in history—and then get in step with God!" (Graham 1965, xvi).

Later in the book and after discussing numerous social problems in the United States, Graham suggests ministering to people requires knowing them. He goes on to say:

This is the reason that I have such an interest in those who are working in the "intercity churches." It is probably the most frustrating ministry in America today—to face teeming areas of people living in substandard housing, thousands of them unemployed. Religious ideas have little meaning for them. Their lives are totally disorganized. The intercity pastor faces all their frustrations and tries to compassionately to enter into their problems. During the last fifteen years the rush of white church members to suburbs has caused such a religious upheaval that a whole new urban ministry has emerged. Religious urban projects are springing up all over the country. To capture the attention of the changing, television-oriented city dweller living in an apartment house requires bold new techniques of evangelism and Christian leadership. (Graham 1965, 179–180)

The emphasis here is on ministry opportunities in cities but this excitement is based on numerous negative descriptors of urban life including comments about housing, jobs, the lack of religious activity, the loss of white residents, and how city residents use their time. Within a text that emphasizes the difficult social conditions in the United States, the urban dweller truly lives in a "world aflame."

This is also a rare recognition by Graham of white flight from cities. Graham includes it in a list of other issues in cities and does so in a particular way. He describes white flight as "a rush of white church members to suburbs." With the departure of these white church members, "a religious upheaval" is underway. There is no mention of the motivations for white flight or whether white congregations also left the city alongside white church members.

Graham was not silent about race in his books. Graham discussed "the race problem" in the United States in multiple texts. In his first best-seller, *Peace with God*, Graham talked about the social responsibilities of Christians. Graham included, "Sixth: *the Christian looks through the eyes of Christ at the race question* and admits that the church has failed in solving this great human problem ... The church should have been the pace-setter" (Graham 1953b, 195, emphasis in original). After admitting this lack of effort, Graham suggested how he would address the issue: "But in the final analysis the only real solution will be found at the foot of the cross where we come together in brotherly love. The closer the people of all races get to Christ and His cross, the closer they will get to one another" (Graham 1953b, 195). Later, Graham said, "The idea of a super race is unBiblical, unScriptural and unChristian"

(Graham 1955a, 23), denounced segregation and said, "the Bible teaches the opposite" (Graham n.d., 127), and illustrated the idea that *"We each want our own way"* by stating "Those who think their race or ethnic background is superior will always have problems getting along with others" (Graham 2006, 206, emphasis in original). He repeated multiple times his refusal to hold segregated meetings starting in 1952 (Graham 1965, 184; 1983, 145; 1988, 191) as he became more aware of "the difficulties, problems and oppressions of black people" after experiencing more of life on his own and attending school with Black students at Wheaton College (Graham 1983, 145).

The solution to race in the United States was to change hearts and wait for God's Kingdom. In 1965 (Graham 1965, 7) he said, "There is only one possible solution to the race problem and that is a vital personal experience with Jesus Christ on the part of both races. In Christ the middle wall of partition has been broken down." In the same book, he said, "There will be a state of complete reconciliation between man and God—between race and race—between nation and nation" in the full Kingdom of God (Graham 1965, 191). He disagreed with those who said "the Civil Rights Acts of 1964 would solve the race issue in the United States" as subsequent evidence demonstrated Americans needed "something deeper than legislation" as a solution would not come "unless the heart is reached" (Graham n.d., 128).

Elsewhere, Graham talked of urban neighborhoods at multiple points. He said he "visited the slums of our inner cities" (Graham 1971, 28) and mentioned urban slums at multiple points (e.g., Graham 1953b, 198; 1977, 145; 1991, 10). Residents in cities around the world "are warned not to go out on the streets at night" (Graham 1991, 220). When extolling the virtues of prayer and its role in revivals, Graham mentioned these revivals happening in cities like Rochester, New York and London (Graham 1978, 219).

Brief mentions of suburban life popped up in Graham's books. He remembered his first pastorate in the suburbs of Chicago (Graham 1984, 35). He considered how suburbanites of Ephesus or Laodicea might have encountered the Roman call to proclaim "Caesar is Lord" (Graham 1983, 33). "Crime, disease, and violence" could be found in "suburbia" as well as in "cities" and "country" (Graham 1971, 39–40).

Graham also considered how teenagers and young adults viewed suburbs. In 1969, Graham spoke of issues facing young people. This included seeing "adult society in which drinking had become a status symbol in the suburbs" (Graham 1969, 38). In 1971, Graham (1971, 15) noted a *Life* magazine article that showed teenagers transformed by Jesus in a wealthy New York suburb. In the same book, Graham told of a father confronted by his son after a speech on "suburban morality":

> Look at yourself, needing a couple of stiff drinks before you have the courage to talk with another human being. Look at you, making it with your neighbor's wife on the sly just to try to prove that you're really alive. Look at you, hooked on your cafeteria of pills, making up dirty names for anybody who isn't in your bag, and messing up the land, the water, and the air for profit and calling this "nowhere scene" the Great Society. And you're trying to tell me how to live? C'mon, man, you've got to be kidding. (Graham 1971, 46–47)

These comments were all aimed at teenagers and young adults who might struggle with suburban life amid societal unrest and existential questions. Suburban life could be marked by immorality and hypocrisy even as conversion could change suburban teenagers.

Perhaps Graham was thinking of suburbs when he provided this description of life in heaven: "In heaven there will be no need for environmentalists to work for better air and water quality, or to decry the destruction of our land for housing developments" (Graham 1987, 246).

Graham occasionally made comparisons between urban and rural life. After describing the beginning of humanity in a garden ("He didn't put him in the middle of a city"), Graham said, "Morally and spiritually, there are temptations in the city that you don't face out in the small village and you don't face in rural areas." Directly after this quote, he noted the shift from rural to urban populations from the turn of the twentieth century to 1969 (Graham 1969, 162).

Graham himself expressed a preference for living in the country. He wrote of growing up on a North Carolina farm, milking the cows before breakfast, and rebelling against God and his family with their regular church attendance (Graham 1971, 41; 1986, 280). Reflecting on what he saw in Korea, Graham contrasted the "quiet study of my home in Montreat, nestled away in the Great Smoky Mountains" and the violence and pain of the Korean War (Graham 1953a, 9). In a discussion of heaven, he said, "My wife and I do not like cities. We do not care for 'mansions.' We love log houses, on the primitive side, with simple comforts" (Graham 1991, 222). His family spent time in the nearby mountains and explored the outdoors (Graham 1981, 163; 1986, vii; 2012, 52). The mountains were not without issues—Graham

(1955b, 62) expressed surprise at finding neighbors in mountain valleys who struggled financially and his wife suffered significant injuries after a fall while constructing a zip line (e.g., Graham 1991, 173)—but he said he longed for their log home in the mountains when he was traveling throughout the world (Graham 1987, 245).

Graham also noted the scale of urbanization around the globe. In the context of discussing homelessness, one longer passage in *Storm Warning* described the incredible population growth in cities:

> Nor is the problem limited to America. It is especially critical in poorer countries. There the trend toward urbanization of the past fifty years has been the largest contributor to the problem of homelessness. Since 1950 the urban population has doubled in most developed countries. In developing countries it has quadrupled. In the last sixty years urbanization has multiplied ten times. According to the *Almanac of the Christian World*, 1990 was the first year in world history where there were more people living in cities than in rural areas. To complicate matters, the United Nations projects that by the year 2000, seventeen of the twenty largest cities in the world will be in Third World nations. All of these trends—urbanization, homelessness, growth in Third World populations—contribute to the plague of hunger in our time. (Graham 1992, 214)

With burgeoning populations in the developing world, Graham highlighted the needs present in these locations. He concluded this section by calling Christians to respond. Graham admitted that "For much of my life I spent little time thinking about the humanitarian responsibilities of the church" (Graham 1992, 218). Noting the abundance in the United States, Graham said, "Christ calls us to share with those in need around the world" and failing to answer Christ's call in this area meant "we will be judged for our failure" (Graham 1992, 218–219).

Graham regularly noted the crime, lawlessness, and unrest present in cities. Graham connected crime to cities, including citing high rates of crimes committed by youths in New York City (Graham 1958, 40), young people running away to cities like New York where "they become prey to all the thugs and con-men and drug merchants and sex perverts and all the others" (Graham 1969, 53), noting "crime is up" and "There is no longer a safety zone in any city" in reference to "every major city in America and Europe" (Graham 1977, 65–66), referencing crime stories and statistics in Detroit,

Los Angeles, and New York City (Graham 1991, 6–7), and receiving letters from fearful people in "the heart of one of our most crime-riddled cities" (Graham 2006, 101).

Crime was not the only issue in cities; so was lawlessness and riots. Graham mentioned riots in San Francisco and Los Angeles in the early 1990s (Graham 1992, 17–20). On the flip side of unrest, Graham highlights hippies founding centers in big cities before spreading throughout the United States (Graham 1971, 122). Those hippies then showed up at a 1969 crusade in large numbers in suburban Anaheim (Graham 1971, 134).

A second theme involves Graham invoking cities in the Bible to make points about cities and societies today. For example, Graham described Paul in Athens in Acts 17 and said, "The city of Athens in Paul's day was not much different from today's carnal culture" (Graham 2015, 167). The city of Corinth was "the sex capital of the ancient world" (Graham n.d., 27) and "the kind of town in which we wouldn't want to raise our families," plus they found the cross foolish (Graham 1977, 109). Graham mentioned Nineveh multiple times as God warned the people and they repented, providing a hopeful example for today (e.g., Graham 1983, 216; 2015, 121). In contrast, Sodom was an example of a lack of spiritual awakening (Graham 1947, 19; 1992, 283). A broader list of Old Testament cities "destroyed by the fires of judgment—Sodom, Babylon, Tyre, Sidon, Nineveh" helped make the comparison that "the same sins of those cities are the sins of the American city tonight and of the American people" (Graham 1969, 4). Similarly, a list of contemporaneous cities to New Testament events—"Rome, Pompeii and Naples"—were "carried" by sin "to ruin" (Graham 1947, 19). The big city was also home to sin in retelling the parable of the Prodigal Son. While preaching in New York City in 1969, Graham set up this parable in such a way that the wayward son wanted to go to New York as "he had heard all about the bright lights" (Graham 1969, 55). But that trip from the country to the city became derailed by dope, alcohol, and women. Graham noted, "It's not easy to live in New York or any of our great metropolitan areas and live the disciplined life for Jesus Christ" (Graham 1969, 65).

Compared to cities on earth full of crime and sin, Graham described heaven as a different kind of city. He regularly shared the details provided in Revelation 21 and 22 (e.g., Graham 2012). It would be a "new creation" with all sorts of new changes including in bodies, names, songs, government, and "social justice for all" (Graham 1971, 253). Put differently, Graham suggested heaven would be the place where "We will be free to become the whole, productive, and happy people God intends us to be" (Graham 1981, 216).

This longer passage from a book about hope contains much overlap with Graham's other discussions of heaven:

> When the Book of Revelation was written, cities were places of refuge, companionship, and security. Today, they speak of crowding, crime, and corruption. Heaven as a city is the former description, not our modern concept of a city. Revelation pictures Heaven as a city, the new Jerusalem. This is the city where we will live forever. It will be large enough to house all believers without being crowded. For centuries women have loved jewels. The New Jerusalem will have gates of pearl, streets of gold, and the foundation of the city walls will be like a display case at Tiffany's, multiplied many times in their magnificence. On Main Street in New Jerusalem, the Tree of Life will be growing. Everyone will have access to it. John describes the Tree of Life as "bearing twelve crops of fruit, yielding its fruit every month. And the leaves of the tree are for the healing of the nations" (Revelation 22, 2). The Tree of Life will accomplish what the United Nations, heads of state, ambassadors, and peace-making missions have never been able to do. Harmony will reign in Heaven. (Graham 1991, 221–222)

Some of these discussions of heaven included reference to Hebrews 11:10—"a city whose builder and maker is God"—and Hebrews 13:14—"Here we have no continuing city" (Graham 1965, 260; 1975, 145; 1992, 394; 2012, 21; 2015, 72). While Christians are on earth, Graham suggested they should care about and act on social problems but remember that their ultimate citizenship is in heaven (Graham 1969, 80; 2002, 305).

A third theme involves a particular city: New York City. Two of Graham's books consist of messages he gave in the city, including a series of 10 messages in June 1969 and three evenings in 2006 at what turned out to be his last Crusade. Graham looked back fondly on his time in the city; he said, "I love New York, and I always have!" as he recalled the 16 weeks he spent there in 1957 (also a draining period that led Graham to believe he might not make it past age 50; see Graham 2011, 7) and a Central Park Crusade in 1991, among the eight crusades that he held in the city (Graham 2005, 23–26). He noted that the 1957 crusade "became our most successful American crusade" and they started "to put our crusades on national television on prime evening hours" (Graham 1987, 193–194). He lamented the September 11, 2001 terrorist attacks on the city (Graham 2002, 278; 2005, 24) and celebrated the city's diversity (Graham 2005, 23–24, 42).

In addition to recalling specific time spent in the city, he used it an example of an important city that needed God. Graham spoke of contrasts found in New York City, and thus across all cities. Across his books, Graham said New York City neighborhoods "are a microcosm of our world" (Graham 2005, 23). It was a city with lots of churches and religious activity (Graham 2005, 25) and where a religious awakening occurred in 1857–1858 (Graham 1978, 212). New York "is the communications, the intellectual and the cultural centers—and certainly the financial center — of the United States" (Graham 1969, 2). Yet New York had a dark side. It was riddled with crime (Graham 1958, 40; 1977, 66; 1991, 6–7), full of idol worship rooted in "materialism, the money, the obsession with sex, the pleasure, the leisure, the fashions, the entertainments, the ambition" (Graham 1969, 2), marked by loneliness and "some of the worst slums of the world side by side with some of the most luxurious places in all the world" (Graham 1969, 2–3), home to many "slaves of sin" (Graham 1969, 63), perhaps "ungovernable" (Graham 1971, 36), and containing crowds marked by faces full of "hopelessness, fear and boredom" (Graham 1983, 20).

In his three 2005 messages delivered in Corona Park in Flushing Meadows, Queens, Graham had relatively little negative to say about the city. He acknowledged that he did not speak as long as he did in the 1957 New York City Crusade (Graham 2005, 40) and he stuck to common themes: a need for hearers to be born-again (based on John 3:1–17), seeking eternal life amid the hurt and rejection people feel (based on Mark 10:17–27), and a final message involving Noah and the Second Coming of Christ. His 1969 messages contained more details about the problems and depravity of the city but ended in a similar place. In the sermon delivered June 22, 1969, Graham spoke of the human issues present in cities, noting that Cain built the first city in the Bible and Noah's day, an era where God issued judgment on the whole earth, was marked by movement to and the construction of cities (Graham 1969, 162).

Conclusion

In 2021, evangelical musician and author Andrew Peterson published a book titled *The God in the Garden*. In the first sentence, he describes it as "a story about place," and he goes on to share his thoughts about trees and places, particularly a sprawling property outside Nashville where he has lived most recently. He describes the joys and tensions of his particular suburban location:

> On the north bank of Mill Creek, there are eighty-six acres for sale, I'd buy it tomorrow if I had a spare three million bucks lying around. It's zoned residential, with the potential for commercial development, which understandably has us Cane Ridgers hot and bothered; the last thing any of us wants is a Dollar General sprouting like a noxious weed in the middle of the valley. I often describe Cane Ridge as "Nashville, with cows." It's one of the last pockets of Davidson County where, in the Valley of Mordu for instance, one can still see things the way they would have been a century ago, with herds of sleek cattle chewing the cud beside a pond. We love being close enough to town to take in a movie or a concert at the Ryman, close enough to be a part of the vibrant cultural life of a good city, and yet far enough away that there's a measure of privacy and a reason for care of the land. I used to think that to have the one, you had to forsake the other, but my mind has changed over the years. Few things are more wonderful to me than a graceful integration of nature and culture, which is essentially what a garden is-and few things are less wonderful to me than the razing of a forest to plaster yet another soulless subdivision onto yet another corner of the land. (Peterson 2021, 159)

Peterson expresses appreciation both for the open land he can experience and the ability to easily access amenities of urban life. He is also concerned about that open land disappearing and becoming more suburban and closed off to public use. While Peterson draws on Christian authors and poets—including Thomas Merton and Wendell Berry—to explore places and his own experiences, the evangelical cultural toolkit regarding places and suburbs as exemplified by Billy Graham offers limited resources.

In 29 books spanning nearly 70 years, Billy Graham said little directly about suburbs. Suburbanization was taking place all around him and the comments in his books suggest suburban communities and residents faced problems like everyone else. In light of the problems of suburbs and cities, he regularly employed an evangelical cultural toolkit emphasizing individualistic repentance and piety in the face of always threatening and destabilizing social conditions. In New York City and other large cities in the United States and around the world, residents faced the consequences of sin: crime, lawlessness, riots and unrest, corruption, threat of nuclear war, and a false security based in technology, science, and human progress. Graham expressed his own preference to return home to country life with family and quiet while also sharing moments of excitement about speaking in and ministering in cities.

In decades of preaching, Graham reinforced and influenced evangelical cultural toolkits about places even if Graham primarily pursued bringing people to personal salvation. Graham's individualistic approach, emphasis of urban problems, and celebration of New York's traits while also celebrating rural life posed few conflicts with an evangelical embrace of individualistic and nuclear-family centered suburbs, suburban spaces perceived as safe and away from urban threats, and suburbs that offered proximity to nature and big cities. Put in other terms, Graham decried suburbs in the same ways he decried other settings: the people living in them faced real issues stemming from a lack of personal faith and virtuous Christian living. The toolkit he deployed then contributed to "the emergence of a political coalition that emphasized family values, patriotism, and fighting crime, which gained great support across the nation by the late 1960s" (Evans 2017, 157). Similarly, Miller (2009, 201) argues that Graham tried later in his career to stand "beyond partisanship and, by the 1990s, above the culture wars" even as his efforts supported Richard Nixon's "southern strategy," the Christian Right, and Republican presidents for which evangelicals voted for in large numbers. Many in this emerging political coalition anchored by evangelicals lived in the growing suburbs and metropolitan regions with rapid suburban growth.

As Graham's career wound down by the early twenty-first century, the cultural toolkit Graham offered for addressing places was not the only one available to evangelicals. Other evangelicals and Christians discussed and employed different toolkits regarding suburbs and places. Several books aimed at suburban evangelicals from evangelical publishers reinforced some of Graham's toolkit with emphases on individual and neighborhood action such as through acting hospitably (Miller 2021). Some evangelicals promoted a different approach to cities, suburbs, and social needs focusing on justice and transformed communities and systems (e.g., Claiborne 2006; Sider et al. 2008; Keller 2012; Yeo and Green 2022) rather than solely on converted individuals and stronger interracial relationships. Other Christian actors also responded to the geographic and social change in the United States with reflection on their cultural and theological approaches to suburbs rooted in Christian scripture and tradition (e.g., Brueggeman 2002; Gorringe 2002; Inge 2003; Jennings 2010; Love-Fordham 2014).

If the American suburbs are now the "settled" places (Swidler 1986) within American society, perhaps significant economic, political, cultural, and social changes in the coming decades will prompt white evangelicals to develop a different toolkit regarding suburbs and places. Or evangelicals could attempt to bring their suburban toolkits to other settings. A study of a church plant in Chicago begun by a suburban congregation (Barron and Williams 2017) illustrates the intersection of suburban toolkits and structural concerns within a big city. When a suburban congregation in northwest Indiana planted a church in Chicago, they aimed to be a diverse congregation that appealed to young adults. However, they did so with a particular image of the city in mind: they emphasized consuming the city and enacted a racialized understanding of what racial diversity in the city looked like (not becoming an "inner-city church"). The suburban leaders of the congregation attracted a good number of attendees but relied on "stereotypical tropes of authenticity, the incorporation of a white middle-class consumer lifestyle centered on the city, and the racialization of urban space" (Barron and Williams 2017, 164). The church competed in Chicago's religious landscape, maintained a white leadership tied to a suburban congregation, and promoted an evangelical view of the world shaped in and reinforced by suburban contexts.

With the cultural toolkits of Billy Graham and evangelicalism writ large contributing to the suburbanization of American evangelicals, the final chapter considers five key findings of the book. Examining Graham's books contributes to one of the key findings: understanding the intertwining of the American suburbs and American evangelicals requires considering the spatial context of the development and deployment of evangelical cultural toolkits. After considering different sets of data, communities, and patterns over time throughout this book, what other important themes stand out for better understanding how evangelicals embraced the American suburbs?

9
Conclusion

In 1995, a cultural phenomenon emerged in an unlikely place. An evangelical publishing house located in the suburbs and known for a particular Bible translation started a series of books about the apocalypse. The *Left Behind* series sold millions of copies as it built on longstanding evangelical emphases: understanding the difficult-to-interpret biblical book of Revelation, a fascination with end times and the apocalypse, and a quick-moving and action-oriented literary approach, all provided by two male authors firmly anchored in evangelical spiritual and political circles (Sutton 2014; Frykholm 2004; Du Mez 2020; Hummel 2023).

The series had multiple connections to the suburbs and evangelicals within them. Tyndale House Publishers is located just north of Wheaton, Illinois in the suburb of Carol Stream on the same street as TEAM (The Evangelical Alliance Mission) headquarters and the former headquarters of the National Association of Evangelicals. The company started with the first popular paraphrase of the Bible, known as *The Living Bible*, and later produced the New Living Translation. As Christian publishing expanded, so did Tyndale (Vaca 2019). But the success of the *Left Behind* series encompassing over a dozen books, tens of millions of copies sold, and a kids book series and graphic novel adaptations, led to profits and building expansions for Tyndale (Cutrer 2000). Tyndale steered the *Left Behind* phenomena from a suburban office building and warehouses near big box stores, strip malls, and single-family homes.

The suburban life of the physical copies of *Left Behind* extended into the plots themselves. One protagonist of the series, airline pilot Rayford Steele, finds himself left at home while his wife and younger son are raptured. Steele and family lived in the northwest suburbs of Chicago where, despite his rise to a successful life marked by a suburban home and steady job, Rayford found the American Dream lacking. From there, Steele helps form the Tribulation Force. This group keeps an eye on and engages in international affairs—the land of Israel and Jerusalem are important places in the series and the antichrist arises from Romania—while navigating a postapocalyptic

Sanctifying Suburbia. Brian J. Miller, Oxford University Press. © Oxford University Press 2025.
DOI: 10.1093/oso/9780197679623.003.0010

Chicagoland region. Whereas C. S. Lewis described a hell that sounded like suburbia at the beginning of *The Great Divorce*, in the *Left Behind* series God's people emerge from postapocalyptic suburbia to take on the charming foreign antichrist who enthralls the global elite in major cities like New York.

The authors of the series were well-known to evangelicals and had their own connections to suburbs and places filled with evangelicals. Tim LaHaye was a Baptist pastor, author, early board member of the Moral Majority, and founder of several evangelical political organizations. LaHaye spent much of his adult life in the San Diego area, pastoring a megachurch for decades that later became a multisite church within the region and founding a Christian college in the San Diego suburb of El Cajon (Peterson 2016). Jerry Jenkins was a prolific Christian author with over 200 titles to his name. He served in different positions at Moody Bible Institute, including as trustee, and resided outside of Colorado Springs (Jent 2019; "Biography" 2024).

Left Behind's popularity occurred during an era of evangelical power and notoriety. The attention paid to evangelicals has not abated as scholars continue to consider what shaped evangelicals and the consequences of evangelical actions. Just as a few examples, historian Kristin du Mez (2020) argues that evangelicals support patriarchy and particular roles for men and women, historian Anthea Butler (2021) concisely summarizes how evangelicals in the United States have always defended whiteness, and sociologist Gerardo Martí (2020) shows how race and a quest for political power came together in evangelical support for Donald Trump for president.

Even with many interested in evangelicals, few consider the role the physical setting of evangelicalism, the spaces where evangelicals live and worship and vote and go about daily life. The *Left Behind* phenomenon took off around the point when a majority Americans resided in suburbs. Popular rock group Green Day commented on this convergence. Their 2004 concept album *American Idiot* considered a fictional figure dubbed the "Jesus of Suburbia." The song "Jesus of Suburbia"—front man Billy Jo Armstrong's favorite song in the band's oeuvre (Chesler 2021)—described this suburban messiah as the product of "love and rage" and with followers depicted as "the kids of war and peace." In the United States at the beginning of the twenty-first century, it was and is hard to pull apart evangelicals and suburbs. These communities built around raising children, private single-family homes, cars and driving, and exclusion of others are not just the backdrop to American evangelicalism; they have helped shape what evangelicalism is today. To reckon with the identities, beliefs, and actions of American evangelicals, the suburbs and their lifestyle are an important part of the equation.

I argue that American evangelicals made the suburbs their sanctified home for multiple reasons as evangelicals and mass suburbia emerged in American life after World War II, even as both had roots in earlier American life. Evangelical cultural toolkits addressing family life, engagement with politics, and an emphasis on individual rather than collective or structural action merged with and were bolstered by the toolkits of American suburbs. Within the burgeoning suburbs, evangelical congregations and organizations offered individual autonomy, an appeal to "orthodox" faith, and family friendly values while protecting and upholding a white, middle-class, nuclear family ideal. Structural and ecological forces shaped both evangelical and suburban toolkits. The suburbs offered white, middle-class space away from racial and social change in cities and society at large. The suburbs were not open to all, and evangelicals competed well within these spaces in establishing congregations and institutions that engaged broader American society from a place of perceived safety and opportunity. The evidence presented in this book, drawing on historical patterns, white flight, case studies of multiple communities as well as the experiences of evangelical organizations, and an analysis of cultural toolkits regarding places and the suburbs, shows how this convergence occurred and continues.

Considering an alternative scenario helps illuminate these suburban patterns. Could the evangelicals in the United States today thrive primarily in big cities? In the early twentieth century, growing population centers might have appeared to the be home for evangelicalism. Rapidly growing cities like New York City, Chicago, and Los Angeles, among others, presented numerous opportunities for mass evangelism, engaging society, and addressing social ills. Prominent early neo-evangelical leaders from the 1940s, like Harold Ockenga and Billy Graham, operated in and spoke regularly in the biggest cities. Evangelicals could have adjusted to the demographic, economic, and social changes in these cities and remained close to influential media, networks, and leaders.

But due to a series of decisions made by organizations, congregations, and individuals, evangelicals embraced and embedded themselves in the suburbs. They eschewed urban centers and more racially diverse populations. They emphasized a particular vision of American life that centered nuclear family life in private spaces. They trained their attention on congregations and a message that appealed to suburbanites who might have found the American land of plenty lacking and sought personal salvation.

To summarize the reasons for and consequences of evangelicals embracing the suburbs, I discuss five takeaways drawing on the analyses across the chapters of this book. These summary points describe what this work adds to studying evangelicals and to considering place and religion.

1: The Spatial Dimensions of Evangelical (and Religious) Life

American evangelicals, like all religious groups, are multifaceted. They can be understood in a variety of ways and researchers and pundits have trained multiple lenses on evangelicals to understand their emergence and ongoing activity. This includes a set of core beliefs evangelicals bundle together (Bebbington 1989), how evangelicals engage with society and social change while trying to maintain subcultural distinctives (Smith 1998), interactions between religious and political beliefs and practices (e.g., Whitehead and Perry 2020), approaches to race and ethnicity (Emerson and Smith 2000; Butler 2021), and perspectives on gender (Du Mez 2020). All together, these dimensions demonstrate what separates evangelicals from other religious adherents and from Americans more broadly.

This text emphasizes the placed dimensions of evangelical life. The lenses of the perspectives briefly described in the preceding paragraph play out in particular ways in particular places. These ideas are not just abstract notions; they have an embodied dimension lived out within particular settings. Places matter, not just as background variables to control for unique places, such as the American South, but as formative social forces in their own right. The suburbs of the United States are intertwined with evangelicalism in ways observers of evangelicalism need to consider in order to make better sense of this group.

Take several regular exemplars of evangelical life in the United States. Start with the interest of evangelicals in societal influence and power. This occurs at the national level such as in offering particular visions of the past and future of the United States and an interest in evangelicals serving in leading roles in the executive, legislative, and judiciary branches. This also plays out at the local level as evangelicals live, work, go to school, worship, and participate in neighborhoods and communities. If power is defined as the ability to carry out one's will even with opposition (Weber 1978), evangelical power is present in numerous settings. At the national level, conservative momentum was boosted by the evangelical suburbanites of southern California in the 1960s and 1970s (McGirr 2001). At least a few of the 1990s Republican leaders supported by evangelicals emerged from suburbs, including Newt Gingrich who hailed from Marietta, Georgia, a growing suburb northwest of Atlanta, and Dennis Hastert, representing the far southwest suburbs of the Chicago region. In addition to national issues, evangelicals are active in municipal issues, school questions, and state legislatures and governorships. Evangelical concerns about national decisions regarding prayer in school (Smith 1998) are linked to more recent concerns about curriculum and books within public schools and public libraries.

Going further, evangelicals attempt to exert power through numerous organizations that have cultural or soft power and that might seek to influence policy. Care about a traditional family structure? Focus on the Family promoted this starting in the late 1970s and its influence at the national level grew out of a location in the suburbs of southern California and then in the growing evangelical center of Colorado Springs. Need an umbrella organization to coordinate and support evangelical efforts? The National Association of Evangelicals chose Wheaton and Carol Stream, Illinois for its headquarters for decades rather than more visible seats of power and influence. Want to engage kids with Bible stories? VeggieTales emerged from the suburbs of Chicago. The numerous evangelical parachurch organizations critical to American religion today (Wuthnow 1998; Scheitle 2010) often operate in evangelical suburban contexts or smaller big cities.

Another way to link evangelicals and suburban places involves considering lived religion or everyday religion (Ammerman 2007; McGuire 2008). The faith of millions of evangelical Americans does not develop solely through sermons on Sunday morning or in affirming particular doctrines. Instead, evangelical faith is formed in regular moments in daily life and in interaction with the social and physical realities of the American suburbs. What does the Bible have to say about troubles in marital relationships or with difficulties with a boss or about how to raise kids? The suburban life offers many small moments for spiritual formation as evangelicals engage with systems and organizations. Does shopping at Hobby Lobby or eating at Chick-fil-A, well-known evangelical corporations often operating in suburbs, enhance spiritual life? Evangelical suburbanites can spend a lot of time in the car, driving from place to place, and listening to Christian radio with both talk and music options providing spiritual reinforcement and learning opportunities. Small groups, whether targeting certain age groups or moms or men or others, meet throughout the week provide opportunities for building relationships and interpreting what God might be doing in one's life. Interactions with neighbors and community members offer opportunities to share God—with evangelism a key component of many evangelical efforts—and/or advocate for particular social and policy positions. And so on.

Living out evangelical faith looks and feels different in suburban contexts where a particular historical and societal trajectory in the United States meets a religious tradition. The religious in the suburbs might not be aware of the way places shape their faith, a concern expressed by religious leaders in the suburban jeremiads of the postwar era (Hudnut-Beumler 1994). When evangelicals do take a step back and recognize the suburbanization of faith, they try to understand what it means and ask difficult questions: Are suburbs really the Promised Land? Are there certain spiritual practices needed to maintain and cultivate a vibrant suburban faith? Is the suburban life too tied up in the possibly problematic notions of the American Dream (Miller 2021)? These questions have lingered for decades and do not have easy answers for a group that has often pursued the American Dream and faith together. But the crux of the questions is an important one: Just how much should religious faith and practice be "pure" as opposed to shaped by every place in which it is introduced and lived? Evangelicals might be amenable to contextualizing their message and means to attract people, but less open to sacrificing and/or rethinking what they consider important aspects of their lives and theology in suburbs that can present challenges to their expressed religious commitments.

By considering the influence of the suburbs on evangelicals both in specific communities and across the United States, this study shows how place matters for understanding religious groups. To know American evangelicals involve addressing their connections to and influence from places, particularly the suburbs.

2: Evangelicals, Suburbs, and Race, Class, and Gender

The suburbs have a deserved reputation as white and wealthy with limited space for a broader range of suburban residents (e.g., Nicolaides 2002; Wiese 2004; Lung-Amam 2017). Even as suburban populations have become more diverse in recent decades in terms of race and ethnicity and social class (Frey 2022; Berube and Kneebone 2013), the whiter, middle-class and above, and family-oriented suburbs appeared attractive to many evangelicals. Even if the suburbs were not perfect Edens for living out an evangelical vision, American cities offered a less palatable alternative with more diversity, greater interest in exploring and leading social and cultural change, and a perceived lower level of interest in the well-being of children and families.

From the beginning of suburbs, evangelicals have expressed interest in them because of what they offer regarding race, class, and gender. From William Wilberforce wanting to protect his wife and children from a growing London to postwar evangelicals leaving cities and developing institutions in the suburbs, evangelicals have liked suburbs in part because of who was there and who was not there. The regular exclusion present in suburbs plus particular roles for men and women in stereotypical postwar suburban life attracted evangelicals.

Two examples discussed earlier in this book help illustrate this. First, Billy Graham led hundreds of crusades and evangelistic events in American communities. The vast majority of these events took place at stadiums and arenas located in major cities. Some of his most famous revivals, such as 1949 in Los Angeles and 1957 in New York City, took place in the largest cities and big arenas even as white Christians and members of other religious traditions fled cities. While these efforts often drew attendees from the entire metropolitan region, Graham needed cities as central locations, homes to sizable stadiums, and media centers in order to hold his meetings. Additionally, cities could be used to illustrate the problems of American culture, ranging from problems with crime, drugs, broken families, and loneliness to possible centers of mass destruction from nuclear war to spiritual depravity. Graham may have connected with powerful leaders in cities, but he looked forward to heaven as the ultimate redeemed city. Contemporaries of Graham saw this disconnect, criticizing the lack of interaction with substantial race and class issues facing cities and American society and failing to interact with and include diverse Christians already present and active in cities (Evans 2017). In other words, engaging society requires at least some engagement with cities as centers of influence and power and Graham took advantage of this. But his approach to the problems of cities as well as their potential followed evangelical patterns of seeking true hope elsewhere—or a heavenly city still to come—and tacitly reinforcing white majorities in suburban areas.

Second, studying communities with notable concentrations of evangelical residents and organizations leads to a question: Are these communities substantially different and/or better off because of the presence of evangelicals? There are numerous markers to consider: The number of churches and parachurch organizations in the community; The presence of particular symbols, such as crosses or Christian flags or particular architectural patterns; Civic engagement; The actions of local politicians regarding local budgets and ordinances; The demographics of the community by race and ethnicity and social class; How open residents and newcomers perceive a community to be regarding residents of different backgrounds and social markers; Levels of economic activity; Measures of well-being at the individual and community levels. Studies of evangelical communities have often focused on political actions and concentrations of particular residents. The scholarly work on Orange County in the postwar era (e.g., McGirr 2001; Luhr 2009; Dochuk 2011) highlights evangelical political and congregational activity in a suburban context. Did this transform day-to-day suburban life for evangelicals or communities? Similarly, is Wheaton quantitatively and qualitatively a different kind of suburb because of its evangelical reputation or is it a slight variation on the wealthier bedroom suburb found throughout the United States? Does Colorado Springs, a sprawling city home to hundreds of evangelical organizations, have a higher quality of life and community spirit enhanced by the presence of evangelicals? Examining how race, class, and gender play out in evangelical suburbs as opposed to other suburbs could help explain these convergences and how exactly they are manifested in daily suburban life.

The approaches evangelicals have to race, class, and gender cannot be separated from the suburban context in which many evangelicals reside. The long-standing critiques of suburbs as homogenous and producing stifling norms echo similar critiques of evangelicals. As evangelicals helped limit racial integration and sustained racial divides with a color-blind approach to race that downplayed structural realities (Emerson and Smith 2000), this matches the approach of many suburbanites who would not speak of racism but instead point to class and lifestyle differences in suburbs (Freund 2007; Heiman 2015).

The ways evangelicals centered a nuclear family with a working husband and supportive wife and mother at home with numerous children underfoot paralleled such emphases in postwar suburbanism. The actions of William Wilberforce, the close links between churches and religious schools as

Christian Reformed Church individuals and churches moved to the Chicago suburbs after World War II (Mulder 2015), and the family values orientation of evangelicals from the late 1970s onward reinforced these connections. Even as feminism emerged in part from well-off suburbs (Friedan 1963), evangelicals idealized a family-friendly suburbia where Christian families could live in peace and show others the benefits of their lives.

Focusing primarily on the national aspects of how evangelicals approach race, class, and gender can obscure the important lower-level, and often suburban, manifestations of these evangelical approaches. When suburban residents and religious leaders express concerns about racial justice in their communities, how do evangelicals respond (Francis 2015)? How do they interact with suburban neighbors who through yard signs promote "liberal creeds" (McIvor 2023) or who practice different faiths (Numrich and Wedam 2015)? When communities face tension and conflict regarding immigration (Vicino 2013), what do evangelicals do? While the national or state level of evangelical activity helps set the broader context, everyday suburban life in the suburbs helps illustrate how evangelicals interact with race, class, and gender.

3: Suburbs and Evangelicals In-Between

Evangelical vitality in the United States exists in part because of a tension between building internal social capital and cohesion while also engaging with American society (Smith 1998). With the emergence of the National Association of Evangelicals in the 1940s, evangelicals pushed against the fundamentalist approach of withdrawal from American society and pursued engaging society, often in particular areas and on particular topics. On the continuum between churches and sects (Troeltsch 1931) or in the different ways Christians viewed God's work and people interacting with culture (Niebuhr 1956), evangelicals attempted to steer a middle path. Or, as evangelicals might put it, they wrestled with how to be in the world but not of it.

If evangelicals as a whole represent this in-between of engagement and withdrawal, the suburbs sit in a similar in-between place among American spaces. From the beginning of American suburbs, the suburbs offered a unique setting with access to growing cities—via railroad, streetcars, and later automobiles—with the potential to approximate a cottage in the woods closer to nature (Archer 2005). Suburbs today also exhibit a continuum of development—ranging from inner-ring suburbs with similar experiences to many urban neighborhoods to suburbs at the edges of metropolitan regions that have much lower population densities and smaller populations. When asked in 2021 where they would prefer to live, Pew Research (Parker, Horowitz, and Minkin 2021) found 46% of Americans said suburbs, 35% said rural areas, and 19% preferred urban areas. Americans may appeal to small town ideals (Thomma 2011; Wuthnow 2013) but often live these out in suburban settings that offer proximity to big cities. Jesus may have lived out his ministry at a three miles per hour walking pace but suburban evangelicals do so at 30 to 60 miles per hour in their vehicles driving place to place (The Ranch Studios 2017).

Both suburbs and evangelicalism took on lives of their own as they developed and grew. Evangelicals became one of the largest religious traditions in the United States by the end of the twentieth century. They engaged society but did so in established ways so that by the early 2020s commentators could highlight more than 40 years of consistent political advocacy and cultural practices. More Americans lived in suburbs than other locations by the 1960s and they became home to half of Americans by the 2000 Census (Hobbs and Stoops 2002). The suburbs are not a new phenomenon; there are more than 60 years of postwar suburban growth plus over 100 years of suburban ideology and communities before that.

What the in-between positions of evangelicalism and suburbia help highlight is that both sit within fields of other actors, institutions, and places. Suburbs and evangelicals are defined by what they are plus what they are not and how they have interacted with other actors. In the American religious landscape, evangelicals are a known commodity in part because of how they interact with other groups. Evangelicals continue to expend much energy in both trying to build internal understandings of themselves as well as marking others as outside the fold (Smith 1998). Social conditions and forces can change, leading to significant swings down the road. For example, evangelicals could oppose a Catholic presidential candidate in 1960 but later join hands with conservative Catholics over abortion and other conservative issues of interest just two decades later and also support a presidential candidate in 2012 who was a member of The Church of Jesus Christ of Latter-day Saints. In contrast, evangelicals have not built deep connections with the Black Protestant tradition; the two groups share numerous theological commitments but emerged from different contexts and emphasize different aspects of faith (Shelton and Emerson 2012). In the future, evangelicals might be defined by how they engage with a growing number of "religious nones" (Smith 2021) who prioritize different values and causes.

The American suburbs are not cities or rural areas, but they have also grown in their own capacities as they have interacted with both. While dependent on big cities for jobs and economic activity for decades, suburbs now have their own economic footing with office parks, economic opportunities, and millions of jobs. Suburbs are not just the stepchildren of cities; the Los Angeles School of urban scholars, drawing upon the unique sprawl of southern California, argued that the suburbs organized the content of the entire region as opposed to a Chicago School model that operated from the city center out (Dear and Flusty 1998). Yet some pockets of the suburbs are more urban—denser, numerous jobs, mixed-use zoning—while others are more rural—larger lots, single-family home dominate, and contain protected open space. Suburbs and cities are now inextricably linked. It is hard to imagine one without the other, leading some to argue that the focus should be on metropolitan regions rather than two separate spaces. Evangelicals who operate in the suburbs cannot escape the fate of big cities as communities, regions, economies, and social conditions are dependent on each other.

This overlap, tension, and differences as being in-between social categories provide rich opportunities for those studying religion and place. The lines between urban and suburban religion might be more blurred than ever with insights from each being helpful to understanding the other. For example, how does place influence faith in religiously diverse Flushing, Queens (Hanson 2016), a neighborhood of New York with single-family homes, to the activity of Catholics and evangelicals in the Mexican community in the big suburb of Santa Ana, California (Calvillo 2020)? Evangelicals and the suburbs might both be in-between but they deserve attention on their own merits, not just because they are somewhere in the middle of important poles.

Furthermore, lack of evangelical residents, congregations, and organizations in the biggest American cities suggests embracing the suburbs leaves a smaller presence in centers of influence and power. Want to have a say in the booming world of technology, social media, and artificial intelligence? Evangelicals are not known for a strong presence in San Francisco, San Jose, and Silicon Valley. Want to influence movies, music, television, and media? Evangelicals are not known for their presence in Los Angeles (though they are in some suburbs as discussed in Chapter 6) or New York City. Want to be in the places where people from different global cultures are interacting? The suburbs are increasingly diverse with more immigrants and racial and ethnic minorities, but evangelicals are not known for being in gateway and arrival cities. Want to be at the center of intellectual debates and innovation? Evangelicals engage in limited ways with the leading research universities that are often located in big cities.

Evangelicals have embraced the in-betweenness of the suburbs and this puts them on the outside of some urban networks, conversations, and capital. Some evangelical leaders may have reached the top of their respective industry or sector (Lindsay 2007), but the religious group as a whole is geographically not in the biggest cities. For a group that wishes to influence society, embracing the suburbs for other reasons leaves them at a disadvantage when so much of the modern world involves activity in urban centers. Perhaps evangelicals can serve as bridges or connectors, helping to link urban and rural areas or religious groups at different ends of engagement with society. Can evangelicals help bring groups together from a suburban position or will their efforts to engage society yet remain distinct as suburbanites consume much of their efforts?

4: Evangelicals Engaging in More Robust Thinking About Suburbs and Places

The introduction to this book is bookended by two different visions of places: singer/songwriter Ben Folds sang of "Jesusland," a sprawling landscape imbued with religion yet needing help, while Audio Adrenaline imagined a "Big House," a massive single-family heavenly home full of family activity. How often would evangelical congregations and adherents encounter places in evangelical worship songs or hymnody?

The worship hit "God of this City," first released in 2007, is one of few recent evangelical songs that tackles this subject. Inspired by the sex tourism they saw in a city in Thailand, a worship band from Northern Ireland named Bluetree wrote the song (Godtube 2010). The chorus speaks to God acting "in this city" and Christians responding to God "in this city." Popular worship artist Chris Tomlin later recorded a version and the song ended up on an album connected to the Passion Conferences. This song illustrates the idea that God can and will redeem any city in the end.

Even as the song speaks of about a city—a rarity in recent Christian music—it does so in generic terms. It says little regarding specific communities or about suburbs. Speaking of "this city" does little to highlight local conditions, the actions of local churches and evangelicals, and the specific ways that evangelicals believe God acted, is acting, and will act within places. For a religious tradition that reveres the biblical story rooted in a particular people in a particular places in a particular time, the evangelical vision of place, people, and time is often vague. The song could fit any American city or community. Evangelicals could imagine God operating in and people responding to him in all sorts of places.

Evangelical cultural toolkits have relatively little to offer in deeply wrestling with suburban contexts or places more broadly. They have often denigrated cities except as contexts for missions. American evangelicals have been quick at times to emphasize heaven, such as Billy Graham speaking of "a city that is to come" (see Chapter 8). Even those evangelicals who ask other evangelicals to consider suburbs as places God cares about and is acting within often propose individual actions such as hospitality and spiritual disciplines rather than addressing community and structural issues (Miller 2021).

Developing an evangelical toolkit that more deeply addresses suburbs and places could involve pursuing multiple perspectives. Theologian Willie James Jennings (2010) explores the intersection of race and place amid a lacking doctrine of creation. Or majority-world evangelical theologians with experiences in Palestine, South Africa, and Latin America can help American evangelicals incorporate place, land, and creation in their thinking and action (Yeo and Green 2021). Theologians in adjacent Christian traditions offer possibilities, ranging from Walter Brueggeman's (1977) emphasis on land in the Old Testament narrative to more sacramental understandings of places (Inge 2004; Gamm 1999). Listening to and learning from evangelicals and other Christians with different experiences compared to white suburban evangelicals could help.

A deeper connection to their suburban communities might also help evangelicals both meet their own goals and answer a persistent critique of the group. Regarding their own goals, evangelicals want to engage society. As one evangelical puts it, "Suburban evangelicals tend to demand a voice in cultural conversations" (O'Brien 2019). However, they often privilege individualistic and anti-structuralist approaches to social issues (Emerson and Smith 2000). Or they want to pursue certain issues and not others (Smith 1998). This leaves limited space for looking out for the good of communities and those in need. When evangelicals discuss themselves as exiles in a country (this is a debated status as they still exert sizable influence and enjoy certain historical and current benefits), they often reference (e.g., Grabill 2014) the prophet Jeremiah's message that God asked them to "seek the peace and prosperity" of the city of Babylon. What if evangelicals in the American suburbs were known less as exclusivist Christians opposed to others and more as people devoted to the good of all in their communities? If evangelicals have received criticism in the past for paying more attention to a future heaven—leading critics to repeat Marx's suggestion that "religion is the opiate of the masses"—or yearning for a "city on a hill" vision, such a move toward seeking the good of the suburbs and specific communities within the suburbs could help anchor evangelicals to current realities in a suburban United States.

To develop a deeper engagement with suburbs and places will require significant work among evangelicals. Yet evangelicals have altered their emphases in the past in interaction with societal change—the modernism versus fundamentalist debates, the postwar era, in the culture wars and political polarization starting in the late twentieth century—and could do so again in a majority-suburban society. Or, as suggested at the end of Chapter 8, changing conditions in the United States—economic, social, cultural, and political change—could help prompt evangelicals to develop different toolkits regarding suburbs and places.

5: Adding Cultural Toolkits to Understanding Places and Religion and Place

As scholars examined urban and suburban places in the United States, they often relied on two theoretical lenses. The first emerged at the University of Chicago in the early twentieth century (Park and Burgess 1925) and highlighted the ecological processes urban development echoes. In competing for land, actors expand out of an urban core. The second developed several decades later as multiple scholars (e.g., Lefebrve 1991 [1974]; Castells 1979; Logan and Molotch 1987; Feagin 1998) emphasized uneven development, economic and social disparities, and powerful actors that shaped urban landscapes in what became known as the political economy approach or new urban paradigm. In these two perspectives, suburbs are then the outworking of actors looking for profit in an expanding metropolis and the result of policies and control of resources in ways that advantage some and limit others.

Those studying religion and place have often adopted an ecological approach. Stressing competition for resources, religious congregations and organizations sought their own ecological niches where they could successfully operate and grow (e.g., Eiesland 2000; Doughtery and Mulder 2009). In recent decades, scholars in multiple fields have contributed to a vibrant corpus of research connecting religion and cities. In a rapidly changing world, cities in the United States continue to be home to religious groups and sites of religious innovation even as more Americans identify as religious nones (Smith 2021). In the broader religious landscape in the United States, evangelicals have competed well for people and resources, including in the growing suburbs.

This study suggests a third theoretical perspective helps illuminate how evangelicals came to embrace the suburbs. In the "unsettled times" (Swidler 1986) evangelicals experienced at multiple points, including a political and social nadir from roughly the mid-1920s to the mid-1940s, evangelicals found the suburbs to a setting where they could exercise agency and pursue their goals. In the postwar era, changing cities in the United States and new policies pushed and pulled evangelicals to the suburbs where they could live out a nuclear family, middle-class life revolving around children. Examining evangelical toolkits and the lifestyle of American suburbs suggests significant overlap that would make it easy for evangelicals to embrace the suburbs and find "settled" (Swidler 1986) space.

Thus, understanding both the American suburbs and American evangelicals requires incorporating work that shows the important context in which the suburbs and evangelicals emerged. Structural factors—competition within a religious landscape, the development and continuation of the suburbs influenced by race, class, and gender— influenced and interacted with an evangelical toolkit that emerged and evolve. Evangelicals as they are known today began in a particular social context with both a set of distinctive theological commitments and a unique approach to suburbs and American society.

While they were not the only Americans or religious group who ended up in the suburbs, evangelicals made choices to embrace this developing setting. They did this in multiple ways. They decried the plight of cities and their ills. The National Association of Evangelicals made its national headquarters in the suburbs of Chicago for decades. Congregations and individuals moved to the suburbs. Evangelical parachurch organizations clustered in suburban locations and sprawling cities. They developed suburban congregations. They supported politicians and policies that provided advantages for suburbanites.

This happened as a smaller number of evangelicals called evangelicals to life in cities (e.g., Sider et al. 2008; Keller 2012a) and others pursued personal and congregational life in big cities (Claiborne 2006; Bielo 2011a; Markofski 2015). Other evangelicals (e.g., Goetz 2006; Hsu 2006; Hales 2018) described the spiritual vacuity of the suburbs and proposed ways evangelicals could revive their faith in comfortable suburban communities.

Evangelicals made homes in the suburbs, developed congregations and organizations there, and often approved of the suburban lifestyle. The agency evangelicals exercised in embracing the suburbs had consequences. Evangelicals made the suburbs their place in ways that shaped evangelical daily life, social concerns, and political activity. The ongoing inequalities of suburbia merged with evangelical tendencies to address race, class, and gender in particular ways. Evangelical suburban faith took on particular forms. But there is limited evidence that evangelicals want to leave the suburbs or see them as significant problems for carrying out their mission. Many American evangelicals see life through a suburban lens.

Less clear is whether evangelicals have altered suburban communities. Not all suburbs in the United States are like Wheaton, a suburb with a religious character and numerous evangelical organizations in the community or nearby. If evangelicals have become suburban, have the suburbs become evangelical? Perhaps the dearth of studies suggesting evangelicals shape suburban settings suggests evangelicals have little to no impact in suburbs. This may be the case. An individual congregation is just one among possibly dozens in a suburb. Even a concentration of evangelicals within a suburb— like Wheaton (see Chapter 5)—or a smaller big city—like Colorado Springs (see Chapter 6)—does not mean they automatically engender goodwill within the community or are perceived as working for the good for the whole community.

Recent studies of religious groups in the suburbs tend to emphasize the ways religious groups and congregations are shaped by and/or engage with the suburbs. For example, Howe (2018) discusses how Muslims hold on to their faith in the western suburbs of Chicago and live a suburban lifestyle. Dugandzic (2022) finds a suburban setting outside Washington, DC provided particular affordances for a traditional Catholic group to take root. Across religious traditions and suburban locations in the Chicago region, Numrich and Wedam (2015) discuss the varied levels of engagement congregations have as they interact with communities and the region.

At the same time, American scholars tend to examine both place and religious faith as background variables as they try to explain societal outcomes. Both factors can pale at times in favor of examining economic, political, and other social forces. Place can be controlled for by considering whether respondents or groups are in urban, suburban, or rural areas. Or controlling for region tries to bracket out unique features across parts of the United States. Religion can also be a background or secondary variable. When considering religion, researchers can factor in religious tradition, church attendance, or other aspects of belief, behavior, and belonging.

Alternatively, those who study the character of communities and places leave little room for religious actors and motivations. Communities and places themselves make particular decisions and deploy particular strategies as they respond to external and internal pressures (Molotch, Freudenburg, and Paulsen 2000; Kaufman and Kaliner 2011; Miller 2013). Are consequential responses to external and internal pressures not guided at all by religious beliefs, behavior, and belonging? Would a suburbia dominated by one religious group look and feel different compared to a more pluralistic community or one with relatively few religious adherents and groups?

Evangelicals say they want to influence the society around them. This has been clear from the beginning of the neo-evangelical activity launched in the early 1940s. Through evangelism and action in social matters, evangelicals hope to lead people around them to Jesus and promote particular values and societal outcomes. In sociological terms, they want to exercise agency and help shape institutions, values, and communities. Are they actually able to do this in suburban settings or in a suburban nation?

Evangelicals follow particular strategies when pursuing social change. One common approach is to emphasize faithful leaders in important positions across sectors (Hunter 2010; Lindsay 2007). Yet Hunter (2010) argues that focusing on individuals may be an evangelical perspective but it does not typically alter societies.

Another approach is to work through congregations and small groups of faithful evangelicals. Evangelist Billy Graham promoted individual conversions who would then join congregations who could then work together to affect society. Geographer Justin Wilford's (2012) study of Saddleback Community Church in Orange County, California discusses the importance of small groups across the region for the influential megachurch. Roughly 50 miles southeast of downtown Los Angeles, the large and influential congregation has a central location but also exists in the many small groups of church attendees spread throughout the vast metropolitan region. The congregation has both centripetal—inside out—and centrifugal—outside in—forces contributing to its stability and presence.

Yet as one of the largest congregations in the United States that also had a well-known pastor who was also a best-selling author, how much did Saddleback influence life in the Los Angeles region? Within Orange County, Saddleback existed among numerous other evangelical congregations. Long-time pastor Rick Warren learned from influential suburban pastor Robert Schuller (Mulder and Martí 2020) and they were not the only ones who found southern California ripe for evangelical activity. Less clear is how Saddleback and similar congregations changed communities and everyday life in the Los Angeles region beyond individual and congregational religious beliefs and practices.

Through a particular history and reaction to and shaping by social forces, evangelicals chose suburbia. Evangelicals came to embrace suburbia because they could compete for resources; race, class, gender, and policies helped push evangelicals to suburbs; and evangelical life, goals, and cultural toolkits often overlapped with that of suburbia and the two became enmeshed. Evangelicals continue to live in and operate organizations in big cities and in rural areas, but as American society and places changed in significant ways, evangelicals adapted by establishing themselves in the growing suburbs.

***

In 1959, sociologist and Catholic priest Andrew Greeley wrote of the difficulties in merging faith and a suburban lifestyle. Greeley (1959, 206) said,

> Two beautiful worlds are growing up in the suburbs. One is the world of the gadget, the lovely world of color TV, deepfreezes, big hi-fis, two cars in the garage and tranquilizing drugs in the medicine cabinet. This world is not of itself bad. The other world is the world of the presumably spiritual: the world of the crowded churches, long lines at the Communion rail, CFM meetings, good will, and noble intentions. This world is not of itself enough. The basic trouble is that few suburbanites see any connection

between the world of the gadget and the world of the spirit. It never occurs to them to ask whether there might not be some incongruity in the St. Christopher Medal and the Cadillac or the penitential ashes of Lent on the side of the Florida swimming pool. The intimate relationship between the Holy Eucharist and the new migrant in the heart of the city is not evident to them. They are not aware of the connection between their own abundance and starvation in India. It is to this basic secularism of Suburbia that the suburbanite prophet must address himself.

According to Greeley, the American suburban life is full of single-family homes, individualism, exclusion, sprawl, driving, consumerism, and looking out for the welfare of one's nuclear family. This posed questions, if not contradictions, for people of faith. Greeley was not alone in voicing his concerns about the mixing of Christian faith in the suburbs in the postwar era (Hudnut-Beumler 1994) or at the beginning of the twenty-first century (Miller 2021).

Yet among American religious groups, evangelicals have appeared to thrive in a suburbanizing country. As Greeley envisioned difficulties reconciling Lent and Cadillacs, what if there was a religious group that did not see many problems pursuing their faith and the suburban dream? What if the nondenominational suburban church down the road grew into a megachurch and became known wide and far for its leader and programs? As the United States became suburban, evangelical congregations, organizations, and residents moved to the suburbs, developed lives and institutions, and celebrated suburban life while simultaneously becoming known for their religious belonging, beliefs, and behaviors and social traits. Greeley expressed concerns about Catholic faith and institutions in a suburbanizing country, but evangelicals have leaned into the suburbs and prospered within them.

The reasons evangelicals became suburban are deeply connected to why Americans in general have embraced suburbs. At the same time, the reasons are also unique to evangelical formation and development. The suburbs offered an opportunity to pursue homeownership and a middle-class life with limited interaction with Black residents and other racial and ethnic minority groups. The suburban emphasis on nuclear family life paralleled a growing evangelical emphasis on a traditional nuclear-family lifestyle with a husband who leads, a wife who follows, and children who grow up with opportunities. In addition to the suburbs offering evangelicals a new space in which to compete for attendees and status, the cultural toolkits of evangelicals—engaging society and trying to hold to beliefs they consider orthodox—aligned better with suburban life than urban or rural life. They did all of this alongside numerous other Americans who had similar goals but different or no religious motivations and practices.

What this means in the third decade of the twenty-first century is that evangelicals are active in suburbia and in promoting a suburban lifestyle and less present or influential in the biggest cities in the United States. With long-term presences in places like Wheaton, some of the suburbs around Los Angeles, and more sprawling cities like Colorado Springs, evangelicals are less present in influential cities like New York, Chicago, San Francisco, Seattle, and Boston. The one city evangelicals can commit to, at least institutionally through the headquarters of the National Association of Evangelicals, is Washington, DC where proximity to power and leaders is hard to pass up.

Thus, the American suburbs are both a promised land for evangelicals and a setting where evangelicals have similar lives to many others. Due to race, class, gender, competition between religious groups, and the development of evangelical cultural toolkits within American suburban contexts, the suburbs became the home to many evangelicals. Whether evangelicals have fully sanctified the suburbs, made them holier places or set apart places, is another matter that many, including evangelicals, could debate. But understanding American evangelicalism requires accounting for the intertwining of religiosity and suburbia that significantly shapes evangelical life.

References

"2010 Standards for Delineating Metropolitan and Micropolitan Statistical Areas." 2010. *Federal Register* 75, no. 123. https://www.govinfo.gov/content/pkg/FR-2010-06-28/pdf/2010-15605.pdf.
Abbott, Carl. 1980. "'Necessary' Adjuncts to its Growth: The Railroad Suburbs of Chicago, 1854–1875." *Journal of the Illinois State Historical Society* 73, no. 2: 117–131.
Adams, James L. 1959. "He'll Try to Bring Christ Into Lives." *The Daily Journal*, September 26.
Alba, Richard D., John R. Logan, and Kyle Crowder. 1997. "White Ethnic Neighborhoods and Assimilation: The Greater New York Region, 1980–1990." *Social Forces* 75, no. 3: 883–912.
Ammerman, Nancy Tatom. 1987. *Bible Believers: Fundamentalists in the Modern World*. New Brunswick, NJ: Rutgers University Press.
Ammerman, Nancy Tatom. 1997. *Congregation & Community*. New Brunswick, NJ: Rutgers University Press.
Ammerman, Nancy T., ed. 2007. *Everyday Religion: Observing Modern Religious Lives*. New York: Oxford University Press.
Anderson, Jeffrey H. 2020. "Classification of Urban, Suburban, and Rural Areas in the National Crime Victimization Survey." Bureau of Justice Statistics. https://bjs.ojp.gov/content/pub/pdf/cusrancvs.pdf.
Archer, John. 2005. *Architecture and Suburbia: From English Villa to American Dream House, 1690–2000*. Minneapolis: University of Minnesota Press.
"A Religious Headquarters; Wheaton to Get $200,000 Home of Theosophists." 1926. *Chicago Daily Tribune*, August 26.
Armor, Samuel. 1921. *History of Orange County, California*. Los Angeles: Historic Record Co.
Asgedom, Mawi. 2002. *Of Beetles and Angels: A Boy's Remarkable Journey from a Refugee Camp to Harvard*. Boston: Little, Brown.
Assemblies of God. 2021. "Statistics." https://ag.org/About/Statistics.
Atkins, Gregory James. 2019. "America's Theopolis: Boosters, Businesses, and Christian Nonprofits in Colorado Springs, 1871–2000." PhD diss., Washington State University.
Badger, Emily, and Nate Cohn. 2020. "Why Trump's Blunt Appeals to Suburban Voters May Not Work." *New York Times*, July 30. https://www.nytimes.com/2020/07/30/upshot/trump-suburban-voters.html.
Baldassare, Mark. 1998. *When Government Fails: The Orange County Bankruptcy*. Berkeley: University of California Press.
Baldassare, Mark, and Cheryl Katz. 1991. "Orange County Annual Survey: 1991 Final Report." http://data.lib.uci.edu/ocas/1991/ocas91.pdf.
Banas, Casey. 1991. "Election Hints Shift In Wheaton Ideology." *Chicago Tribune*, November 7.
Barr, Beth Allison. 2021. *The Making of Biblical Womanhood: How the Subjugation of Women Became Gospel Truth*. Grand Rapids, MI: Brazos Press.
Barron, Jessica M., and Rhys H. Williams. 2017. *The Urban Church Imagined: Religion, Race, and Authenticity in the City*. New York: New York University Press.
Bassman, Herbert J, ed. 1995. *Riverside Then and Now: A History of Riverside, Illinois*. Riverside, IL: Riverside Historical Commission.
Bauer, John T. 2012. "U.S. Religious Regions Revisited." *The Professional Geographer* 64, no. 4: 521–539.
Baumgartner, M. P. 1988. *The Moral Order of a Suburb*. New York: Oxford University Press.

Baxter, Albert. 1891. *History of the City of Grand Rapids, Michigan.* New York: Munsell & Company.
Bean, Lydia. 2014. *The Politics of Evangelical Identity: Local Churches and Partisan Divides in the United States and Canada.* Princeton, NJ: Princeton University Press.
Bebbington. D. W. 1989. *Evangelicalism in Modern Britain: A History From the 1730s to the 1980s.* Boston: Unwin Hyman.
Bechtel, Paul M. 1984. *Wheaton College: A Heritage Remembered, 1860–1984.* Wheaton, IL: H. Shaw Publishers.
Beebe, Ralph. 1991. "Chapter Six—1969 to 1982." https://digitalcommons.georgefox.edu/cgi/viewcontent.cgi?referer=https://duckduckgo.com/&httpsredir=1&article=1009&context=heritage_honor.
Bellah, Robert N. 1967. "Civil Religion in America." *Daedalus* 96, no. 1: 1–21.
Bendroth, Margaret Lamberts. 2005. *Fundamentalists in the City: Conflict and Division in Boston's Churches.* New York: Oxford University Press.
Bentz Thompson Rietow. 2021. "Woodale Church—Eden Prairie, MN." http://btr-architects.com/projects/worship/wooddale-church-eden-prairie-mn.
Berger, Bennett M. 1960. *Working-Class Suburb: A Study of Auto Workers in Suburbia.* Berkeley: University of California Press.
Bergler, Thomas E. 2012. *The Juvenilization of American Christianity.* Grand Rapids, MI: Wm. B. Eerdmans Publishing Co.
Berwanger, Eugene H. 2007. *The Rise of the Centennial State: Colorado Territory, 1861–76.* Urbana: University of Illinois Press.
Beuka, Robert. 2004. *SuburbiaNation: Reading Suburban Landscape in Twentieth-Century American Fiction and Film.* New York: Palgrave Macmillan.
Bielefield, Wolfgang, and James C. Murdoch. 2004. "The Locations of Nonprofit Organizations and Their For-Profit Counterparts: An Exploratory Analysis." *Nonprofit and Voluntary Sector Quarterly* 33, no. 2: 221–246.
Bielo, James S. 2011a. "City of Man, City of God: The Re-Urbanization of American Evangelicals." *City & Society* 23, no. S1: 2–23.
Bielo, James S. 2011b. "Purity, Danger, and Redemption: Notes on Urban Missional Evangelicals." *American Ethnologist* 38, no. 2: 267–280.
Billingsley, Lloyd. 1990. *From Mainline to Sideline: The Social Witness of the National Council of Churches.* Washington, DC: Ethics and Public Policy Center.
Biola University. 2007. *Biola University: Rooted for One Hundred Years.* La Mirada, CA: Biola University.
Biola University. 2019. "Life in La Mirada." https://studenthub.biola.edu/la-mirada.
Bishop, Bill. 2008. *The Big Sort: Why the Clustering of Like-Minded America is Tearing Us Apart.* Boston: Houghton Mifflin.
Bjork-James, Sophie. 2021. *The Divine Institution: White Evangelicalism's Politics of the Family.* New Brunswick, NJ: Rutgers University Press.
Blanchard, Rufus. 1882. *History of Du Page County, Illinois.* Chicago: O. L. Baskin & Co., Historical Publishers.
Bluestone, Daniel. 1991. *Constructing Chicago.* New Haven, CT: Yale University Press.
Blumhofer, Edith Waldvogel. 1985. *Assemblies of God: A Popular History.* Springfield, MO: Gospel Publishing House.
Brady, Jeff. 2005. "Colorado Springs a Mecca for Evangelical Christians." *NPR,* January 17. http://www.npr.org/templates/story/story.php?storyId=4287106.
Bratt, James D. 1984. *Dutch Calvinism in Modern America: A History of a Conservative Subculture.* Grand Rapids, MI: Wm. B. Eerdmans Publishing Co.
Brenneman, Robert, and Brian J. Miller. 2020. *Building Faith: A Sociology of Religious Structures.* New York: Oxford University Press.
Brooks, David. 2000. *Bobos in Paradise: The New Upper Class and How They Got There.* New York: Simon & Schuster.

Brueggemann, Walter. 2002. *The Land: Place as Gift, Promise and Challenge in Biblical Faith.* Minneapolis: Fortress Press.

Brumback, Carl. 1961. *Suddenly...from Heaven: A History of the Assemblies of God.* Springfield, MO: Gospel Publishing House.

Bucholtz, Shawn. 2020. "Urban. Suburban. Rural. How Do Households Describe Where They Live?" *PD&R Edge*, August 3. https://www.huduser.gov/portal/pdredge/pdr-edge-frm-asst-sec-080320.html.

Buck, Stephen James. 1992. *Political and Economic Transformation in the Civil War Era: DuPage County, Illinois, 1830–1880.* PhD diss., Northern Illinois University.

Buggeln, Gretchen. 2015. *The Suburban Church: Modernism and Community in Postwar America.* Minneapolis: University of Minnesota Press.

Burge, Ryan. 2018. "ryanburge/reltrad." https://github.com/ryanburge/reltrad.

Burge, Ryan. 2019. "Why Do Evangelicals Support Trump? Blame the Suburbs." *Religion News Service.* https://religionnews.com/2019/07/30/why-do-evangelicals-support-trump-blame-the-suburbs/.

Burrows, Edwin G., and Mike Wallace. 1999. *Gotham: A History of New York City to 1898.* New York: Oxford University Press.

Butler, Anthea D. 2021. *White Evangelical Racism: The Politics of Morality in America.* Chapel Hill: University of North Carolina Press.

Butler, Jon. 2020. *God in Gotham: The Miracle of Religion in Modern Manhattan.* Cambridge, MA: The Belknap Press of Harvard University Press.

Cadge, Wendy. 2008. "De Facto Congregationalism and the Religious Organizations of Post-1965 Immigrants to the United States: A Revised Approach." *Journal of the American Academy of Religion* 76, no. 2: 344–374.

Call, Keith. 2006. *Wheaton.* Charleston, SC: Arcadia Publishing.

Calvillo, Jonathan. 2020. *The Saints of Santa Ana: Faith and Ethnicity in a Mexican Majority City.* New York: Oxford University Press.

Cantrell, Randolph L., James F. Krile, and George A. Donohue. 1983. "Parish Autonomy: Measuring Denominational Differences." *Journal for the Scientific Study of Religion* 22, no. 3: 276–287.

Capps, Kriston. 2018. "Do Millennials Prefer Cities or Suburbs? Maybe Both." *Bloomberg CityLab*, July 30. https://www.bloomberg.com/news/articles/2018-07-30/do-millennials-prefer-cities-or-suburbs-maybe-both.

Capps, Kriston. 2020. "Trump Targets Efforts to Desegregate U.S. Suburbs." *Bloomberg*, July 2. https://www.bloomberg.com/news/articles/2020-07-02/trump-targets-efforts-to-desegregate-u-s-suburbs.

Carpenter, Joel A. 1997. *Revive Us Again: The Reawakening of American Fundamentalism.* New York: Oxford University Press.

Castells, Manuel. 1979. *The Urban Question.* Cambridge, MA: MIT Press.

Cavalcanti, H. B. 2007. *Gloryland: Christian Suburbia, Christian Nation.* Westport, CT: Praeger.

Chatterley, Greg. 2018a. "From Norway to Carol Stream: Ethnic Protestant Foundations of White Evangelicalism." American Association of Religion Conference, Denver, November 18.

Chatterley, Greg. 2018b. "'White' Evangelicalism: Suburbanization, Religion and Raced Social Order." American Association of Religion Conference, Denver, November 17.

Chaves, Mark. 2004. *Congregations in America.* Cambridge, MA: Harvard University Press.

Chaves, Mark, Joseph Roso, Anna Holleman, and Mary Hawkins. 2021. *Congregations in 21st Century America.* Durham, NC: Duke University, Department of Sociology. https://sites.duke.edu/ncsweb/files/2022/02/NCSIV_Report_Web_FINAL2.pdf.

Chesler, Josh. 2021. "Billy Joe Armstrong Really Thinks Green Day's Best Song is 'Jesus of Suburbia.'" *Spin*, April 26. https://www.spin.com/2021/04/billie-joe-armstrong-green-day-best-jesus-suburbia/.

Chicago Fact Book Consortium. 1984. *Local Community Fact Book Chicago Metropolitan Area*. Chicago: The Chicago Review Press.

Chicago Fact Book Consortium. 1995. *Local Community Fact Book Chicago Metropolitan Area 1990*. Chicago: Academy Chicago Publishers.

Chinni, Dante, and James Gimpel. 2010. *Our Patchwork Nation: The Surprising Truth about the "Real" America*. New York: Gotham Books.

Christakis, Nicholas A. and James H. Fowler. 2009. *Connected: The Surprising Power of our Social Networks and How They Shape our Lives*. New York: Little, Brown and Co.

Cimino, Richard, Nadia A. Mian, and Weishan Huang, eds. 2013. *Ecologies of Faith in New York City: The Evolution of Religious Institutions*. Bloomington: Indiana University Press.

City of La Mirada. 2020. "History of La Mirada." https://www.cityoflamirada.org/about-us/history.

City of Wheaton. 1991. "City of Wheaton: Resident Information Guide." Center for History archives, Wheaton, IL.

Cizik, Richard. 2005. "A History of the Public Policy Resolutions of the National Association of Evangelicals." In *Toward an Evangelical Public Policy: Political Strategies for the Health of the Nation*, ed. Ronald J. Sider and Diane Knippers, 35–63. Grand Rapids, MI: Baker Books.

Claiborne, Shane. 2006. *Irresistible Revolution: Living as an Ordinary Radical*. Grand Rapids, MI: Zondervan.

Clark, Terry Nichols. 2011. "The New Chicago School: Notes Toward a Theory." In *The City Revisited: Urban Theory from Chicago, Los Angeles, New York*, ed. Dennis R. Judd and Dick Simpson, 220–241. Minneapolis: University of Minnesota Press.

Coffman, Elesha. 2013. *The Christian Century and the Rise of the Protestant Mainline*. New York: Oxford University Press.

"Colorado Springs Evangelicals." 2013. Religion & Ethics Newsweekly, February 22. http://www.pbs.org/wnet/religionandethics/2013/02/22/february-22-2013-colorado-springs-evangelicals/14792/.

"Community Profile." 1994. Center for History archives, Wheaton, IL.

Conn, Harvie M. 1994. *The American City and the Evangelical Church: A Historical Overview*. Grand Rapids, MI: Baker Books.

Conn, Stephen. 2014. *Americans Against the City: Anti-Urbanism in the Twentieth Century*. New York: Oxford University Press.

Coon, David R. 2014. *Look Closer: Suburban Narratives and American Values in Film and Television*. New Brunswick, NJ: Rutgers University Press.

Cragun, Ryan T., Stephanie Yeager, and Desmond Vega. 2012. "Research Report: How Secular Humanists (and Everyone Else) Subsidize Religion in the United States." *Free Inquiry* 32, no. 4: 39–46.

Cronon, William. 1991. *Nature's Metropolis: Chicago and the Great West*. New York: Norton.

Cruz, Wilfredo. 2007. *City of Dreams: Latino Immigration to Chicago*. Lanham, MD: University Press of America.

Curtis, Jesse. 2021. *The Myth of Colorblind Christians: Evangelicals and White Supremacy in the Civil Rights Era*. New York: New York University Press.

Cutler, Irving. 1996. *The Jews of Chicago: From Shtetl to Suburb*. Urbana: University of Illinois Press.

Cutler, Irving. 2006. *Chicago: Metropolis of the Mid-Continent*. 4th ed. Carbondale: Southern Illinois University Press.

Cutrer, Corrie. 2000. "Left Behind Series Puts Tyndale Ahead." *Christianity Today*, November 13. https://www.christianitytoday.com/ct/2000/november13/20.26.html.

Davis, Charles L., II. 2017. "Louis Sullivan and the Physiognomic Translation of American Character." *Journal of the Society of Architectural Historians* 76, no. 1: 63–81.

Dear, Michael, and Steven Flusty. 1998. "Postmodern Urbanism." *Annals of the Association of American Geographers* 88, no. 1: 50–72.

"Decades of Progress 1945–1965." n.d. Center for History Exhibit, Wheaton, IL.

DeKruyter, Arthur H., and Quentin J. Schultze. 2008. *The Suburban Church: Practical Advice for Authentic Ministry*. Louisville: Westminster John Knox Press.

Demerath, N. J. III, Peter Dobkin Hall, Terry Schmitt, and Rhys H. Williams, eds. 1998. *Sacred Companies: Organizations Aspects of Religion and Religious Aspects of Organizations*. New York: Oxford University Press.

Diamond, Etan. 2000. *And I Will Dwell in Their Midst: Orthodox Jews in Suburbia*. Chapel Hill: University of North Carolina Press.

Diamond, Etan. 2003. *Souls of the City: Religion and the Search for Community in Postwar America*. Bloomington: Indiana University Press.

Dickerson, Dennis C. 2020. *The African Methodist Episcopal Church: A History*. New York: Cambridge University Press.

Dickinson, Greg. 2015. *Suburban Dreams: Imagining and Building the Good Life*. Tuscaloosa: University of Alabama Press.

Dillon, Michelle, and Sarah Savage. 2006. "Values and Religion in Rural America: Attitudes Toward Abortion and Same-Sex Relations." *Carsey Institute*. https://scholars.unh.edu/cgi/viewcontent.cgi?article=1011&context=carsey.

Dochuk, Darren. 2003. "'Praying for a Wicked City': Congregation, Community and the Suburbanization of Fundamentalism." *Religious and American Culture: A Journal of Interpretation* 13, no. 2: 167–203.

Dochuk, Darren. 2011. *From Bible Belt to Sunbelt: Plain-Folk Religion, Grassroots Politics, and the Rise of Evangelical Conservatism*. New York: Norton.

Doughtery, Kevin D., and Mark T. Mulder. 2009. "Congregational Responses to Growing Urban Diversity in a White Ethnic Denomination." *Social Problems* 56, no. 2: 335–356.

Douglass, H. Paul. 1925. *The Suburban Trend*. New York: Century.

Drake, St. Clair, and Horace R. Cayton. 1945. *Black Metropolis: A Study of Negro Life in a Northern City*. New York: Harcourt, Brace and Company.

Du Mez, Kristin Kobes. 2020. *Jesus and John Wayne: How White Evangelicals Corrupted a Faith and Fractured a Nation*. New York: Liveright Publishing Corporation.

Duany, Andres, Elizabeth Plater-Zyberk, and Jeff Speck. 2000. *Suburban Nation: The Rise of Sprawl and the Decline of the American Dream*. New York: North Point Press.

Dugandzic, Audra. 2022. "Reconnecting Religion and Community in a Small City How Urban Amenities Afford Religious Amenities." *Sociology of Religion* 83, no. (4): 434–458.

Dungey, Diane. 1985. "After Dry Spell, Liquor to Quench Wheaton's Thirst." *Daily Herald*, November 3.

Dunn, Joshua M. 2014. "The Paradoxes of Politics in Colorado Springs." *The Forum* 12, no. (2): 329–342.

Duranton, Gilles, and Diego Puga. 2004. "Micro-Foundations of Urban Agglomeration Economies." In *Handbook of Regional and Urban Economics: Cities an Geography*, ed. J. Vernon Henderson and Jacques-Francois Thisse, 2064–2117. Amsterdam: Elsevier B.V.

Edgerton, Michael. 1983. "A New Silicon Valley? Du Page County Thinks So." *Chicago Tribune*, April 10.

Ehrenhalt, Aaron. 2012. *The Great Inversion and the Future of the American City*. New York: Knopf.

Eiesland, Nancy. 2000. *A Particular Place: Urban Restructuring and Religious Ecology in a Southern Exurb*. New Brunswick, NJ: Rutgers University Press.

Eiesland, Nancy L., and R. Stephen Warner. 1997. "Ecology: Seeing the Congregation in Context." In *Studying Congregations: A New Handbook*, ed. Nancy T. Ammerman, Jackson W. Carroll, Carl S. Dudley, and William McKinney, 40–77. Nashville: Abingdon Press.

Elisha, Omri. 2011a. *Moral Ambition: Mobilization and Social Outreach in Evangelical Megachurches*. Berkeley: University of California Press.

Elisha, Omri. 2011b. "Taking the (Inner) City for God: Ambiguities of Urban Social Engagement Among Conservative White Evangelicals." In *The Fundamentalist

City: Religion and Urbanism in the New Global Order, ed. Nezar AlSayyad and Mejgan Massoumi, 236–256. New York: Routledge.

Emerson, Michael O., and Christian Smith. 2000. *Divided by Faith: Evangelical Religion and the Problem of Race in America*. New York: Oxford University Press.

Eskridge, Larry. 2013. *God's Forever Family: The Jesus People Movement in America*. New York: Oxford University Press.

"Evangelical Association Will Relocate to Azusa." 1999. *Los Angeles Times*, September 17.

"Evangelicals Dedicate New Headquarters." 1962. *Chicago Tribune*, October 10.

Evans, Curtis. 2017. "A Politics of Conversion: Billy Graham's Political and Social Vision." In *Billy Graham: American Pilgrim*, ed. Andrew Finstuen, Anne Blue Wills, and Grant Wacker, 143–160. New York: Oxford University Press.

"Excitement in DuPage County Over the Removal of the County Seat from Naperville to Wheaton." 1867. *Chicago Daily Tribune*, June 6.

Executive Committee, ed. 1942. *Evangelical Action! A Report of the Organization of the National Association of Evangelicals for United Action*. Boston: United Action Press.

Feagin, Joe R. 1998. *The New Urban Paradigm: Critical Perspectives on the City*. Lanham, MD: Rowman & Littlefield.

"Feel Greatest Impact of Crusade Coming." 1959a. *The Daily Journal*, October 10.

Fegelman, Andrew, and Ray Gibson. 1985. "Wheaton to Vote on Ending Liquor Ban." *Chicago Tribune*, January 3.

Fernandez, Lilia. 2012. *Brown in the Windy City: Mexicans and Puerto Ricans in Postwar Chicago*. Chicago: University of Chicago Press.

Finke, Roger, and Rodney Stark. 2005. *The Churching of America, 1776–2005: Winners and Losers in our Religious Economy*. New Brunswick, NJ: Rutgers University Press.

Fischer, Claude S., and Michael Hout. 2006. *Century of Difference: How America Changed in the Last One Hundred Years*. New York: Russell Sage Foundation.

Fishman, Robert. 1987. *Bourgeois Utopias: The Rise and Fall of Suburbia*. New York: Basic Books.

Florida, Richard L. 2017. *The New Urban Crisis: How Our Cities are Increasing Inequality, Deepening Segregation, and Failing the Middle Class—and What We Can Do About It*. New York: Basic Books.

"Focus on Family Is Offered $4 Million for Colorado Move." 1990. *Los Angeles Times*, August 9. https://www.latimes.com/archives/la-xpm-1990-08-09-ga-448-story.html.

Folds, Ben. 2019. *A Dream about Lightning Bugs: A Life of Music and Cheap Lessons*. New York: Ballantine Books.

Foote, Wilbur Fiske. 1918. *History of Colorado Volume 1*. Chicago: S. J. Clarke Publishing Company.

Form, William, and Joshua Dubrow. 2008. "Ecology of Denominational Fundamentalism in a Metropolis." *City & Community* 7, no. 2: 141–162.

Fourth Presbyterian Church. 2023. "History of Fourth Presbyterian Church." www.fourthchurch.org/about/history/index.html.

Francis, Leah Gunning. 2015. *Ferguson & Faith: Sparking Leadership & Awakening Community*. St. Louis, MO: Chalice Press.

Frey, William. 2015. *Diversity Explosion: How New Racial Demographics are Remaking America*. Washington, DC: Brookings Institution Press.

Frey, William H. 2022. "Today's Suburbs are Symbolic of America's Rising Diversity: A 2020 Census Portrait." The Brookings Institution. https://www.brookings.edu/research/todays-suburbs-are-symbolic-of-americas-rising-diversity-a-2020-census-portrait/.

Friedan, Betty. 1963. *The Feminine Mystique*. New York: Norton.

Freund, David M. P. 2007. *Colored Property: State Policy and White Racial Politics in Suburban America*. Chicago: University of Chicago Press.

Frykholm, Amy Johnson. 2004. *Rapture Culture: Left Behind in Evangelical America*. New York: Oxford University Press.

Gallagher, Sally K. 2003. *Evangelical Identity and Gendered Family Life*. New Brunswick, NJ: Rutgers University Press.
Gamm, Gerald. 1999. *Urban Exodus: Why the Jews Left Boston and the Catholics Stayed*. Cambridge, MA: Harvard University Press.
Gans, Herbert J. 1967. *The Levittowners*. New York: Pantheon Books.
Garreau, Joel. 1991. *Edge City: Life on the New Frontier*. New York: Doubleday.
Gary-Wheaton Bank. n.d. "The Brothers Wheaton." Center for History archives, Wheaton, IL.
Gill, Jo. 2013. *The Poetics of the American Suburbs*. New York: Palgrave Macmillan.
Glotzer, Paige. 2020. *How the Suburbs Were Segregated: Developers and the Business of Exclusionary Housing, 1890–1960*. New York: Columbia University Press.
Godtube. 2011. "The Story Behind God of This City." https://www.godtube.com/watch/?v=JECE1CNU.
Goetz, David. 2006. *Death By Suburb: How to Keep the Suburbs from Killing Your Soul*. San Francisco: HarperSanFrancisco.
Gorringe, T. J. 2002. *A Theology of the Built Environment: Justice, Empowerment, Redemption*. New York: Cambridge University Press.
Gotham, Kevin Fox, and Miriam Greenberg. 2014. *Crisis Cities: Disaster and Redevelopment in New York and New Orleans*. New York: Oxford University Press.
Gottdiener, Mark. 1977. *Planned Sprawl: Private and Public Interests in Suburbia*. Beverly Hills, CA: Sage Publications.
Gottleib, Alan, and Virginia Culver. 1992. "Evangelical Influx Splits Colorado City." *Chicago Tribune* November 20. http://articles.chicagotribune.com/1992-11-20/news/9204160320_1_religious-groups-colorado-springs-residents-evangelical-groups.
Gordon-Conwell Theological Seminary. 2023. "Pivot Update: Gordon-Conwell Will Stay on the Hamilton Campus." December 15. https://www.gordonconwell.edu/news/pivot-gordon-conwell-will-stay-hamilton/.
Gould, Gordon. 1959. "A Crusader Returns to Wheaton." *Chicago Tribune*, September 27.
Grabill, Stephen. 2014. "The Big Picture." *The Gospel Coalition*, July 8. https://www.thegospelcoalition.org/article/the-big-picture/.
Graham, Billy. 1947. *Calling Youth to Christ*. Grand Rapids, MI: Zondervan.
Graham, Billy. 1953a. *I Saw Your Sons at War: The Korean Diary of Billy Graham*. Minneapolis: The Billy Graham Evangelistic Association.
Graham, Billy. 1953b. *Peace with God*. Garden City, NY: Doubleday.
Graham, Billy. 1955a. *The 7 Deadly Sins*. Grand Rapids, MI: Zondervan.
Graham, Billy. 1955b. *The Secret of Happiness: Jesus' Teaching on Happiness as Expressed in the Beatitudes*. Garden City, NY: Doubleday.
Graham, Billy. 1958. *Billy Graham Talks to Teen-agers*. Wheaton, IL: Miracle Books.
Graham, Billy. 1965. *World Aflame*. Garden City, NY: Doubleday.
Graham, Billy. 1969. *The Challenge: Sermons from Madison Square Garden*. Garden City, NY: Doubleday.
Graham, Billy. 1971. *The Jesus Generation*. Minneapolis: World Wide Publications.
Graham, Billy. 1975. *Angels: God's Secret Agents*. Garden City, NY: Doubleday.
Graham, Billy. 1977. *How to Be Born Again*. Waco, TX: Word Publishers.
Graham, Billy. 1978. *Holy Spirit: Activating GOD'S Power in Your Life*. Waco, TX: Word Books.
Graham, Billy. 1981. *Till Armageddon: A Perspective on Suffering*. Waco, TX: Word Books.
Graham, Billy. 1983. *Approaching Hoofbeats: The Four Horsemen of the Apocalypse*. Waco, TX: Word Books.
Graham, Billy. 1984. *A Biblical Standard for Evangelicals*. Minneapolis: World Wide Publications.
Graham, Billy. 1986. *Unto the Hills*. Waco, TX: Word Books.
Graham, Billy. 1987. *Facing Death and the Life After*. Waco, TX: Word Books.
Graham, Billy. 1988. *Answers to Life's Problems*. Dallas: Word Publishing.
Graham, Billy. 1991. *Hope For the Troubled Heart*. Dallas: Word Publishing.

Graham, Billy. 1992. *Storm Warning*. Dallas: Word Publishing.
Graham, Billy. 2002. *Hope for Each Day*. Nashville: Thomas Nelson.
Graham, Billy. 2003. *The Key to Personal Peace*. Nashville: W Publishing Group.
Graham, Billy. 2005. *Living in God's Love: The New York Crusade*. New York: G. P. Putnam's Sons.
Graham, Billy. 2006. *The Journey: How to Live by Faith in an Uncertain World*. Nashville: W Publishing Group.
Graham, Billy. 2011. *Nearing Home: Life, Faith, and Finishing Well*. Nashville: Thomas Nelson.
Graham, Billy. 2012. *The Heaven Answer Book*. Nashville: Thomas Nelson.
Graham, Billy. 2013. *The Reason for My Hope: Salvation*. Nashville: W Publishing Group.
Graham, Billy. 2015. *Where I Am: Heaven, Eternity, and Our Life Beyond the Now*. Nashville: W Publishing Group.
Graham, Billy. n.d. *Billy Graham Answers Your Questions*. Minneapolis: World Wide Publications.
Grammich, Clifford, Erica J. Dollhopf, Mary L. Gautier, Richard Houseal, Dale E. Jones, Alexei Krindatch, Richie Stanley, and Scott Thumma. 2023. *2020 U.S. Religion Census: Religious Congregations & Adherents Study*. Association of Statisticians of American Religious Bodies. Archived by The Association of Religion Data Archives, Pennsylvania State University.
Granberg-Michaelson, Wesley. 2011. *Unexpected Destinations: An Evangelical Pilgrimage to World Christianity*. Grand Rapids, MI: Wm. B. Eerdmans Publishing Co.
Greeley, Andrew M. 1959. *The Church and the Suburbs*. Glen Rock, NJ: Deus Books.
Green, Joel B., Jeannine K. Brown, and Nicholas Perrin, eds. 2013. *Dictionary of Jesus and the Gospels*. Downers Grove, IL: InterVarsity Press.
Griffin, Jean Latz, and Art Barnum. 1985. "Wheaton Votes to Pop Cork After 50-Year Dry Spell." *Chicago Tribune*, April 3.
Grossman, Cathy Lynn. 2018. "Billy Graham Wrote a LOT of books. Here's a List, Including His Last on Heaven." *USA Today*, February 21. https://www.usatoday.com/story/news/nation/2018/02/21/billy-graham-books-autobiography/858796001/.
Grossman, James R. 1989. *Land of Hope: Chicago, Black Southerners, and the Great Migration*. Chicago: University of Chicago Press.
Grossman, James R., Ann Durkin Keating, and Janice L. Reiff, eds. 2004. *Encyclopedia of Chicago*. Chicago: University of Chicago Press.
Gundersen, Valborg J. 1966. *Long Shadow: The Living Story of a Layman and His Lord*. Minneapolis: Beacon Publications.
Gustafson, Anita Olson. 2003. "North Park: Building a Swedish community in Chicago." *Journal of American Ethnic History* 22, no. 2: 31–49.
Hales, Ashley. 2018. *Finding Holy in the Suburbs: Living Faithfully in the Land of Too Much*. Downers Grove, IL: InterVarsity Press.
Hamilton, Michael S. 1994. "The Fundamentalist Harvard: Wheaton College and the Continuing Vitality of American Evangelicalism, 1919–1965." PhD diss., University of Notre Dame.
Hanlon, Bernadette. 2010. *Once the American Dream: Inner-Ring Suburbs of the Metropolitan United States*. Philadelphia: Temple University Press.
Hanson, R. Scott. 2016. *City of Gods: Religious Freedom, Immigration, and Pluralism in Flushing, Queens*. New York: Empire States Editions.
Haralovich, Mary Beth. 1992. "Sit-coms and Suburbs: Positioning the 1950s Homemaker." In *Private Screenings*, ed. Lynn Spigel and Denise Mann, 111–141. Minneapolis: University of Minnesota Press.
Hartford Institute for Religion Research. 2021. "Database of Megachurches in the U.S." http://hartfordinstitute.org/megachurch/database.html.
Hatch, Nathan O. 1989. *The Democratization of American Christianity*. New Haven, CT: Yale University Press.
Haug, Sonja. 2008. "Migration Networks and Migration Decision-Making." *Journal of Ethnic and Migration Studies* 34, no. 4: 585–605.

Hayden, Dolores. 2003. *Building Suburbia: Green Fields and Urban Growth, 1820–2000*. New York: Vintage Books.

Haynes, Bruce D. 2001. *Red Lines, Black Spaces: The Politics of Race and Space in a Black Middle-Class Suburb*. New Haven, CT: Yale University Press.

Heath, Thomas. 1994. "In Colorado Springs, Religious Groups Have the Right of Way." *Washington Post*, December 25, A3.

Heiman, Rachel. 2015. *Driving After Class: Anxious Times in an American Suburb*. Berkeley: University of California Press.

Heise, Kenan. 1989. "Robert Van Kampen; Served on Billy Graham Association Board." *Chicago Tribune*, November 23.

Heltzel, Peter Goodwin. 2009. *Jesus and Justice: Evangelicals, Race, and American Politics*. New Haven, CT: Yale University Press.

Henry, Carl F. H. 1947. *Uneasy Conscience of Modern Fundamentalism*. Grand Rapids, MI: Wm. B. Eerdmans Publishing Co.

"Henry's Story." 2021. Carl F. H. Henry Institute for Evangelical Engagement. https://www.henryinstitute.org/henrys-story/.

Herberg, Will. 1955. *Protestant, Catholic, Jew: An Essay in American Religious Sociology*. Garden City, NY: Doubleday.

Hirsch, Arnold R. 1983. *Making the Second Ghetto: Race and Housing in Chicago, 1940–1960*. New York: Cambridge University Press.

Hirsch, Arnold R. 1998. *Making the Second Ghetto: Race and Housing in Chicago, 1940–1960*. Chicago: University of Chicago Press.

Hirt, Sonia A. 2014. *Zoned in the USA: The Origins and Implications of American Land Use Planning*. Ithaca, NY: Cornell University Press.

"History Timeline." 2021. Wooddale Church. https://wooddale.org/about/history-timeline/.

Hobbs, Frank and Nicole Stoops. 2002. *Demographic Trends in the 20th Century*. Washington, DC: US Census Bureau. http://www.census.gov/prod/2002pubs/censr-4.pdf.

Hochschild, Arlie Russell. 2016. *Strangers in Their Own Land: Anger and Mourning on the American Right*. New York: The New Press.

Holli, Melvin G., and Peter d'A. Jones, eds. 1994. *Ethnic Chicago: A Multicultural Portrait*. Grand Rapids, MI: W. B. Eerdmans Publishing Co.

Hoover, Edward Malone. 1948. *The Location of Economic Activity*. New York: McGraw Hill.

Hopfensperger, Jean. 2019. "Minnesotan Retires as Head of National Association of Evangelicals." *StarTribune*, December 28. https://www.startribune.com/minnesotan-retires-as-head-of-national-assocation-of-evangelicals/566513712/.

Houston, Jack. 1978. "Wheaton: A Place for the True Believer." *Chicago Tribune*, June 8.

Howe, Justine. 2018. *Suburban Islam*. New York: Oxford University Press.

Hsu, Albert Y. 2006. *The Suburban Christian: Finding Spiritual Vitality in the Land of Plenty*. Downers Grove, IL: InterVarsity Press.

Hudnut-Beumler, James David. 1994. *Looking for God in the Suburbs: The Religion of the American Dream and its Critics, 1945–1965*. New Brunswick, NJ: Rutgers University Press.

Hummel, Daniel G. 2023. *The Rise and Fall of Dispensationalism: How the Evangelical Battle over the End Times Shaped a Nation*. Grand Rapids, MI: Wm. B. Eerdmans Publishing Co.

Hunter, James Davison. 1991. *Culture Wars: The Struggle to Define America*. New York: Basic Books.

Hunter, James Davison. 2010. *To Change the World: The Irony, Tragedy, and Possibility of Christianity in the Late Modern World*. New York: Oxford University Press.

Huq, Rupa. 2013. *Making Sense of Suburbia Through Popular Culture*. London: Bloomsbury.

Iannaccone, Laurence C. 1992. "Religious Markets and the Economics of Religion." *Social Compass* 39, no. 1: 123–131.

"In Brief." 2002. *Washington Post*, May 4.

Inge, John. 2003. *A Christian Theology of Place*. Burlington, VT: Ashgate.

InterVarsity. 2021. "The U.S. Racial Crisis and World Evangelism." https://urbana.org/message/us-racial-crisis-and-world-evangelism.

Jackson, Kenneth T. 1985. *Crabgrass Frontier: The Suburbanization of the United States.* New York: Oxford University Press.

Jennings, Willie James. 2010. *The Christian Imagination: Theology and the Origins of Race.* New Haven, CT: Yale University Press.

Johnson, Dirk. 1993. "Rise of Christian Right Splits a City." *New York Times*, February 14. http://www.nytimes.com/1993/02/14/us/rise-of-christian-right-splits-a-city.html.

Jones, Kim. 2009. "Audio Adrenaline Releasing Final Album on August 1." About.com. https://web.archive.org/web/20090616024610/http://christianmusic.about.com/od/upcomingreleases/a/AAfinalalbum801.htm.

Judd, Dennis R., and Dick Simpson, eds. 2011. *The City, Revisited: Urban Theory from Chicago, Los Angeles, and New York.* Minneapolis: University of Minnesota Press.

Jurca, Catherine. 2001. *White Diaspora: The Suburb and the Twentieth-Century American Novel.* Princeton, NJ: Princeton University Press.

Karnes, Kimberly, Wayne McIntosh, Irwin L. Morris, and Shanna Pearson-Merkowitz. 2007. "Mighty Fortresses: Explaining the Spatial Distribution of American Megachurches." *Journal for the Scientific Study of Religion* 46, no. 2: 261–268.

Kass, John. 1985. "Boycott Shuts Store, 'Porn' Issue Remains." *Chicago Tribune*, January 13.

Kaufman, Jason, and Matthew E. Kaliner. 2011. "The Re-Accomplishment of Place in Twentieth Century Vermont and New Hampshire: History Repeats Itself, Until It Doesn't." *Theory and Society* 40, no. 2: 119–154.

Keating, Ann Durkin. 2002. *Building Chicago: Suburban Developers and the Creation of a Divided Metropolis.* Urbana: University of Illinois Press.

Keating, Ann Durkin. 2005. *Chicagoland: City and Suburbs in the Railroad Age.* Chicago: University of Chicago Press.

Keating, Ann Durkin. 2012. *Rising Up from Indian Country: The Battle of Fort Dearborn and the Birth of Chicago.* Chicago: University of Chicago Press.

Keller, Timothy. 2012a. *Center Church: Doing Balanced, Gospel-Centered Ministry in Your City.* Grand Rapids, MI: Zondervan.

Keller, Timothy. 2012b. "A Theology of Cities." CRU Press. https://www.cru.org/content/dam/cru/legacy/2012/02/A_Theology_of_Cities.pdf.

Keller, Timothy. 2016. *Serving a Movement: Doing Balanced, Gospel-centered Ministry in Your City.* Grand Rapids, MI: Zondervan.

Kelly, David. 2004. "In Colorado, a Wellspring of Conservative Christianity." *Los Angeles Times*, July 6. http://articles.latimes.com/2004/jul/06/entertainment/et-kelly6.

Kennedy, John W. 1999. "NAE Mulls Move to Azusa." *Christianity Today* 43, no. 10: 22.

Kenney, Martin, and Urs Von Burg. 1999. "Technology, Entrepreneurship and Path Dependence: Industrial Clustering in Silicon Valley and Route 128." *Industrial and Corporate Change* 8, no. 1: 67–103.

Kidd, Thomas J. 2019. *Who Is an Evangelical? The History of a Movement in Crisis.* New Haven, CT: Yale University Press.

King, David P. 2019. *God's Internationalists: World Vision and the Age of Evangelical Humanitarianism.* Philadelphia: University of Pennsylvania Press.

Kisiel, Caroline M., and Brian J. Miller. 2023. "Property and Racial Exclusion in Illinois: Patterns and Practices from Colonial Slavery to Suburban Marginalization, 1720s-2010s." *Journal of the Illinois State Historical Society* 116, no. 4: 9–47.

Kitagawa, Evelyn M., and Karl E. Taeuber, eds. 1963. *Local Community Fact Book Chicago Metropolitan Area 1960.* Chicago: Chicago Community Inventory.

Kling, Rob, Spencer Olin, and Mark Poster, eds. 1991. *Postsuburban California: The Transformation of Orange County Since World War II.* Berkeley: University of California Press.

Kneebone, Elizabeth, and Alan Berube. 2013. *Confronting Suburban Poverty in America.* Washington, DC: Brookings Institution Press.

Knoblauch, Marion, ed. 1951. *DuPage County: A Descriptive and Historical Guide*. Wheaton, IL: DuPage Title Company.

Korver-Glenn, Elizabeth. 2022. *Race Brokers: Housing Markets and Racial Segregation in 21st Century Urban America*. New York: Oxford University Press.

Kotkin, Joel. 2016. "It Wasn't Rural 'Hicks' Who Elected Trump: The Suburbs Were—And Will Remain—the Real Battleground." *Forbes*, November 22. https://www.forbes.com/sites/joelkotkin/2016/11/22/donald-trump-clinton-rural-suburbs/#273cc0c838b5.

Kristof, Nicholas. 2008. "Evangelicals a Liberal Can Love." *New York Times*, February 3.

Kruse, Kevin M. 2005. *White Flight: Atlanta and the Making of Modern Conservatism*. Princeton, NJ: Princeton University Press.

Kushner, David. 2009. *Levittown: Two Families, One Tycoon, and the Fight for Civil Rights in America's Legendary Suburb*. New York: Walker & Co.

Kye, Samuel H. 2018. "The Persistence of White Flight in Middle-Class Suburbia." *Social Science Research* 72: 38–52.

Lacy, Karyn R. 2007. *Blue-Chip Black: Race, Class, and Status in the New Black Middle Class*. Berkeley: University of California Press.

Lang, Robert E., and Jennifer B. LeFurgy. 2007. *Boomburbs: The Rise of America's Accidental Cities*. Washington, DC: Brookings Institution Press.

Larsen, Timothy. 2007. "Defining and Locating Evangelicalism." In *The Cambridge Companion to Evangelical Theology*, ed. Timothy Larsen and Daniel J. Trier, 1–14. New York: Cambridge University Press.

Lassiter, Matthew D. 2006. *The Silent Majority: Suburban Politics in the Sunbelt South*. Princeton, NJ: Princeton University Press.

Lausanne Committee for World Evangelization. 1978. "The Pasadena Consultation: Homogeneous Unit Principle (LOP 1)." https://lausanne.org/content/lop/lop-1 (accessed June 10, 2021).

Lausanne Movement. 2022. "The Cape Town Commitment." https://lausanne.org/content/ctc/ctcommitment.

League of Women Voters. 1956. "Wheaton Profile." DuPage County Historical Museum archives, Wheaton, IL.

Lee, Andrew. 2006. "Christian Groups in Colorado Springs." The Martin Marty Center for Advanced Study of Religion. http://divinity.uchicago.edu/sightings/christian-groups-colorado-springs-andrew-lee.

Lee, Shayne, and Phillip Sinitiere. 2009. *Holy Mavericks: Evangelical Innovators and the Spiritual Marketplace*. New York: New York University Press.

Lefebvre, Henri. 1991 [1974]. *The Production of Space*. Translated by Donald Nicholson-Smith. Cambridge, MA: Blackwell.

Leibman, Nina C. 1995. *Living Room Lectures: The Fifties Family in Film and Television*. Austin: University of Texas Press.

Lepillez, Jean-Marc. 1981. "Graduate Student Recounts Wheaton's Battle to Remain Dry." *The Daily Journal*, November 11.

Lester, Ross. 2017. "My Life as a Suburban Church Planter." July 19. https://rosslester.com/2017/07/19/my-life-as-a-suburban-church-planter/.

Letter from Vern Kiebler to Mayor Bob Martin. n.d. Center for History archives, Wheaton, IL.

Lewis, C. S. 1946. *The Great Divorce*. New York: Macmillan.

Li, Wei. 2009. *Ethnoburb: The New Ethnic Community in Urban America*. Honolulu: University of Hawai'i Press.

LifeWay Research. 2015. "NAE LifeWay Research Evangelical Beliefs Research Definition." http://lifewayresearch.com/wp-content/uploads/2015/11/NAE-LifeWay-Research-Evangelical-Beliefs-Research-Definition-Methodology-and-Use.pdf.

Lindsell, Harold. 1951. *Park Street Prophet: A Life of Harold John Ockenga*. Wheaton, IL: Van Kampen Press.

Lindsay, D. Michael. 2007. *Faith in the Halls of Power: How Evangelicals Joined the American Elite*. New York: Oxford University Press.
Livezey, Lowell W. 2000. *Public Religion and Urban Transformation: Faith in the City*. New York: New York University Press.
Logan, John R., and Harvey L. Molotch. 1987. *Urban Fortunes*. Berkeley: University of California Press.
Loveland, Anne C., and Otis B. Wheeler. 2003. *From Meetinghouse to Megachurch: A Material and Cultural History*. Columbia: University of Missouri Press.
Love-Fordham, April. 2014. *James in the Suburbs: A Disorderly Parable of the Epistle of James*. Eugene, OR: Resource Publications.
Low, Setha M. 2003. *Behind the Gates: Life, Security, and the Pursuit of Happiness in Fortress America*. New York: Routledge.
Lowe, David Garrard. 2010. *Lost Chicago*. Chicago: University of Chicago Press.
Luhr, Eileen. 2009. *Witnessing Suburbia: Conservatives and Christian Youth Culture*. Berkeley: University of California Press.
Luhr, Eileen. 2012. "Marketing Religion." In *Clones, Fakes, and Posthumans: Cultures of Replication*, ed. Philomena Essed and Gabriele Schwab, 153–168. New York: Rodopi.
Luhrmann, T. M. 2012. *When God Talks Back: Understanding the American Evangelical Relationship with God*. New York: Knopf.
Lung-Amam, Willow S. 2017. *Trespassers? Asian Americans and the Battle for Suburbia*. Berkeley: University of California Press.
Lydens, Z. Z., ed. 1966. *The Story of Grand Rapids*. Grand Rapids, MI: Kregel Publications.
Maas, David E., and Charles W. Weber. 1976. *DuPage Discovery 1776–1976*. Wheaton, IL: DuPage County Bicentennial Commission.
Macek, Steve. 2006. *Urban Nightmares: The Media, the Right, and the Moral Panic Over the City*. Minneapolis: University of Minnesota Press.
Magnuson, Norris. 1977. *Salvation in the Slums: Evangelical Social Work, 1865–1920*. Metuchen, NJ: The Scarecrow Press, Inc.
Mahler, Jonathan. 2005. "The Soul of the New Exurb." *New York Times*, March 27. http://leighhouse.typepad.com/blog/files/soul_of_the_new_exurb.pdf.
Mann, Leslie. 2008. "Timeless Wheaton Ages Gracefully." *Chicago Tribune*, November 21. https://www.chicagotribune.com/chi-wheaton-profile_chomes_1121_nov21-story.html.
Mapes, Lynn G., and Anthony Travis. 1976. *Pictorial History of Grand Rapids*. Grand Rapids, MI: Kregel Publications.
"Maria Miranda." 2017. Richlandsource. https://www.richlandsource.com/obituaries/maria-miranda/article_e91fc5da-d9df-11e6-bc2f-277bdc594907.html.
Markoe, Lauren. 2013. "Cash-Strapped National Council of Churches to Move to D.C." *The Christian Century*, February 18. https://www.christiancentury.org/article/2013-02/cash-strapped-national-council-churches-move-dc.
Markofski, Wes. 2015. *New Monasticism and the Transformation of American Evangelicalism*. New York: Oxford University Press.
Marsden, George M. 1987. *Reforming Fundamentalism: Fuller Seminary and the New Evangelicalism*. Grand Rapids, MI: Wm. B. Eerdmans Publishing Co.
Marsden, George M. 2006. *Fundamentalism and American Culture*. 2nd ed. New York: Oxford University Press.
Marsh, Margaret. 1990. *Suburban Lives*. New Brunswick, NJ: Rutgers University Press.
Marshall, Alfred. 1895. *Principles of Economics*. London: Macmillan.
Martí, Gerardo. 2020. *American Blindspot: Race, Class, Religion, and the Trump Presidency*. Lanham, MD: Rowman & Littlefield.
Martínez, Jessica, and Gregory A. Smith. 2016. "How the Faithful Voted: A Preliminary 2016 Analysis." *Pew Research Center*, November 9. https://www.pewresearch.org/fact-tank/2016/11/09/how-the-faithful-voted-a-preliminary-2016-analysis/.

Massey, Douglas S., and Nancy A. Denton. 1993. *American Apartheid: Segregation and the Making of the Underclass.* Cambridge, MA: Harvard University Press.

Massey, Douglas S., and Brendan P. Mullan. 1984. "Processes of Hispanic and Black Spatial Assimilation." *American Journal of Sociology* 89, no. 4: 836–873.

Mather, Mark, Kelvin Pollard, and Linda A. Jacobsen. 2011. *First Results from the 2010 Census.* Population Reference Bureau. http://www.prb.org/pdf11/reports-on-america-2010-census.pdf.

Mathews, Mary Beth Swetnam. 2006. *Rethinking Zion: How the Print Media Placed Fundamentalism in the South.* Knoxville: University of Tennessee Press.

Matthews, Arthur H. 1992. *Standing Up, Standing Together: The Emergence of the National Association of Evangelicals.* Carol Stream, IL: National Association of Evangelicals.

Matsumoto, Noriko. 2018. *Beyond the City and the Bridge: East Asian Immigration in a New Jersey Suburb.* New Brunswick, NJ: Rutgers University Press.

McAdams, Jake. 2019. "'Can I Get a Yee-Haw and an Amen': The Texas Cowboy Church Movement." In *Lone Star Suburbs: Life on Texas's Metropolitan Frontier*, ed. Paul J. P. Sandul and M. Scott Sosebee, 149–165. Norman: University of Oklahoma Press.

McCabe, Brian J. 2016. *No Place Like Home: Wealth, Community, and the Politics of Homeownership.* New York: Oxford University Press.

McClain, Jordan M., and Amanda S. McClain. 2016. "Narrative Themes about Post-Band Solo Work in Media Coverage of Ben Folds's *Rockin' the Suburbs* (2001)." In *All By Myself: Essays on the Single-Artist Rock Album*, ed. Steve Hamelman, 149–162. Lanham, MD: Rowman & Littlefield.

McGirr, Lisa. 2001. *Suburban Warriors: The Origins of the New American Right.* Princeton, NJ: Princeton University Press.

McGowin, Emily Hunter. 2018. *Quivering Families: The Quiverfull Movement and Evangelical Theology of the Family.* Minneapolis: Fortress Press.

McGreevy, John T. 1996. *Parish Boundaries: The Catholic Encounter with Race in the Twentieth-Century Urban North.* Chicago: University of Chicago Press.

McGuire, Meredith B. 1988. *Ritual Healing in Suburban America.* New Brunswick, NJ: Rutgers University Press.

McGuire, Meredith B. 2008. *Lived Religion: Faith and Practice in Everyday Life.* New York: Oxford University Press.

McIvor, Méadhbh. 2023. "Liberal Creeds: Signs of Belief in the US Suburbs." *American Religion* 4, no. 2: 1–16.

McKibben, Bill. 2022. *The Flag, the Cross, and the Station Wagon: A Graying American Looks Back at His Suburban Boyhood and Wonders What the Hell Happens.* New York: Henry Holt and Company.

McLear, Patrick E. 1980. "The Galena and Chicago Union Railroad: A Symbol of Chicago's Economic Maturity." *Journal of the Illinois State Historical Society* 73, no. 1: 17–26.

McMahon, Eileen M. 1995. *What Parish Are You From? A Chicago Irish Community and Race Relations.* Lexington: University Press of Kentucky.

McRoberts, Omar M. 2003. *Streets of Glory: Church and Community in a Black Urban Neighborhood.* Chicago: University of Chicago Press.

Mehler, Neil H. 1990. "Churches' Growth Felt in Wheaton." *Chicago Tribune*, July 24.

Melkonian-Hoover, Ruth M., and Lyman A. Kellstedt. 2019. *Evangelicals and Immigration: Fault Lines Among the Faithful.* Cham: Palgrave Macmillan.

Mendieta, Eduardo. 2009. "Fundamentalism and Antiurbanism: The Frontier Myth, the Christian Nation, and the Heartland." In *Fleeing the City: Studies in the Culture and Politics of Antiurbanism*, ed. Michal J. Thompson, 209–229. New York: Palgrave Macmillan.

Meyer, Stephen Grant. 2000. *As Long as They Don't Move Next Door: Segregation and Racial Conflict in American Neighborhoods.* Lanham, MD: Rowman & Littlefield.

Miller, Brian J. 2012. "Competing Visions of the American Single-Family Home: Defining McMansions in the New York Times and Dallas Morning News, 2000–2009." *Journal of Urban History* 38, no. 6: 1094–1113.

Miller, Brian J. 2013. "Not All Suburbs are the Same: The Role of Character in Shaping Growth and Development in Three Chicago Suburbs." *Urban Affairs Review* 49, no. 5: 652–677.

Miller, Brian J. 2016a. "Measuring Religion in Different Spatial Contexts: How Surveys Involving Religion Inconsistently Determine Locations." *Review of Religious Research* 58, no. 2: 285–304.

Miller, Brian J. 2016b. "A Small Suburb Becomes a Boomburb: Explaining Suburban Growth in Naperville, Illinois." *Journal of Urban History* 42, no. 6: 1135–1152.

Miller, Brian J. 2017a. "From I Love Lucy in Connecticut to Desperate Housewives' Wisteria Lane: Suburban TV Shows, 1950–2007." *Sociological Focus* 50, no. 3: 277–290.

Miller, Brian J. 2017b. "Growing Suburbs, Relocating Churches: The Suburbanization of Protestant Churches in the Chicago Region, 1925–1990." *Journal for the Scientific Study of Religion* 56, no. 2: 342–364.

Miller, Brian J. 2018. "A McMansion for the Suburban Mob Family: The Unfulfilling Single-family Home of The Sopranos." *Journal of Popular Film and Television* 46, no. 4: 207–218.

Miller, Brian J. 2019. "'Would Prefer a Trailer Park to a Large [Religious] Structure': Suburban Responses to Proposals for Religious Buildings." *The Sociological Quarterly* 60, no. 2: 265–286.

Miller, Brian J. 2020. "Religious Freedom and Local Conflict: Religious Buildings and Zoning Issues in the New York City Region, 1992–2017." *Sociology of Religion* 81, no. 4: 462–484.

Miller, Brian J. 2021. "Faith in the Suburbs: Evangelical Christian Books about Suburban Life." In *The Routledge Handbook of Religion and Cities*, ed. Katie Day and Elise M. Edwards, 119–135. New York: Routledge.

Miller, Brian J. 2022. "From 'Jungles of Terror' to 'God Will Begin a Healing in This City': Billy Graham and Evangelicals on Cities and Suburbs. *Journal of Urban History* 48, no. 2: 302–318.

Miller, Brian J., and David B. Malone. 2019. "Race, Town, and Gown: A White Christian College and a White Suburb Address Race." *Journal of the Illinois State Historical Society* 112, no. 3: 293–316.

Miller, Brian J., and Benjamin E. Norquist. 2021. "Christian Colleges in the Locational Wilderness: The Locations of CCCU Institutions." *Christian Higher Education* 20, no. 4: 223–239.

Miller, Kent D. 2002. "Competitive Strategies of Religious Organizations." *Strategic Management Journal* 23: 435–456.

Miller, Stephen P. 2009. *Billy Graham and the Rise of the Republican South*. Philadelphia: University of Pennsylvania Press.

Mirola, William A. 1999. "Shorter Hours and the Protestant Sabbath: Religious Framing and Movement Alliances in Late-Nineteenth-Century Chicago." *Social Science History* 23, no. 3: 395–433.

Mishkin, Shana, Allana Akhtar, and Prachi Bhardwaj. 2018. "This is the Best Place to Live in Every State." *Money*, December 17. https://money.com/this-is-the-best-place-to-live-in-every-state/.

Moberg, David O. 2007 [1972]. *The Great Reversal; Evangelism Versus Social Concern*. Eugene, OR: Wipf and Stock Publishers.

Molotch, Harvey. 1969. "Racial Integration in a Transition Community." *American Sociological Review* 34, no. 6: 878–893.

Molotch, Harvey. 1972. *Managed Integration: Dilemmas of Doing Good in the City*. Berkeley: University of California Press.

Molotch, Harvey, William Freudenburg, and Kristin E. Paulsen. 2000. "History Repeats Itself, but How? City Character, Urban Tradition, and the Accomplishment of Place." *American Sociological Review* 65: 791–823.

Monkkonen, Eric H. 1988. *America Becomes Urban: The Development of U.S. Cities and Towns, 1780–1980*. Berkeley: University of California Press.

Moody Bible Institute. 2021. "William Henry Houghton." https://library.moody.edu/archives/biographies/william-henry-houghton/.

Moore, Jean. 1974. *From Tower to Tower: A History of Wheaton, Illinois*. Wheaton, IL: Gary-Wheaton Bank.

Moore, Jean. 1984. *Building Your Own Town—The Carol Stream Story*. Carol Stream, IL: Carol Stream Historical Society.

Moore, Jean, and Hiawatha Bray. 1989. *DuPage at 150 and Those Who Shaped Our World*. Wheaton, IL: DuPage Sesquicentennial Steering Committee.

Morgan, David. 2002. "Protestant Visual Culture and the Challenges of Urban America during the Progressive Era." In *Faith in the Market: Religion and the Rise of Urban Commercial Culture*, ed. John M. Giggie and Diane Winston, 37–56. New Brunswick, NJ: Rutgers University Press.

Mulder, Mark Timothy. 2004. "A Dissonant Faith: The Exodus of Reformed Dutch Churches From the South Side of Chicago." PhD diss., University of Wisconsin-Milwaukee.

Mulder, Mark T. 2012. "Evangelical Church Polity and the Nuances of White Flight: A Case Study from the Roseland and Englewood neighborhoods in Chicago." *Journal of Urban History* 38, no. 1: 16–38.

Mulder, Mark T. 2015. *Shades of White Flight: Evangelical Congregations and Urban Departure*. New Brunswick, NJ: Rutgers University Press.

Mulder, Mark T., and Amy Jonason. 2017. "White Evangelical Congregations in Cities and Suburbs: Social Engagement, Geography, Diffusion, and Disembeddedness." *City & Society* 29, no. 1: 104–126.

Mulder, Mark T., and Gerardo Martí. 2020. *The Glass Church: Robert H. Schuller, the Crystal Cathedral, and the Strain of Megachurch Ministry*. New Brunswick, NJ: Rutgers University Press.

Mulder, Mark T., Aida I. Ramos, and Gerardo Marti. 2017. *Latino Protestants in America: Growing and Diverse*. Lanham, MD: Rowman & Littlefield Publishers.

Mulder, Mark T., and James K. A. Smith. 2009. "Subdivided by Faith? An Historical Account of Evangelicals and the City." *Christian Scholar's Review* 38, no. 4: 415–434.

Muller, Peter O. 1981. *Contemporary Suburban America*. Englewood Cliffs, NJ: Prentice-Hall, Inc.

Mundey, Peter. 2009. "The 'Neo-Parish': Willow Creek's Middle Ground between Small Groups and Mega Worship." MA thesis, University of Notre Dame.

Murch, James Deforest. 1956. *Cooperation without Compromise: A History of the National Association of Evangelicals*. Grand Rapids, MI: Wm. B. Eerdmans Publishing Co.

Murphy, Alexandra K. 2010. "The Symbolic Dilemmas of Suburban Poverty: Challenges and Opportunities Posed by Variations in the Contours of Suburban Poverty." *Sociological Forum* 25.3: 541–569.

Myatt, William. 2016. "God in Gotham: Tim Keller's Theology of the City." *Missiology: An International Review* 44, no. 2: 182–183.

Nash, Dennison. 1968. "A Little Child Shall Lead Them: A Statistical Test of an Hypothesis That Children Were the Source of the American 'Religious Revival.'" *Journal for the Scientific Study of Religion* 7, no. 2: 238–240.

Nash, Dennison, and Peter L. Berger. 1962. "The Child, the Family, and the 'Religious Revival' in Suburbia." *Journal for the Scientific Study of Religion* 2, no. 1: 85–93.

National Association of Evangelicals. 1942. *Evangelical Action! A Report of the Organization of the National Association of Evangelicals for United Action*. Boston: United Action Press.

National Association of Evangelicals. c1975. "Presenting Evangelical Center." Brochure. Special Collections Wheaton College, National Association of Evangelicals files, Box 13 Folder 5.

National Association of Evangelicals. 1992. "Forward in Faith: 50 Years of Evangelical Cooperation." Special Collections Wheaton College, National Association of Evangelicals files, Box 185 Folder 3.

National Association of Evangelicals. 1999. "Special Meeting of Board of Directors Minutes September 13, 1999." Special Collections Wheaton College, National Association of Evangelicals files, Box 86 Folder 112.

National Association of Evangelicals. 2015. "NAE, LifeWay Research Publish Evangelical Beliefs Research Definition." https://www.nae.net/evangelical-beliefs-research-definition/.

National Association of Evangelicals. 2021. "History." https://www.nae.net/about-nae/history/.

Neal, Zachary P. 2013. *The Connected City: How Networks Are Shaping the Modern Metropolis.* New York: Routledge.

Nesbitt, Charles F. 1961. "The Bethany Tradition in the Gospel Narratives." *Journal of Bible and Religion* 29, no. 2: 119–124).

Neumann, David J. 2019. "Domestic Security: Defending the Evangelical Home in the Southern California Sunbelt." *Journal of Religious History* 43, no. 1: 83–107.

Nicolaides, Becky. 2002. *My Blue Heaven: Life and Politics in Working-Class Suburbs of Los Angeles.* Chicago: University of Chicago Press.

Niebuhr, H. Richard. 1956. *Christ and Culture.* New York: Harper & Row.

Noll, Mark A. 1994. *The Scandal of the Evangelical Mind.* Grand Rapids, MI: Wm. B. Eerdmans Publishing Co.

Noll, Mark A. 2003. *The Rise of Evangelicalism: The Age of Edwards, Whitefield, and the Wesleys.* Downers Grove, IL: InterVarsity Press.

Noll, Mark A. 2019. *A History of Christianity in the United States and Canada.* 2019. Grand Rapids, MI: Wm. B. Eerdmans Publishing C.

Noll, Mark A., David W. Bebbington, and George M. Marsden, eds. 2019. *Evangelicals: Who They Have Been, Are Now, and Could Be.* Grand Rapids, MI: Wm. B. Eerdmans Publishing Co.

Numrich, Paul D. 1997. "Recent Immigrant Religions in a Restructuring Metropolis: New Religious Landscapes in Chicago." *Journal of Cultural Geography* 17, no. 1: 55–76.

Numrich, Paul D., and Elfriede Wedam. 2015. *Religion and Community in the New Urban America.* New York: Oxford University Press.

O'Brien, Brandon J. 2019. *Not From Around Here: What Unites Us, What Divides Us, and How We Can Move Forward.* Chicago: Moody Publishers.

Okulicz-Kozaryn, Adam. 2017. "Unhappy Metropolis (When American City is Too Big)." *Cities* 61: 144–155.

Olson, Gordon L., ed. 1989. *Themes in Grand Rapids History.* Grand Rapids, MI: Public History Press.

Orange County Board of Supervisors. 1965. *Orange County's Diamond Jubilee.* Santa Ana, CA: Orange County Board of Supervisors.

Orfield, Myron. 2002. *American Metropolitics: The New Suburban Reality.* Washington, DC: Brookings Institution Press.

Orsi, Robert A., ed. 1999. *Gods of the City: Religion and the American Urban Landscape.* Bloomington, IN: Indiana University Press.

Orthodox Presbyterian Church. 2021. "Fighting the Good Fight: A Brief History of the Orthodox Presbyterian Church." https://opc.org/books/fighting/pt1.html.

Oyakawa, Michelle. 2019. "Racial Reconciliation as a Suppressive Frame in Evangelical Multiracial Churches." *Sociology of Religion* 80, no. 4: 496–517.

Padoongpatt, Tanachai Mark. 2015. "'A Landmark for Sun Valley': Wat Thai of Los Angeles and Thai American Suburban Culture in 1980s San Fernando Valley." *Journal of American Ethnic History* 34, no. 2: 83–114.

Park, Robert E., and Ernest W. Burgess. 1925. *The City.* Chicago: University of Chicago Press.

Parker, Kim, Juliana Horowitz, Anna Brown, Richard Fry, D'Vera Cohn, and Ruth Igielnik. 2018. "What Unites and Divides Urban, Suburban and Rural Communities." Pew Research

Center. https://www.pewresearch.org/social-trends/wp-content/uploads/sites/3/2018/05/Pew-Research-Center-Community-Type-Full-Report-FINAL.pdf.

Parisi, Domenico, Daniel T. Lichter, and Michael C. Taquino. 2019. "Remaking Metropolitan America? Residential Mobility and Racial Integration in the Suburbs." *Socius*. https://doi.org/10.1177/2378023119854882.

Parker, Kim, Juliana Menasce Horowitz, and Rachel Minkin. 2021. "Americans Are Less Likely than Before COVID-19 to Want to Live in Cities, More Likely to Prefer Suburbs." Pew Research Center. https://www.pewresearch.org/social-trends/2021/12/16/americans-are-less-likely-than-before-covid-19-to-want-to-live-in-cities-more-likely-to-prefer-suburbs/.

Payne, Leah. 2024. *God Gave Rock and Roll to You: A History of Contemporary Christian Music.* New York: Oxford University Press.

Peters, Marjorie Herlache, ed. 1981. *DuPage County, Illinois, Churches and Their Records.* Lombard, IL: Lombard Suburban Genealogical Society.

Peterson, Andrew. 2021. *The God in the Garden: Thoughts on Creation, Culture, and the Kingdom.* Nashville: B&H Publishing Group.

Pew Research. 2015. "Religious Landscape Study." https://www.pewforum.org/religious-landscape-study/.

Philbrick, Richard. 1962. "Graham Heard by 116,000; Rally is Largest for Evangelist in N. America." *Chicago Tribune*, June 18.

Pierce, Victoria. 2000. "World Relief Set to Relocate Its Wheaton Headquarters." *Daily Herald*, July 11.

Pilgrim Baptist Church. 2011. "Rebuild Pilgrim Baptist Church." web.archive.org/web/20150324060919/http://rebuildingprilgrim.org/.

Plowman, Edward E. 1986. "Hispanic Christians in the United States." *Christianity Today*, January 17.

Porter, Michael E. 1996. "Competitive Advantage, Agglomeration Economies, and Regional Policy." *International Regional Science Review* 19, no. (2): 85–94.

Portes, Alejandro, and Min Zhou. 1993. "The New Second Generation: Segmented Assimilation and its Variants." *ANNALS of the American Academy of Political and Social Science* 530, no. 1: 74–96.

Price, Jay M. 2013. *Temples for a Modern God: Religious Architecture in Postwar America.* New York: Oxford University Press.

Pritchard, E. R. 1897. *Illinois of To-Day and Its Progressive Cities.* Chicago: Illinois of To-day.

"Prohibition Information." n.d. Brochure. The Citizens to End Prohibition. In Archives of Center for History in Wheaton.

Pruter, Robert, and Richard A. Thompson, eds. *DuPage Roots: Then and Now.* 2022. Wheaton, IL: DuPage County Historical Society.

Putnam, Robert D., and David E. Campbell. 2010. *American Grace: How Religion Divides and Unites Us.* New York: Simon & Schuster.

Rabey, Steve. 1991. "Head for the Mountains." *Christianity Today* 35, no. 14: 47.

"Racial Change." 1984. Editorial. *Chicago Tribune*, August 3.

Ranch Studios. 2017. *Godspeed: The Pace of Being Known.* https://vimeo.com/200206468.

Reardon, Patrick. 1983. "'Wet' Issue Uncorks a War for Wheaton." *Chicago Tribune*, March 13.

Redeemer Churches & Ministries. 2022. "Redeemer History." https://www.redeemer.com/learn/about_us/redeemer_history/.

Reed, Atavia. 2022. "Bronzeville's Pilgrim Baptist Church Gets $2 Million to Rebuild, Create National Museum of Gospel Music." *Block Club Chicago*, June 17. https://blockclubchicago.org/2022/06/17/bronzevilles-pilgrim-baptist-church-gets-2-million-to-rebuild-create-national-museum-of-gospel-music/.

Reformed Church in America. 2017. "Brief Outline of RCA History." https://www.rca.org/resources/rca-basics/brief-outline-rca-history.

"Religious Groups: Reformed/Presbyterian." 2017. Association of Religion Data Archives. http://www.thearda.com/denoms/Families/F_91.asp.

"Remember When Railroad Ran on Geneva Rd.?" 1959b. *The Daily Journal*, August 22.

Rivera, John. 2001. "Hoping to Bridge a Great Divide." *The Baltimore Sun*, January 25.

Riverside. 2023. "The History of Riverside." https://www.riverside.il.us/568/The-History-of-Riverside.

Riverside Presbyterian Church. 2023. "History of Riverside Presbyterian Church." https://www.rpcusa.org/history.

Roberts, Kyle B. 2016. *Evangelical Gotham: Religion and the Making of New York City, 1873–1860*. Chicago: University of Chicago Press.

Rodkin, Dennis. 2018. "These Chicago Suburbs Are Seeing White Flight." *Crain's Chicago Business*, March 14. https://www.chicagobusiness.com/article/20180314/CRED0701/180319958/chicago-suburbs-seeing-white-flight.

Rosell, Garth M. 2008. *The Surprising Work of God: Harold John Ockenga, Billy Graham, and the Rebirth of Evangelicalism*. Grand Rapids, MI: Baker Academic.

Rosenberg, Lee, and Saralee Rosenberg. 1993. *50 Fabulous Places to Raise Your Family*. Hawthorne, NJ: Career Press.

Rosenthal, Erich. 1960. "This Was North Lawndale: The Transplantation of a Jewish Community." *Jewish Social Studies* 22, no. 2: 67–82.

Rosenthal, Stuart S. and William C. Strange. 2004. "Evidence on the Nature and Sources of Agglomeration Economies." In *Handbook of Urban and Regional Economics: Cities an Geographies*, ed. J. Vernon Henderson and Jacques-Francois Thisse, 2110–2171. Amsterdam: Elsevier.

Rothstein, Richard. 2017. *The Color of Law: A Forgotten History of How our Government Segregated America*. New York: Liveright Publishing Corporation.

Rowley, Stephen. 2015. *Movie Towns and Sitcom Suburbs: Building Hollywood's Ideal Communities*. London: Palgrave MacMillan.

Ruotsila, Markku. 2016. *Fighting Fundamentalist: Carl McIntire and the Politicization of American Fundamentalism*. New York: Oxford University Press.

Rusk, David. 2013. *Cities Without Suburbs: A Census 2010 Perspective*. Washington, DC: Woodrow Wilson Center Press.

Sahagun, Louis. 1994. "Rise of Religious Groups Divides Conservative Town." *Los Angeles Times*, July 6.

Salamon, Sonya. 2003. *Newcomers to Old Towns: Suburbanization of the Heartland*. Chicago: University of Chicago Press.

Sandul, Paul J. P. 2019. "Texas Suburbia Rising." In *Lone Star Suburbs: Life on Texas's Metropolitan Frontier*, ed. Paul J. P. Sandul and M. Scott Sosebee, 3–48. Norman: University of Oklahoma Press.

Santana, Marco. 2011. "Once-dry Wheaton holds first Ale Fest." *Daily Herald*, August 5. https://www.dailyherald.com/20110805/news/once-dry-wheaton-holds-first-ale-fest/.

Sassen, Saskia. 2001. *The Global City: New York, London, Tokyo*. Princeton, NJ: Princeton University Press.

Saxenian, AnnaLee. 1996. "Inside-Out: Regional Networks and Industrial Adaptation in Silicon Valley and Route 128." *Cityscape* 2, no. 2: 41–60.

Scheitle, Christopher P. 2010. *Beyond the Congregation: The World of Christian Nonprofits*. New York: Oxford University Press.

Scheitle, Christopher P., Erica J. Dollhopf, and John D. McCarthy. 2017. "Spiritual Districts: The Origins and Dynamics of US Cities with Unusually High Concentrations of Parachurch Organizations." *Social Science History* 41, no. 3: 505–532.

Scheitle, Christopher P., and Kevin D. Dougherty. 2008. "The Sociology of Religious Organizations." *Sociology Compass* 2, no. 3: 981–999.

Scheitle, Christopher P., and John D. McCarthy. 2018. "The Mobilization of Evangelical Protestants in the Nonprofit Sector: Parachurch Foundings Across U.S. Counties, 1998–2016." *Journal for the Scientific Study of Religion* 57, no. 2: 238–257.

Schmeltzer, John. 1986. "'Vatican' of Religious Publishing Thrives: College's Talent Pool is Suburban Area Focal Point." *Chicago Tribune*, August 29.

Schmidt, Leone. 1989. *When the Democrats Ruled DuPage*. Warrenville, IL: L. Schmidt.

Schwarze, Pat. 1984. "Chamber Plans Blitz; To Pass Petitions for Liquor Referendum on Saturday." *The Wheaton Leader*, November 14.

Schultz, William John. 2017. "Garden of the Gods: Colorado Springs and the Fate of the Culture Wars." PhD diss., Princeton University.

Seeley, John R., R. Alexander Sim, and Elizabeth W. Loosley. 1956. *Crestwood Heights: A Study of the Culture of Suburban Life*. New York: Basic Books.

Sellers, Jeff M. 2002. "NAE Goes to Washington." *Christianity Today* 46, no. 7: 17.

Sellers, Jefferey M. 2013. "Places, Institutions and the Political Ecology of US Metropolitan Areas." In *The Political Ecology of the Metropolis*, ed. Jefferey M. Sellers, Daniel Kübler, Melanie Walter-Rogg, and R. Alan Walks, 37–86. Colchester: ECPR Press.

Shanahan, Ed. 2020. "How Trump Is Using Westchester to Stir Up Suburban Fears." *New York Times*, September 3. https://www.nytimes.com/2020/09/03/nyregion/trump-westchester-housing.html.

Sharlet, Jeff. 2005. "Soldiers of Christ: Inside America's Most Powerful Megachurch." *Harper's Magazine* May: 41–54.

Shellnut, Kate. 2017. "Tim Keller Stepping Down as Redeemer Senior Pastor." *Christianity Today*, February 26. https://www.christianitytoday.com/news/2017/february/tim-keller-stepping-down-nyc-redeemer-senior-pastor.html.

Shellnut, Kate. 2019. "National Association of Evangelicals' New President Hopes to Bring Together a Movement in Crisis." *Christianity Today*, October 17. https://www.christianitytoday.com/news/2019/october/national-association-evangelicals-walter-kim-president-nae.html.

Shelton, Jason E., and Michael O. Emerson. 2012. *Blacks and Whites in Christian America: How Racial Discrimination Shapes Religious Convictions*. New York: New York University Press.

Shibley, Mark A. 1998. "Contemporary Evangelicals: Born-Again and World Affirming." *ANNALS of the American Academy of Political and Social Science* 558, no. 1: 67–87.

Shippey, Frederick A. 1964. *Protestantism in Suburban Life*. New York: Abingdon Press.

Sider, Ronald J., John M. Perkins, Wayne L. Gordon, and F. Albert Tizon. 2008. *Linking Arms, Linking Lives: How Urban-Suburban Partnerships Can Transform Communities*. Grand Rapids, MI: Baker Books.

Silliman, Daniel. 2022. "Gordon-Conwell to Sell Main Campus, Move to Boston." *Christianity Today*, May 17. https://www.christianitytoday.com/news/2022/may/gordon-conwell-sell-campus-financial-enrollment-struggle.html.

Silliman, Daniel. 2023. "Died: Tim Keller, New York City Pastor Who Modeled Winsome Witness." *Christianity Today*, May 19. https://www.christianitytoday.com/news/2023/may/tim-keller-dead-redeemer-new-york-pastor-cancer.html?utm_source=ground.news&utm_medium=referral.

Silk, Mark, and Andrew Walsh. 2008. *One Nation, Divisible: How Regional Religious Differences Shape American Politics*. Lanham, MD: Rowman & Littlefield Publishers.

Silverstone, Roger. 1994. *Television and Everyday Life*. London: Taylor and Francis.

Singer, Audrey, Susan W. Hardwick, and Caroline B. Brettell, eds. 2008. *Twenty First Century Gateways: Immigrant Incorporation in Suburban America*. Washington, DC: Brookings Institution Press.

Sinha, Jill Witmer, Amy Hillier, Ram A. Cnaan, and Charlene C. McGrew. 2007. "Proximity Matters: Exploring Relationships Among Neighborhoods, Congregations, and the Residential Patterns of Members." *Journal for the Scientific Study of Religion* 46, no. 2: 245–260.

Sisson, Patrick. 2016. "Millennials Look to the Suburbs, Not Cities, for First Homes." *Curbed*. https://archive.curbed.com/2016/6/21/11956516/millennial-first-time-home-trends-suburbs.

Skinner, Tom. 1970. "The U.S. Racial Crisis and World Evangelism (1970)." InterVarsity Urbana. https://urbana.org/transcript/us-racial-crisis-and-world-evangelism-1970 (accessed May 24, 2023).

Smith, Christian. 1998. *American Evangelicalism: Embattled and Thriving*. Chicago: University of Chicago Press.

Smith, Gregory A. 2021. "About Three-in-Ten U.S. Adults Are Now Religiously Unaffiliated." Pew Research. https://www.pewresearch.org/religion/2021/12/14/about-three-in-ten-u-s-adults-are-now-religiously-unaffiliated/.

Sobieraj, Sandra. 2002. "Bush Sets Goal on Home Ownership." Associated Press, June 17. https://apnews.com/27408f4c4ca707f6f93a403486edc157.

Sparks, Paul, Tim Soerens, and Dwight J. Friesen. 2014. *The New Parish: How Neighborhood Churches are Transforming Mission, Discipleship and Community*. Downers Grove, IL: IVP Books.

Spigel, Lynn. 2001. *Welcome to the Dreamhouse: Popular Media and Postwar Suburbs*. Durham, NC: Duke University Press.

Spillman, Lyn. 2012. *Solidarity in Strategy: Making Business Meaningful in American Trade Associations*. Chicago: University of Chicago Press.

Spillman, Lyn. 2020. *What Is Cultural Sociology?* Medford, MA: Polity.

Sprague, Marshall. 1971. *One Hundred Plus: A Centennial Story of Colorado Springs*. Colorado Springs: Colorado Springs Centennial, Inc.

Stammer, Larry B. 2001. "The Nation; Evangelical Group Chief Resigns Post." *Los Angeles Times*, June 21.

Stark, Rodney. 1996. *The Rise of Christianity: A Sociologist Reconsiders History*. Princeton, NJ: Princeton University Press.

Starr, Kevin. 2009. *Golden Dreams: California in an Age of Abundance, 1950–1963*. New York: Oxford University Press.

"Statistics on Crusade." 1959c. *The Daily Journal*, October 5.

Steensland, Brian, Jerry Z. Park, Mark D. Regnerus, Lynn D. Robinson, W. Bradford Wilcox, and Robert D. Woodberry. 2000. "The Measure of American Religion: Toward Improving the State of the Art." *Social Forces* 79: 291–324.

Stellway, Richard J. 1990. *Christiantown, USA*. New York: Haworth Press.

Stetzer, Ed, and Ryan P. Burge. 2015. "Reltrad Coding Problems and a New Repository." *Politics and Religion* 9, no. 1: 187–190.

Stewart, Beverly. 1989. "Church Outreach, Suburban Zoning Often at Odds." *Chicago Tribune*, February 24.

Stott, Anne. 2012. *Wilberforce: Family and Friends*. New York: Oxford University Press.

Strachan, Owen. 2015. *Awakening the Evangelical Mind: An Intellectual History of the Neo-Evangelical Movement*. Grand Rapids, MI: Zondervan.

Strhan, Anna. 2015. *Aliens and Strangers? The Struggle for Coherence in the Everyday Lives of Evangelicals*. Oxford: Oxford University Press.

Sugrue, Thomas J. 1996. *The Origins of the Urban Crisis: Race and Inequality in Postwar Detroit*. Princeton, NJ: Princeton University Press.

Sullivan, Barbara. 1989. "Conservatism, Football Bring Out Worshippers." *Chicago Tribune*, April 8.

Sutton, Matthew Avery. 2014. *American Apocalypse: A History of Modern Evangelicalism*. Cambridge, MA: The Belknap Press of Harvard University Press.

Sutton, Matthew Avery. 2024. "Redefining the History and Historiography on American Evangelicalism in the Era of the Religious Right." *Journal of the American Academy of Religion*. https://doi.org/10.1093/jaarel/lfae063.

Swartz, David R. 2012. *Moral Minority: The Evangelical Left in an Age of Conservatism*. Philadelphia: University of Pennsylvania Press.

Swartz, Lisa Weaver. 2023. *Stained Glass Ceilings: How Evangelicals Do Gender and Practice Power*. New Brunswick, NJ: Rutgers University Press.

Swidler, Ann. 1986. "Culture in Action: Symbols and Strategies." *American Sociological Review* 51, no. 2: 273–286.

Swidler, Ann. 2001. *Talk of Love: How Culture Matters*. Chicago: University of Chicago Press.

Swierenga, Robert P. 1980. "Local-Cosmopolitan Theory and Immigrant Religion: The Social Bases of the Antebellum Dutch Reformed Schism." *Journal of Social History* 14, no. 1: 113–135.

Swierenga, Robert P. 2002. *Dutch Chicago: A History of the Hollanders in the Windy City*. Grand Rapids, MI: Wm. B. Eerdmans Publishing Co.

Swierenga, Robert P. 2004. "The Western Michigan Dutch." Paper presented to the Holland Genealogical Society, Holland, MI, December 11. http://www.swierenga.com/hgspap1204.html.

Swierenga, Robert P., and Elton J. Bruins. 1999. *Family Quarrels in the Dutch Reformed Churches in the Nineteenth Century: The Pillar Church Sesquicentennial Lectures*. Grand Rapids, MI: Wm. B. Eerdmans Publishing Co.

Swint, Sharon. 2010. *Remembering Colorado Springs*. New York: Turner Publishing Company.

Taylor, Graham Romeyn. 1915. *Satellite Cities: A Study of Industrial Suburbs*. New York: D. Appleton and Company.

Teaford, Jon C. 1997. *Post-Suburbia: Government and Politics in the Edge Cities*. Baltimore: Johns Hopkins University Press.

Teaford, Jon C. 2008. *The American Suburb: The Basics*. New York: Routledge.

Thiessen, Joel, and Sarah Wilkins-Laflamme. 2020. *None of the Above: Non-Religious Identity in the US and Canada*. New York: New York University Press.

Thomma, Steven. 2011. "Small-Town America—the Myth and the Reality." *McClatchy Newspapers*, August 21. https://www.mcclatchydc.com/news/nation-world/national/article24694813.html.

Thompson, Richard A. 1985. *DuPage Roots*. Wheaton, IL: DuPage County Historical Society.

Thumma, Scott, and Warren Bird. 2008. "Changes in American Megachurches: Tracing Eight Years of Growth and Innovation in the Nation's Largest-Attendance Congregations." Leadership Network and Hartford Institute for Religion Research. http://www.hirr.hartsem.edu/megachurch/Changes%20in%20American%20Megachurches%20Sept%2012%202008.pdf.

Thumma, Scott, and Warren Bird. 2015. "Recent Shifts in America's Largest Protestant Churches: Megachurches 2015 Report." http://www.hartfordinstitute.com/megachurch/2015_Megachurches_Report.pdf.

Thumma, Scott, and Dave Travis. 2007. *Beyond Megachurch Myths: What We Can Learn from America's Largest Churches*. San Francisco: Jossey-Bass.

Timmerman, John J. 1975. *Promises to Keep: A Centennial History of Calvin College*. Grand Rapids, MI: Calvin College and Seminary with Wm. B. Eerdmans Publishing Co.

Tomkins, Stephen. 2010. *The Clapham Sect: How Wilberforce's Circle Transformed Britain*. Oxford: Lion.

Tosh, John. 1999. *A Man's Place: Masculinity and the Middle-Class Home in Victorian England*. New Haven, CT: Yale University Press.

Tranby, Eric, and Douglas Hartmann. 2008. "Critical Whiteness Theories and the Evangelical 'Race Problem': Extending Emerson and Smith's *Divided by Faith*." *Journal for the Scientific Study of Religion* 47, no. 3: 341–359.

Troeltsch, Ernst. 1931. *The Social Teaching of the Christian Churches*. Translated by Olive Wyon. New York: Macmillan.

Tuttle, Charles R. 1874. *History of Grand Rapids: With Biographical Sketches*. Grand Rapids, MI: Tuttle & Cooney.

US Census Bureau. 2001. "Ranking Tables for Metropolitan Areas: Population in 2000 and Population Change from 1990 to 2000." https://www.census.gov/data/tables/2000/dec/phc-t-03.html"https://www.census.gov/data/tables/2000/dec/phc-t-03.html.

US Census Bureau. 2002. "Demographic Trends in the 20th Century." http://www.census.gov/prod/2002pubs/censr-4.pdf.
US Census Bureau. 2023. "QuickFacts: Lexington town, Middlesex County, Massachusetts." https://www.census.gov/quickfacts/fact/table/lexingtontownmiddlesexcountymassachusetts/HSD410221.
US Department of Commerce. 1990. "1990 Census of Population; General Population Characteristics; Illinois." ftp://ftp2.census.gov/library/publications/1992/dec/cp-1-15.pdf (accessed February 9, 2015).
Vaca, Daniel. 2019. *Evangelicals Incorporated: Books and the Business of Religion in America*. Cambridge, MA: Harvard University Press.
Vanderstel, David G. 1983. *The Dutch of Grand Rapids, Michigan, 1848–1900: Immigrant Neighborhood and Community Development in a Nineteenth Century City*. PhD diss., Kent State University.
Vermeulen, Timotheus. 2014. *Scenes from the Suburbs: The Suburb in Contemporary US Film and Television*. Edinburgh: Edinburgh University Press.
Vermurlen, Brad. 2020. *Reformed Resurgence: The New Calvinist Movement and the Battle Over American Evangelicalism*. New York: Oxford University Press.
Vescey, George. 1978. "Chicago Suburb is 'Vatican of Evangelicals': A Corporate 'Christian Ghetto.'" *New York Times*, July 21.
Vicino, Thomas. 2013. *Suburban Crossroads: The Fight for Local Control of Immigration Policy*. Lanham, MD: Lexington Books.
Wacker, Grant. 2014. *America's Pastor: Billy Graham and the Shaping of a Nation*. Cambridge, MA: Harvard University Press.
Wacker, Grant. 2017. "Introduction." In *Billy Graham: America Pilgrim*, ed. Andrew S. Finstuen, Grant Wacker, and Anne Blue Willis, 1–20. New York: Oxford University Press.
Wacker, Grant. 2019. *One Soul at a Time: The Story of Billy Graham*. Grand Rapids, MI: Wm. B. Eerdmans Publishing Co.
Wallace, Elizabeth. 2003. *Colorado Springs*. Chicago: Arcadia Publishing.
Warf, Barney, and Morton Winsberg. 2010. "Geographies of Megachurches in the United States." *Journal of Cultural Geography* 27, no. 1: 33–51.
Warikoo, Natasha Kumar. 2022. *Race at the Top: Asian Americans and Whites in Pursuit of the American Dream in Suburban Schools*. Chicago: University of Chicago Press.
Warner, Sam Bass. 1978. *Streetcar Suburbs: The Process of Growth in Boston, 1870–1900*. Cambridge, MA: Harvard University Press.
Warner, R. Stephen. 2007. "The Role of Religion in the Process of Segmented Assimilation." *ANNALS of the American Academy of Political and Social Science* 612, no. 1: 100–115.
Warner, W. Lloyd, and D. Martin. 1967. "Big Trade and Business Associations." In *The Emergent American Society, Vol. 1*, ed. W. L. Warner, 314–346. New Haven, CT: Yale University Press.
Weber, Max. 1930. *The Protestant Ethic and the Spirit of Capitalism*. Translated by Talcott Parsons. New York: Scribner.
Weber, Max. 1978. *Economy & Society*. Edited by Guenther Roth and Claus Wittich. Berkeley: University of California Press.
Weinstein, Michael L., and Davin Seay. 2006. *With God on our Side: One Man's War Against an Evangelical Coup in America's Military*. New York: Thomas Dunne Books.
Wellman, James K. Jr. 1999. *The Gold Coast Church and the Ghetto: Christ and Culture in Mainline Protestantism*. Urbana: University of Illinois Press.
Wellman, James K., Katie E. Corcoran, and Kate J. Stockly. 2020. *High on God: How Megachurches Won the Heart of America*. New York: Oxford University Press.
"Wheaton." 2022. Niche. https://www.niche.com/places-to-live/wheaton-dupage-il/.
Wheaton Bible Church. 2022. "About Wheaton Bible." https://wheatonbible.org/about/wheaton-bible-church/about-wheaton-bible/.
Wheaton Public Library. 2021. "The First Civil Rights March in Wheaton." https://www.youtube.com/watch?v=1DcjLVcSPMU.

Wheaton Suburban Living. 2003. "Wheaton." *Wheaton Suburban Living*, March/April, 90–101.
The White House. 2003. "President Bush Signs American Dream Downpayment." https://geor gewbush-whitehouse.archives.gov/news/releases/2003/12/20031216-9.html.
Whitehead, Andrew L., and Samuel L. Perry. 2020. *Taking America Back for God: Christian Nationalism in the United States*. New York: Oxford University Press.
Whyte, William H., Jr. 1956. *The Organization Man*. New York: Simon and Schuster.
Wiese, Andrew. 2004. *Places of Their Own: African American Suburbanization in the Twentieth Century*. Chicago: University of Chicago Press.
Wilcox, W. Bradford. 2009. "How Focused on the Family? Evangelical Protestants, the Family, and Sexuality." In *Evangelicals and Democracy in America—Volume 1: Religion and Society*, ed. Steven Brint and Jean Reith Schroedel, 251–275. New York: Russell Sage Foundation.
Wilford, Justin G. 2012. *Sacred Subdivisions: The Postsuburban Transformation of American Evangelicalism*. New York: New York University Press.
Wilkerson, Isabel. 2010. *The Warmth of Other Suns: The Epic Story of America's Great Migration*. New York: Random House.
Willard, W. Wyeth. 1950. *Fire on the Prairie*. Wheaton, IL: Van Kampen Press.
Williams, George G. 1959. "Billy Sunday 'Pitched' Fire and Brimstone Here." *The Daily Journal*, October 3.
Wilson, William Julius. 1996. *When Work Disappears: The World of the New Urban Poor*. New York: Knopf.
Winchester, Daniel, and Jeffrey Guhin. 2019. "Praying 'Straight from the Heart': Evangelical Sincerity and the Normative Frames of Culture in Action." *Poetics* 72: 32–42.
Winston, Diane H. 1999. *Red-Hot and Righteous: The Urban Religion of the Salvation Army*. Cambridge, MA: Harvard University Press.
Winter, Gibson. 1961. *The Suburban Captivity of the Churches: An Analysis of Protestant Responsibility in the Expanding Metropolis*. Garden City, NY: Doubleday.
Wirth, Louis, and Eleanor H. Bernert, eds. 1949. *Local Community Fact Book of Chicago*. Chicago: University of Chicago Press.
Woodard, Colin. 2011. *American Nations: A History of the Eleven Rival Regional Cultures of North America*. New York: Penguin Books.
Woodward, Kenneth. 1976. "Born Again!" *Newsweek*, October 25, 68–76.
Wuthnow, Robert. 1988. *The Restructuring of American Religion: Society and Faith Since World War II*. Princeton, NJ: Princeton University Press.
Wuthnow, Robert. 2007. *After the Baby Boomers: How Twenty- and Thirty-Somethings are Shaping the Future of American Religion*. Princeton, NJ: Princeton University Press.
Wuthnow, Robert. 2013. *Small-Town America: Finding Community, Shaping the Future*. Princeton, NJ: Princeton University Press.
Wyckoff, William. 1999. *Creating Colorado: The Making of a Western American Landscape*. New Haven, CT: Yale University Press.
Yeo, K. K., and Gene L. Green, eds. 2021. *Theologies of Land: Contested Land, Spatial Justice, and Identity*. Eugene, OR: Cascade Books.
Zelinsky, Wilbur. 1961. "An Approach to the Religious Geography of the United States: Patterns of Church Membership in 1952." *Annals of the Association of American Geographers* 51, no. 2: 139–193.
Zelinsky, Wilbur. 2001. "The Uniqueness of the American Religious Landscape." *The Geographical Review* 91, no. 3: 565–585.
Zelinsky, Wilbur, and Stephen A. Matthews. 2011. *The Place of Religion in Chicago*. Chicago: Center for American Places.

Index

For the benefit of digital users, indexed terms that span two pages (e.g., 52–53) may, on occasion, appear on only one of those pages.

Tables and figures are indicated by an italic *t* and *f* following the page number.

ACCC. *See* American Council of Christian Churches
Acts 29 global conference, 25
Addams, Jane, 44–45
African Methodist Episcopal (AME), 10, 63–64, 66–68, 69, 77–78
alcohol, Wheaton, Illinois, 112–14
American Beauty (film), 2
American cities
   American Protestantism, 42
   cities as centers of worship, 40
   and Clapham, England, 41–42
   and early European settlement, 39–40
   and English religious movements, 40–41
   plans for communities outside cities, 40
   Roman roots of, 40
   single-family homes, 42
American Community Survey, 114–15
American Council of Christian Churches (ACCC), 87–88
American Dream, 2–3
   communities idealized in, 13
   seeking out, 14
   suburban faith and critiques, 25–27
   suburbs as part of, 4
   support for, 19
American Idiot, 183–84
American suburbs, 36–37
   adding to theories of religion and place, 32–36
   convergence of evangelicals and, 23–30
   criticism of, 14
   cultural affinities, 29–30
   defining suburbs and evangelicals, 16–22
   "greyness" of, 14
   megachurches and, 23–25
   overview, 14–16
   politicians and, 27–29
   previous studies of, 30–32
   suburban faith and critiques, 25–27

American Theosophical Society, 111
Ammerman, Nancy T., 125
Anderson, Leith, 38–39, 81–82
anti-urban sentiments, 29–30
Assemblies of God, 84, 92
Audio Adrenaline, 8
Azusa Pacific University, 132–33

Baker, 131–32
bedroom suburbs, 18
Berry, Wendell, 179
Bethany, suburb connection to, 38–39
Beyond the Congregation: The World of Christian Nonprofits (Scheitle), 124
Bible Belt, 3–4, 8–44, 51–52, 99, 103–4, 160–61
Bible Presbyterian Church, 87–88
Bielo, James, 147
Billy Graham Center, 118
Billy Graham Evangelistic Association, 166–67
Biola University, 37
Biola University: Rooted for One Hundred Years (Biola University), 37
Black protestants, 12, 20–21, 149–56, 157, 158–59
Bluetree, 193
Board Members (NAE), locations of, 89–92, 90*t*
books
   analysis of, 167–71
   Billy Graham on suburbs and other places in, 171–78
boomburbs, 18
Boston Missionary Training Institute, 57–58
Brethren Church (Argentina), 91–92
Brooklyn, 42–43
Bureau of Justice Statistics, 17
Burge, Ryan, 144
Brueggemann, Walter, 194
Bush, George W., 2, 27–29, 52–53
Buswell, J. O., 88–89
Butler, Anthea, 165, 183

228 INDEX

Calvary Chapel, 31
Cambridge evangelicals, 98–99
Cantrell, Randolph L., 73–74
Cape Town Commitment, 57
Carter, Jimmy, 27, 52–53
Catholics, 20
Cavalcanti, H. B., 30
CCCU. *See* Council for Christian Colleges & Universities
CCM. *See* Contemporary Christian Music
Chatterley, Greg, 93–94
Chaves, Mark, 107–8
Chicago Church Federation, 63
Chicago, Illinois, evangelicals leaving
 church location patterns, 63–64, 65*t*
 churches in Chicago metropolitan region, 65*t*
 in decades leading up to twentieth century, 79–80
 evangelicals, Protestants, and whiteflight, 77–78
 example of congregation development, 60–63
 patterns in white flight, 66–77
Chicago Race Riot, 60–61
Christian Century, 21–22, 61
Christianity Today, 21–22, 98, 142
Christian Reformed Church (CRC), 62, 63–64, 84, 125–26, 189–90
Christiantown, USA. *See* Wheaton, Illinois
Church Federation of Great Chicago, 63, 76, 77
Church of Jesus Christ of Latter-day Saints, 3
cities, theology of, 143
City of God (Augustine), 101
Civil War, 42–43
Claiborne, Shane, 160–61
Clapham, England, 41–42
clusters
 Colorado Springs, Colorado, 128–30
 comparisons across four clusters, 135–37
 East Los Angeles County, California, 132–34
 ecological perspective on, 138
 explaining, 123–27, 137–40
 Grand Rapids, Michigan, 130–32
 influence of, 137–40
 Orange County, California, 132–34
 start and continuation of, 140–41
 studying, 127–28
 Wheaton, Illinois, 134–35
Colorado Springs, Colorado, 11–12, 122–23, 128–30
Colorado Springs' Economic Development Corporation, 123
Columbus, Ohio, congregations in, 33–34

communities, 160–61
 community history of Wheaton, Illinois, 109–14
 differences in population size, 152
 Evangelical Epicenters, 146
 factors shaping types of, 159–60
 Mormon Outposts, 146
 moving from cities and rural areas to suburbs, 156–60
 Nonaffiliated in, 159–60
 over time, 148–56
 patterns of mobility, 156–57
 race-place intersection, 157–58
 religious communities across types of, 145–48
 rural communities, 86, 109
 SRCBELT community types, 149–52, 151*t*, 155, 155*t*
 studying, 189
 types over time, 152–56
 Urban Monastery, 147–48
 where evangelicals live, 142–45
 XNORCSIZ community types, 149, 150*t*, 154–55, 154*t*
competition, religions and, 32–34
Congregational Christian, 63–64
congregations
 competing for attendees, 125–26
 evangelical congregations, 10–11, 22, 29, 33–34, 51–52, 53–54, 56, 79–80, 97–98, 101–2, 121, 126, 184, 193, 199
 Presbyterian congregations, 60, 69–70
 Protestant congregations, 58–59, 63, 64, 77, 78, 108–9
 RCA concentrations, 67, 72–73
 white congregations, 35, 172
connection between religion and suburbs, studying
 deepness articulation, 4–5
 evangelicals as group, 5
 making case, 8–13
 personal component, 5–6
 seeking out data, 7–8
 urban sociology, 6
 Wheaton, Illinois, 6–7
Conservative Congregational Christian Conference, 82
conservative Protestants, 14–15, 20–22, 25–26, 31, 35–36, 48, 49–50, 61, 77–78, 98, 146
Contemporary Christian Music (CCM), 8
Conwell School of Theology, 57–58
Cook County, Illinois, 63–64, 65*t*, 74–75
Council for Christian Colleges & Universities (CCCU), 36

Cox, Harvey, 52
Cracks in the Picture Window (novel), 2
CRC. *See* Christian Reformed Church
critiques and faith, suburban, 25–27
Crystal Cathedral, 31
cultural affinities, 29–30
cultural toolkits, 9, 35–36
    Billy Graham and, 167–71
    Billy Graham as evangelical
        exemplar, 166–67
    Billy Graham illustrating, 178–81
    components of, 163–65
    example of, 162–63
    understanding places and religion and
        place, 195–99

Dacula, Georgia, 33
Darwin, Charles, 44–45
data, previous studies of evangelicals and
    suburbs, 30–32
*Death by Suburb: How to Stop the Suburbs from
    Killing Your Soul* (Goetz), 30
Declaration of Seven Divine Freedoms, 49
delegates (NAE), locations of, 85
    difference in regions, 86
    hailing from cities, 85–86
    hailing from communities of under 50,000
        people, 86
    significant attendees, 86–89
Diamond, Etan, 33, 50–51
Dictionary of Jesus and the Gospels, 38
Disciples of Christ, 63–64
Dobson, James, 52–53, 122, 123
Dollhopf, Erica J., 31, 124, 137, 147
Doughtery, Kevin, 33
Dugandzic, Audra, 146, 197–98
DuPage County, Illinois, 63–64, 65*t*, 74–75,
    76, 109–11
Durkheim, Emile, 143
Dutch immigrants, coming of, 135

East Los Angeles County, California, 132–34
ECFA. *See* Evangelical Council for Financial
    Accountability
ecological theory, 32–34, 78, 97–98, 125, 138, 196
    marketplace argument (Wheaton,
        Illinois), 108–9
edge cities, 18
Eerdmans, 131–32
Eiesland, Nancy, 33, 146
Eisenhower, Dwight D., 49, 100
ELCA. *See* Evangelical Lutheran Church of
    America

Elisha, Omri, 147
Emerson, Michael O., 164
Encyclopedia of Chicago, 114
Episcopal, 63–64
ethnoburbs, 54
*Evangelical Action! A Report of the Organization
    of the National Association of Evangelicals
    for United Action*, 85
Evangelical Council for Financial
    Accountability (ECFA), 127–28
Evangelical Epicenters, 146
Evangelical Free Church of America, 84
Evangelical Lutheran Church of America
    (ELCA), 73–74, 74*f*–75*f*
evangelicals, 200–1
    adapting to suburbs, 51–52
    adding to theories of religion and
        place, 32–36
    and American Dream in suburbs, 14–37
    beliefs of, 20–21
    books about apocalypse, 182–85
    communities serving as homes for, 142–61
    complexity and variation, 22
    convergence in Wheaton, Illinois, 105–9
    cultural affinities between suburban life and
        life of, 29–30
    cultural toolkits of, 162–81
    defining, 16–22
    engaging in more robust thinking, 193–98
    epicenters for, 31
    growth through early 1960s, 47–52
    leaving Chicago for suburbs, 60–80
    marking 1976 as critical year for
        evangelicals, 52–53
    megachurches and, 23–25
    megachurches and organizations, 81–102
    modern evangelical history, 21–22
    naming and praying for, 1–2
    neo-evangelicals, 49–50
    organizational structure of, 22
    and other religious traditions across
        community types, 145–48
    parachurch organizations, 122–41
    as politicians, 27–29
    as powerful internationalists, 28
    previous studies of, 30–32
    race, class, and gender in suburbs, 187–90
    road to studying, 4–8
    short history of, 38–59
    spatial dimensions of life of, 185–87
    suburban faith and critiques, 25–27
    suburbs and evangelicals history, 57–59
    suburbs and evangelicals in-between, 190–93

230 INDEX

evangelicals (cont.)
  theological distinctions, 21
  in Wheaton, Illinois, 103–21
Evans, Curtis, 167

Fair Housing Act of 1968, 55
faith and critiques, suburban, 25–27
Falwell, Jerry, 52–53
FCC. See Federal Communication Commission
Federal Communication Commission (FCC), 98
50 Fabulous Places to Raise Your Family, 117
First Baptist Church, 110–11
First Methodist Episcopal Church, 110–11
Fishman, Robert, 41
Focus on the Family, 122–23
Folds, Ben, 1–2, 8, 193
Fourth Presbyterian Church, 60–61
Freudenberg, William, 105
Friedan, Betty, 49
First Great Awakening, 42
Fuller, Charles, 99
Fuller Evangelical Association, 91–92
Fuller Seminary, 99
fundamentalism, 44–46
  American fundamentalism, 36, 88
  revivalist individualism, 49–50
Fundamentals, The (Stewart), 37

Gallup, George, 20, 52–53
Garden Grove Community Church, 25, 122
Gary, Erastus, 109–10
Gary Methodist Episcopal Church, 110–11
Gary-Wheaton Bank, 95, 111–12
General Association of Regular Baptist Churches, 131–32
General Social Survey, 12, 144, 145, 156
geography, evangelicals and, 3–4
Gingrich, Newt, 186
God-filled life, vision of, 30
God in the Garden, The (Peterson), 178–79
"God of this City" (song), 193–94
Goetz, David, 30
Gone Girl (novel), 2
Gordon-Conwell Seminary, 57–59
Graham, Billy, 21–22, 27, 46–47, 50, 94, 98, 111–12, 117, 161, 163, 188, 194, 198–99
  analyzing books of, 167–71
  comparisons between urban and rural life, 174–75
  consistency about needs of communities, 171
  on crime, lawlessness, and unrest, 175–76
  discussing suburbs and cities, 171
  on discussions of heaven, 176–77
  and evangelical cultural toolkits, 167–71
  as evangelical exemplar, 166–67
  illustrating cultural toolkits, 178–81
  making points about cities and societies today, 176
  mentioning suburban life, 173
  on ministry opportunities, 171–72
  and New York City, 177–78
  on race problem, 172–73
  recognizing white flight, 172
  on suburbs and other places in books of, 171–78
  talks of visiting "slums of our inner cities," 173
  on teenagers and young adults, 173–74
Grand Rapids, Michigan, 11–12, 33–34, 130–32
Great Depression, 17–18, 47–48, 101
Great Divorce, The (Lewis), 14–15
Great Migration, 46
Greeley, Andrew, 25–26, 199–200
Green Day, 183–84
Green, Joel B., 38–39
Growth machine theory. See political economy theory
Gunderson, Carl A, 93–94, 135

Haggard, Ted, 81, 129
Hartman, Douglas, 165
Hastert, Dennis, 186
headquarters (NAE), locations of, 92–93
  in California, 95–96
  in Illinois, 93–95
  importance of NAE in multiple locations, 97–100
  in Washington, DC, 96–97
Henry, Carl F. H., 21–22, 101
Hindus, 19
history, evangelicals and suburbs, 57–59
  American cities, 39–42
  entering twenty-first century, 52–57
  growing American urbanism, 42–47
  modernism, 42–47
  overview, 38–39
  postwar growth through early 1960s, 47–52
  religious fundamentalism, 42–47
  suburban retreats, 39–42
Hochschild, Arlie, 143
Hollywood, 95, 100
homeownership, 28, 46, 47–48, 54, 200–1
homeownership gap, 28
Houghton, William Henry, 88–89
Houston, Texas, 53–54

Howe, Justine, 197–98
Hunter, James, 164–65, 198
Hybels, Bill, 25

Immigrants in suburbs, 19, 54, 55, 158–59, 192–93
Immigration Act of 1924, 46
Immigration and Nationality Act 1965, 19, 54
in-between, suburbs and evangelicals, 190–93
individual virtue, 45
inner-ring suburbs, 18
International Pentecostal Holiness Church, 84

Jennings, Willie James, 162–63, 194
Jesusland, evangelicals in
    making case for evangelical-suburbs connection, 8–13
    naming and praying for suburban evangelicals, 1–2
    religion and suburbs, 2–4
    road to studying suburbs and evangelicals, 4–8
Jews, 3, 12, 19, 26, 44, 46, 49, 50–51, 68–69, 78, 79–80, 125–26, 149–56
John 14: 2– 4, 8–9

Keller, Tim, 3–4, 56–57, 142–43, 161
Kerry, John, 2
Kim, Walter, 87
Kingdom of God, 36, 82, 101, 173
Kregel, 131–32

Lake County, Illinois, 63–64, 65t, 74–75
Leave It to Beaver (film), 2
Left Behind (series), 182–85
LeShana, David, 91
Lester, Ross, 25–26
Lewis, C. S., 14–15
liquor referendum, Wheaton, Illinois, 112–14
Living Bible, The, 118–19, 182
location changes (Chicago region), studying, 63–64, 65t
locations (NAE), importance of
    Cambridge evangelicals, 98–99
    desired sphere of influence, 100
    interplay between suburban and urban locations, 98
    metropolitan regions, 97–98
    places in South, 99–100
Look magazine, 116
Los Angeles, California, 11–12
Louis XVI, king, 40
Luhr, Eileen, 108

Lutheran Church Missouri Synod, 62, 74–75, 75f

Machen, J. Gresham, 88
mainline Protestants, 12, 20–21, 33–34, 51, 108–9, 149–56, 157
majority white community (Wheaton, Illinois), 114–16
Mannoia, Kevin, 95, 96, 100
Markofski, Wes, 147–48
Marsden, George, 36
Marshall, Alfred, 124–25
Martí, Gerardo, 140, 165, 183
Massachusetts Bay Colony, 40
mass media, depiction of suburbs by, 48–49
Matthews, Stephen A., 99
McIntire, Carl, 49–50, 87–88
McKibben, Bill, 79–80
McMahon, Eileen M., 146
McRoberts, Omar, 126–27
megachurches, 23–25, 185–86
    overview, 81–84
men
    mass media depiction of, 48
    and start of suburbanization, 46
Merton, Thomas, 179
Methodists, 67, 73–74
metropolitan statistical area (MSA), 16–17
middle class, 1–2, 15, 17–18, 24–25, 29, 43, 44
militant evangelicalism, 46–47
Miranda, Juan Carlos, 91–92
Miranda, Maria, 91–92
Missouri Synod Lutherans, 62, 74–75
Moberg, David, 25–26
modernism, 44–46
Molotch, Harvey, 105
Money, 81
Moody Bible Institute, 45, 61, 89, 93–94
Moody, Dwight, 45
Moral Majority, rise of, 23
moral minimalism, prevalence of, 107–8
Mormon Outposts, 146
MSA. *See* metropolitan statistical area
Mulder, Mark, 33, 78, 140
Muslims, 19, 55, 125–26, 197–98

NAE. *See* National Association of Evangelicals
National Association of Evangelicals (NAE), 10–11, 38, 80, 101–2, 129, 196–97
    Board Member locations, 89–92, 90t
    formation of, 82–84
    headquarters locations, 92–97
    importance of NAE in multiple locations, 97–100

National Association of Evangelicals (NAE) (*cont.*)
  interplay between suburban and urban locations, 98
  location patterns among delegates of, 85–89
  location(s) of, 84–85
  overview, 81–84
  places in South, 99
National Bible Institute, 88–89
Nazarene Church, 22
neo-evangelicals, 49–50
new evangelicalism, 86–87
New Living Translation, 182
Newsweek, 20
New York City, Billy Graham and, 177–78
New York Times, 6–7, 103–4
Nixon, Richard M., 52–53, 180
Nonaffiliated, 159–60
Norquist, Ben, 36
Norwegian Evangelical Free Church, 93–94
nuclear families, 4, 11, 15–16, 25, 29
Numrich, Paul, 126–27, 197–98

Ockenga, Harold, 49–50, 86–87, 99, 184
Olmstead, Frederick Law, 61–62
Omri, Elisha, 147
Open Bible Standard Churches, 84
Orange County, California, 11–12, 132–34
  studies of suburbs in, 31
Origin of Species, The (Darwin), 44–45
Orthodox Jews, 3
Orthodox Presbyterian Church, 88–89
Over the Hedge (film), 1
Oyakawa, Michelle, 165

parachurch organizations, 140–41, 189
  agglomerations and, 123–27
  clusters in four locations, 127–35
  comparisons across four clusters, 135–37
  evangelical organizations and, 123–27
  explaining clusters, 123–27, 137–40
  how population mix affects creation of, 126
  influence of clusters, 137–40
  overview, 122–23
  studying evangelical clusters, 127–28
Park Street Church, 87
Paulsen, Krista, 105
PCA. *See* Presbyterian Church of America
Peace with God (Graham), 172–73
Peterson, Andrew, 178–79
Pew Research, 3–4, 190–91
Pew Research Religious Landscape Study, 3–4, 20

Pilgrim Baptist Church, 60–61
Pitt, William, 40–41
place
  adding to theories of religion and, 32–36
  understanding places and religion and, 195–99
Pledge of Allegiance, 49
political economy theory, 34–35, 195–96
politicians, evangelicals as, 27–29
postwar era, 11–12, 19, 26, 35–36, 63, 99, 115, 118–19, 121, 135, 147, 187, 189, 195, 196
postwar growth (through early 1960s)
  congregations moving to suburbs, 50–51
  conservative Protestants during, 49–50
  evangelicals adapting to, 51–52
  factors contributing to, 47–48
  increase in religious activity and affiliation, 49
  mass media depicting suburbs, 48–49
  revivalist individualism of fundamentalists, 49–50
  suburbs during, 48
poverty, 55
Presbyterian Church of America (PCA), 87, 88–89, 142
Presbyterians, 67, 73–74
previous studies of evangelicals and suburbs, 30–32
Princeton Theological Seminary, 88
Protestants, 20
  Black protestants, 12, 20–21, 149–56, 157, 158–59
  conservative Protestants, 14–15, 20–22, 25–26, 31, 35–36, 48, 49–50, 61, 77–78, 98, 146
  mainline Protestants, 12, 20–21, 33–34, 51, 108–9, 149–56, 157

race-place intersection, 157–58
railroads, 42
Rauschenbach, Walter, 44–45
Reagan, Ronald, 27, 100
Redeemer Presbyterian Church, 142
Reformed Church in America (RCA), 140
religion
  adding to theories of, 32
  cultural toolkits, 35–36
  development of settlement patterns, 34–35
  religious actors in growth machines, 34
  religious competition, 32–34
  suburbs and, 2–4
  understanding places and, 195–99
religious denomination (Chicago region), studying, 63–64, 65t

religious marketplace theory. *See* ecological theory
religious nones, 55–56, 144, 191–92
religious traditions
  across community types, 145–48
  and community types over time, 152–56
  and community types will all GSS cases, 149–52
  in different kinds of communities over time, 148
  moving from cities and rural areas to suburbs, 156–60
religious traditions, across community types
  anti-urban biases, 147
  competition and change, 146
  engagement in big cities, 147–48
  particular concentrations, 146–47
  urban neighborhoods, 145–46
Reltrad, 144–45
Republican Party, 21
research, previous studies of evangelicals and suburbs, 30–32
revivalist individualism of fundamentalists, 49–50
Robertson, Pat, 52–53
Rockin' the Suburbs, 1–2
Ruotsila, Markku, 88

Saddleback Community Church, 31, 56, 122, 198–99
Scheitle, Christopher, 31, 124–25, 137, 138, 147
Schuller, Robert, 31, 140, 199
science, embrace of, 44–46
Scopes Monkey Trial, 45–46
SDA. *See* Seventh-day Adventist
Second Great Awakening, 42
Secular City, The (Cox), 52
seeker-sensitive churches, 126
segmented assimilation, 158
Serving a Movement: Doing Balanced, Gospel-Centered Ministry in Your City (Keller), 142
settlement patterns, development of, 34–35
Seventh-day Adventist (SDA), 63–64
Simple Way, 160–61
single-family homes, 2–3, 5–7, 11, 14, 15, 17–18, 19–20, 28, 29–30, 38–39, 42, 43–44, 48, 54, 111, 114–15, 182, 183–84, 192, 200
Skinner, Tom, 49–50
Smith, Christian, 164
SMSA. *See* Standard Metropolitan Statistical Area
soccer moms, 54

social class. *See* middle class
Songs for Silverman, 1
Sopranos, The (show), 2
spatial assimilation, 55
spatial dimensions, evangelical life, 185
  considering lived/everyday religion, 186–87
  megachurches, 185–86
  societal influence and power, 185–86
spatialization, race and ethnicity, 157–58
Spilman, Lyn, 125
spiritual districts, examining, 124–25
St. John's Lutheran, 110–11
St. Michael's Catholic Church, 110–11
Standard Metropolitan Statistical Area (SMSA), 144–45
Stark, Rodney, 40
Stewart, Lyman, 37
Storm Warning (Graham), 175
Strachan, Owen, 98–99, 143
Suburban Church: Practical Advice for Authentic Ministry, The (Anderson), 38
suburban communities, 5, 6, 18, 26. *See also* communities
suburban familism, 46
suburban retreats. *See* American cities
suburbs, 200–1
  adding to theories of religion and place, 32–36
  American Dream and evangelicals in, 14–37
  becoming firmly part of American society, 20
  books about apocalypse, 182–85
  in books of Billy Graham, 171–78
  Census Bureau designation, 16–17
  changing, 162–81
  changing social conditions, 19
  complexity and variation, 22
  cultural affinities between evangelical life and life in, 29–30
  cultural component of, 17–18
  defining, 16–22
  engaging in more robust thinking about, 193–98
  evangelical politicians and, 27–29
  evangelicals adapting to, 51–52
  geography defining, 17
  growth through early 1960s, 47–52
  impacting big cities, 19–20
  kinds of communities of, 18
  leaving Chicago for, 60–80
  megachurches and, 23–25
  methodology defining, 17
  modern day-to-day suburban life, 18–19
  moving from cities and rural areas to, 156–60

suburbs (*cont.*)
  naming and praying for evangelicals in, 1–2
  parachurch organizations in, 122–41
  previous studies of, 30–32
  race, class, and gender in, 187–90
  religion and, 2–4
  road to studying, 4–8
  short history of, 38–59
  spiritual pastiche in, 55–56
  suburban faith and critiques, 25–27
  suburbs and evangelicals in-between, 190–93
  waves of development, 19
  in Wheaton, Illinois, 103–21
Sun Belt, 4, 31, 53–54, 124
Sunday, Billy, 46–47, 110–11
Swidler, Ann, 163

Taylor, Ken, 118–19
TEAM (The Evangelical Alliance Mission), 182
The Navigators, 122–23, 129
Theosophical Society in America, 114
Third Lausanne Congress, 57
Thornton, Henry, 41
Time, 52
Tomlin, Chris, 193
toolkits, cultural, 35–36
Torah, 50–51
totem, concept, 143
Tranby, Eric, 165
Trinity Episcopal, 110–11
triple melting pot, 49
Trump, Donald, 143, 165, 183
twentieth century, leaving. *See* twenty-first century, entering
twenty-first century, entering
  emphasis on cities, 57
  evangelicals adapting to changing suburbs, 56–57
  marking 1976 as critical year for evangelicals, 52–53
  poverty, 55
  shift in religious life, 52
  Southerners incorporated into evangelicalism, 53–54
  spiritual pastiche in suburbs, 55–56
  US established as suburban country, 54–55
Tyndale House Publishers, 96–97, 118–19, 182

Uneasy Conscience of Modern Fundamentalism, The (Henry), 101
United States
  establishment as suburban country, 54–55
  growing urbanism in, 42–47
  increase in religious activity and affiliation in, 49
  as pluralistic country, 123–24
  postwar growth through early 1960s, 47–52
  search for religious resources in, 33
  suburb statistics in, 4
"United Towns," commercial, 120–21
unsettled times, evangelicals and, 196
urbanism, growth of
  affecting men and women, 54
  commercial interests, 44
  embrace of science, 44–46
  evangelical Protestant life in Boston, 46–47
  expanding frontier, 43
  growth through immigration and annexation, 42–43
  immigrants, 46
  railroads, 43
  religious shifts, 44
  rise of suburban residents, 43–44
  split between modernism and fundamentalism, 44–46
Urban Monastery, 147–48
urban settlement patterns, Chicago School model of, 33
urbanization. *See* urbanism, growth of
US Census Bureau, 4, 15, 79
  suburb designation, 16–17

Van Kampen, Robert C., 94, 135
Vatican of evangelicals. *See* Wheaton, Illinois

Warner, W. Lloyd, 125
War Relief Commission, 96
Warren, Rick, 31, 199
Wayside Chapel. *See* Wooddale Church
Weber, Max, 108
Wedam, Elfriede, 126–27, 197–98
Wesleyan Methodist Congregation, 110–11
Wheaton Bible Church, 115–16
Wheaton College, 103–4, 111–12, 113–14, 117–18, 134–35
Wheaton Evangelical Free Church, 94
Wheaton, Illinois, 11–12, 103
  Cluster of evangelicals studied in, 134–35
  community and religious history of, 109–14
  community character of, 105–9
  cultural meaning-making, 107–8
  daily lives of evangelicals in, 116–19
  evangelical convergence in, 105–9
  evangelical leaders leading majority to suburbs, 107
  examining idea of place character, 105–6

explaining concentration of evangelicals in, 114–20
influence of religion in suburban character, 106–7
liquor referendum in, 112–14
as majority white and wealthy community, 114–16
marketplace argument, 108–9
NAE headquarters in, 92–97
negative view of concertation of evangelicals in, 114
network development, 119–20
postwar concentration of evangelical organizations, 112
religious character of, 103–5
unique character of, 6–7
"United Towns" advertisement, 120–21
Wheaton, Warren and Jesse, 109–10
white flight
   AME congregations, 66–69
   changing demographics, 72–73
   in Chicago region, 77–78
   congregational autonomy across denominations, 73–74
   congregations in older and newer suburbs, 74–77
   conservative Protestant denominations, 67
   Dutch Reformed denominations, 70–73
   ethnic composition, 67–72
   factors at work, 67
   general pattern, 67
   mainline Protestant denominations, 67
   organizational structure of denominations, 73–77
   Presbyterian congregations, 69–70
   RCA congregations, 72–73
   SDA congregations, 69
   strong ethnic ties, 70
Whyte, William, 17–18
Wilberforce, William, 10, 40–41, 189–90
Wilford, Justin, 198–99
Will County, Illinois, 63–64, 65t, 74–75
Willow Creek Association, 23, 56
Willow Creek Community Church, 23
   and Chicago suburbs, 24
   embracing and adapting to changing suburbs, 56
   and expanding suburban populations, 24
   geographic location and interaction with suburban life, 23–24
   history of, 23
Winter, Gibson, 25–26
Winthrop, John, 40
women
   mass media depictions of, 48–49
   and start of suburbanization, 46
Wooddale Church, 81–82
Word Books, 166–67
World Aflame (Graham), 171
World's Parliament of Religions, 61
World War II, 17–18, 19, 189–90
Wuthnow, Robert, 157

Young Life, 123, 129

Zondervan, 131–32, 166–67
zoning, 19, 48, 79, 138–39, 192